T0331073

# ETHICAL OMNIVORES

This book provides a detailed overview of ethical omnivorism, as well as the philosophical foundations of this movement and diet.

Many eaters are concerned about the impact that their food choices have on the environment, animals, and human health. Ethical omnivorism is at once a new food ethic, diet, and global movement aimed at providing a flexible path for eaters committed to bringing about lasting change one meal at a time. While publications in food ethics are largely dominated by vegetarian titles, this book explores the viability of omnivorism, a dietary choice which is not devoid of animal products, but one which embraces eating local, eating organic, and eating humanely raised food products. In doing so, this diet builds on the local food movement's desire to know where food comes from and stresses the importance of maintaining high animal welfare and environmental standards. Overall, this book provides a foundational overview of ethical omnivorism as a food movement and guidance for those interested in eating ethically, while recognizing that many factors influence dietary choices.

This book will be of great interest to students and scholars of food studies, food, agriculture and animal ethics, environmental philosophy, and those more widely interested in making ethical food choices.

**Samantha Noll** is the Ryan-Bordander Chair and Associate Professor in the School of Politics, Philosophy, and Public Affairs (PPPA) at Washington State University, USA. She publishes widely on topics in food and environmental ethics and the application of emerging technologies in agriculture and is the co-author/editor of the *Field Guide to Formal Logic* (2020) and the *Routledge Handbook of Philosophy of the City* (Routledge, 2019).

# Routledge Studies in Food, Society and the Environment

# ETHICAL OMNIVORES

## Better Eating for Everyone

*Samantha Noll*

Cover image: Copyright Getty Images

First published 2025
by Routledge
4 Park Square, Milton Park, Abingdon, Oxon OX14 4RN

and by Routledge
605 Third Avenue, New York, NY 10158

*Routledge is an imprint of the Taylor & Francis Group, an informa business*

*British Library Cataloguing-in-Publication Data*
A catalogue record for this book is available from the British Library

ISBN: 978-1-032-10409-6 (hbk)
ISBN: 978-1-032-10404-1 (pbk)
ISBN: 978-1-003-21518-9 (ebk)

DOI: 10.4324/9781003215189

Typeset in Optima
by Newgen Publishing UK

*This book would not have been possible without the support of my dissertation director and mentor, Paul B. Thompson. Thank you for encouraging me even when I was a bright-eyed and bushy-tailed first year graduate student, passionate about food and agriculture. Your support throughout the years is a gift.*

# CONTENTS

# ACKNOWLEDGMENTS

I want to thank Shane Epting for all his support over the years. You're my rock and philosophy brother. Keep being awesome! Thank you, Emily LaRosa, for providing many comments on the manuscript. Your discerning insights and fearless feedback made this a better book. Your encouragement means the world to me. Finally, I want to express my gratitude to Dan Curtis, may you never stop being a powerful advocate for wild public lands. All my scholarly brothers and sisters at the NEH Institute on Aldo Leopold made this book possible, as well.

# 1

# THE ETHICAL OMNIVORE DIET

It was a beautiful day on the farm. Playful and happy pigs ran up to a farm tour, "hamming" it up in front of the smiling visitors with cellphones ready to snap selfies. Unlike their relatives in large industrial operations, these pigs were raised on pasture, enjoying grass and sunlight from birth. The Michigan State University (MSU) Student Organic Farm produces a wide range of foodstuffs on its ten acres, from delicate hot-house veggies (such as winter spinach, baby lettuce, tomatoes, etc.) to heartier field crops, such as grains, potatoes, and corn. In this diverse environment, pigs, chickens, cows, and other livestock are raised in an integrated farming system, where vegetable and animal production are done in a balanced and sustainable way. As part of this system, the pigs provide much needed fertilizer and soil tillage, while the chickens oversee pest control, eating larvae from the fields. Unlike the area where I grew up, dotted with large operations, the air was crisp and sweet and there were few flies in sight. Farm tours, like the one described, are part of MSU's initiative to educate the community about where their food comes from. It was started in 1999 to train students how to grow food sustainably and to provide hands-on experience working in agriculture. By the time I arrived, it had become a thriving operation, where diverse communities come together to grow and learn about food.

The pigs made quite an impression on the tour group, which was made up of students and community members who wanted to know more about sustainable agriculture. Standing in the pasture that day, surrounded by the bronze-haired pigs literally glinting in the sun (duroc pigs are golden-brown after all), I was surprised at the size of the group and at the quality of their questions. They were genuinely interested in sustainable agriculture and concerned about how current farming practices could impact the quality

DOI: 10.4324/9781003215189-1

and healthiness of their food. The visitor's stomachs ultimately placed them on this path of learning, as dietary choices have profound impacts beyond the plate. They were from diverse backgrounds but were all asking the same question: What should I eat?

Ethical omnivores' answer to the question "what should I eat?" guides this book. The following pages provide a detailed discussion of their diet, or one way that a group of concerned eaters choose to live their lives. They embrace a diet where the consumption of vegetables, meat, dairy, and eggs is acceptable provided that these products can be: (a) traced back to an organic farm and (b) are sustainably and ethically raised and harvested. The farm above is one example of this type of production system, but according to the USDA (2020), there are over 16,500 registered organic farms in the United States alone and this number is growing. Both Canada and Europe are experiencing similar growth, as the numbers of farms and hectares of organic farmland are on the rise (Vecchio 2009; Pierre 2023). The idea that good food is produced through good farming and animal husbandry is not new. Ethical omnivorism is a diet driven by the desire to embrace once deeply rooted food and agricultural traditions—traditions that are being challenged by the twin forces of industrial agriculture and the power of fad diets to radically change what we think of as "good" food. This diet is one among many that come up in Internet searches, but embracing a thoughtful omnivore diet has a long history. Knowing this history is important to understand the modern ethical omnivore diet and social movement. It's not the same thing as a fad diet. Thoughtful eating has been going on for centuries. The chapter places ethical omnivorism into historical context, before ending with overviews of each chapter going forward.

## What Should I Eat?

There are many ways to answer the question, "what should I eat?" and some answers may conflict with an ethical omnivore diet. Today, entire food movements are driven by thoughtful eaters, who want to change the world one meal at a time. These are as diverse as the people and communities who make them up. For instance, the Slow Food Movement focuses on preventing the disappearance of food traditions and heritage seeds and breeds. Supporters want us to slow down and think deeply about what's on our plate and how it got there (Donati 2005). Similarly, local food movements prioritize eating fruits, vegetables, and other products produced within your community or at least close by. The dietary tradition that has enjoyed a particularly long history is vegetarianism. Individuals adopted plant-based diets, since at least the Ancient Greeks. Notably, Pythagoras (580 BCE), the great philosopher and mathematician, argued that animals should be treated as kindred creatures (Zwart 2000). Not only did he abstain from eating meat, but his followers did as well. Prior to Pythagoras, vegetarianism was practiced by religious groups in Egypt and by some Babylonians (Hargreaves et al. 2021). This complex history prompted the scholar Laura Wright (2021) to argue that vegetarians are not simply following a specific diet. Rather, these food movements are at once a diet, "an ethical system, a religious imposition… a mode of social reform, an agricultural imperative, a way of viewing social relations among humans and between humans and nonhuman animals, and ecological necessity…" (1). Laura B. DeLind (2011) makes similar claims about the local food movement, as it is also at once a diet, social movement, economic strategy, and panacea for a struggling global food system. For many eaters, diets are social identities that reflect the values that they hold dear, such as a determination to limit our ecological footprint, reduce animal harm, support local communities, etc. Ethical omnivorism has its own rich history, as it is grounded in The Organic Agriculture Movement, which embraces the idea that good food begins with good farming. Like other food movements, it is also at once a diet, an ethical system, a mode of social reform, and an agricultural and ecological imperative. Ethical omnivores care about the environment, their local communities, animal welfare, and future generations. Each of these themes will be discussed in detail in this book.

Due to this complexity, it should be noted that "ethical omnivore movement" and "ethical omnivore diet" will be used interchangeably, throughout the book, as both are deeply connected. A movement is a loosely organized social campaign in support of a specific social goal, including dietary goals. People come together because they want to bring about change. For example, local food advocates often want to support rural towns, by buying foodstuffs that are produced within a hundred miles. Money stays in the community, as people exchange those dollars for various services (Thompson 2023). One dollar given to a farmer could support a barber, who then supports a local diner, and so forth. Individual members of movements feel connected, as they pursue a shared vision of a better world, driven by shared values. Within this context, a diet is a manifestation of a social movement's values. We buy products that align with what we care about and do not eat those foods that violate our ethics. In this way, vegetarian eaters opt out of animal production by eating only vegetables. Ethical omnivores similarly opt out of conventional agricultural systems, by buying organic and wild-harvested foodstuffs.

Food movements of all varieties have taken root around the globe. Over the last 20 years, we have seen an increase in public interest in food systems and the ethical implications of production. These are all driven by people who want to eat better and make the world a better place through their choices. The diverse ways that we answer the question "what should I eat?" points to (sometimes conflicting) values that influence our food choices. The ethical omnivore movement is only one way that people answer this question. This book discusses what it means to be an ethical omnivore. It highlights conflicts and commonalities between this path and other diets, such as vegetarianism and veganism, in later chapters. Eaters care about many issues and food choices reflect this normative diversity. Readers may not all agree with this diet, as it embraces eating a wide range of foods, including animal products. However, it is important to remember that eaters thoughtfully reflecting on food choices are all on personal food journeys, grappling with how their choices impact the world. Like harvesting potatoes late in the growing season, this book is intended to unearth the bountiful history of the ethical omnivore diet and explore the deeply held commitments guiding it.

People have been grappling with dietary questions for thousands of years and there are many ways to answer them. For example, the quest to identify better dietary choices was of great social importance for historical societies, from the Ancient Greeks to Medieval and Renaissance communities throughout Europe (Zwart 2000). This is not surprising, especially when you can eat almost anything and when some food could have dire health consequences. The Ancient Greeks thought that eating well was an important part of living a good life (Young 1985). A key component of morality for the Greeks is developing virtues or "habits" that help us perform well, no matter the circumstances. Ultimately, the goal of life is to flourish the best that we can, as humans. In all situations, we can act excessively or deficiently, but a wise person finds the "golden mean," or the middle path between the two. And, there is no better opportunity to develop these habits then when we're deciding what to eat. Several times a day, we are faced with the choice to eat "better" or "worse," to make choices that are best for us, including what we eat, how much, and even when we do so. At a barbeque, for example, the platters of grilled and basted delicacies might tempt one to overeat, but this would be overly giving in to desires to excessively eat all the delicious dishes. Alternatively, that relative (you know the one) who doesn't eat anything is also acting immorally if they're not eating enough to sustain themselves in nature. Finding the middle path between eating too much and eating too little is cultivating virtue. In this case, it's cultivating the virtue of temperance, or self-restraint, where we learn through trial and error to make food choices in line with what's best for us. While today we are reticent to assign blame to eating, as there are social stigmas attached to the act, the Greeks thought that the development of good habits was a journey, where the goal is to improve over a lifetime. Our habits are informed by our culture, but they're also deeply personal. The only way to act appropriately in all situations is to have a wide range of experiences, including acting in excess and in deficit. This helps us to calibrate future choices for ourselves and, as we consciously make better ones, good habits slowly form. We are making choices for us, as part of living our own good life, and others can tend to their own gardens, to paraphrase Voltaire.

But what is "better" eating? How do we answer this seemingly simple but difficult question? For the Ancient Greeks, eating well centered on using reason to find balance when eating, as with all human pursuits (Zwart 2000; Young 1985). To train ourselves using reason is to find the middle path between overindulgence and unjustifiably denying ourselves. To maintain health and train our habits, food became an item of major concern, for which no universal recipes could be forwarded. Rather, eaters had to discover the best daily regimen through trial and error. Each and every day, an individual develops their tastes and pattern of eating habits that suits their physical makeup. Self-observation and reflection are useful for the modern eater. This foundation of self-reflection is an important aspect of the ethical omnivore diet. When everything editable is potentially on the menu, there are many choices. But not all these choices are equal. Some foods are better than others, especially if our goal is *eudemonia*, or flourishing across a lifetime. This is the joy and challenge of being an omnivore. On the one side, you have a veritable cornucopia of food choices waiting to tickle your tastebuds. All those delectable morsels of sugar and fat and tasty sweets are fair game, not to mention wine and other alcoholic beverages. (The Greeks wrote about drinking in moderation, too.) The other side of the coin is that you need to practice restraint if you're going to live a flourishing life. Eating habits can literally kill you. Some of the leading causes of death in modern times include heart disease, cancer, and diabetes. And, all these ailments are at least partially linked to dietary choices. To live well then, one needs to make thoughtful food decisions and eat in moderation.

But, on the other hand, eating a moderate or "balanced" diet doesn't take us very far in modern society, beyond the recommendation to eat a mixture of food types, such as fruits and vegetables. In the quest to find a satisfying answer, eaters have bought many books, read many articles, watched countless documentaries, and even grilled family members and friends on the topic. The desire to determine what it means to eat well has been taken up by experts of many stripes, giving lectures and spilling so much ink on the topic that several readers are more confused than when we started reading about diets. Yet, the quest goes on for thoughtful eaters. Just look at the numbers of diet-related Internet searches. According to Google search data, there are an average of 88 million Google searches relating to dietary questions monthly (Voakes 2011). If eating a balanced diet was enough, then we wouldn't be obsessed with trying out new ways of eating. For many of us, recommendations can also be confusing. Just a quick look at Internet search results highlights the diverse ways that eaters can answer this question. Enjoy fish, fruit, grains, and olives? Try the Mediterranean diet, inspired by the eating habits of people who live near the Mediterranean Sea. Want to avoid grains, dairy, processed foods, and sugars? The Paleo or "caveman" diet might be a good fit. Enjoy foods rich in fat and protein? Then, Keto might work. Vegetarian or vegan diets might also be appealing if you want to cut-out all meat products. There is even a carnivore diet for dedicated meat lovers. The nutritional pros and cons of each of these (and more) are hotly debate online.

Eating is one of the most basic activities, yet we now require an impressive amount of expert help to eat well. Modern nutritional science provides much of this advice. We've been obsessed with how eating can impact health for a long time. *Santorio Sanctorius* (1561–1636), the famous renaissance physician and founding father of Nutritional Science, spent 30 years of his life on a scale, measuring how eating impacted body weight. According to the food historian Hub Zwart (2000), he spent his life:

> carefully measuring the effects of food intake and other daily habits on body weight. He faithfully registered what happened (quantitatively speaking) when he was eating, drinking, sleeping, and having intercourse, and by doing so he discovered, for example, that having breakfast leads to a gaining body weight
>
> *(120)*

If it weren't for this insanely dedicated researcher, our current obsession with food intake and weight would be unthinkable. Fast forward to roughly 100 years ago and modern nutritional science was born (Mozaffarian et al. 2018).

Since its inception, nutritional science made lasting changes to what is on our plate, as food recommendations guided governmental policy and, subsequently, individual food-choices throughout the years. For example, the early focus on combating dietary deficiencies prior to the 1950s morphed into campaigns against sugar and fat, as well as targeted efforts to address the "protein gap" through the production of protein enriched foods. Fast forward again to the 1980s when dietary guidelines were nutrient focused and emphasized eating foods low in fat, cholesterol, and saturated fats. In 1990s, fats, once thought to be the enemy, resurfaced as beneficial in Mediterranean and vegetarian diets, where foods rich in healthy fats from nuts, beans, and plant oils were emphasized. Today, the benefits of fermented foods are championed, as gut microbiota enters the nutritional spotlight as a major player on the food-scene. Couple these radically changing recommendations with the rise of a billion-dollar diet industry, and it is no surprise that eaters are having trouble answering the question "what should I eat?"

According to the food writer Michael Pollan (2006), a perfect storm of expert advice, books on the next "big" diet, and scientific studies hold so much public sway that product labels and supermarket shelves can be changed within weeks of a new dietary fad taking root. We find ourselves navigating a food-scene marked by new "food pyramids" and recommendations, as they are revised and revised again due to new scientific information. And, we are faced with making choices in a context where supermarket shelves are stuffed with food products touting their health benefits with dubious labels, as the diet industry continues to play on food-related desires to remove billions of dollars from the wallets of concerned eaters. For example, it is common to spot foodstuffs vying for your attention with confusing labels such as "all natural," "gluten-free," "fat-free," "guilt-free" etc. I even spotted packages of chicken in the meat department proudly sporting a "gluten free" label. Companies tend to use healthy sounding claims to mislead eaters into thinking that products are healthier than they are. Thus, concerns about what we should eat are not surprising, as this cornucopia of products with competing food labels provide the perception of excessive choice.

It is this perception that informs Michael Pollan's (2006) framing of dietary choice as an "omnivores dilemma," where eaters spend a lot of time devoted to figuring out which, of the many foods on offer, we *should* eat. These decisions will inevitably stir up anxiety, especially when you can eat almost anything. The number of food product recalls due to *Salmonella* contaminations alone highlight risks associated with eating products such as peanuts, spinach, and beef. Many eaters in the Western world have a vast number of food choices, some of which could lead you down the dark road of food-related illnesses, such as diabetes and heart disease. Deciphering food labels, identifying which are connected to certifications, thoroughly inspecting ingredient lists, and paying attention to the nutritional facts label are all important components of making informed food choices. However, for ethical omnivores, these are simply first steps towards determining what we should eat, as they do not challenge the fundamental assumption that foodstuffs in the store can be treated as separate from the farmers and agricultural systems who produced them.

## From Fad Diets to Responsible Agriculture

The visitors at the Michigan State Organic farm were certainly worried about making good food choices, but they also recognized the fundamental connection between what is on their plate and what is done on the farm. They followed this path, from the fork to the field, to make better informed food choices, as they personally confronted this dilemma. I appreciate how Michael Pollan frames the concerns of eaters, as they attempt to navigate our vast and complex food system. This framing helps to highlight the unique commitments that guide the ethical omnivore diet. As a larger segment of the population moves away from farming, there is a growing disconnect between food production and consumption. In 1920, for example, approximately 30% of the population worked on a farm versus 1.3% today (Hirschman and Mogford 2009). But as Wendel Berry (1977) argues, a "sane and healthy agriculture requires an informed urban constituency" (xi). And, for ethical omnivores, so do sane and healthy eaters. This work and a bevy of other popular books and articles helped to launch an international ethical omnivore movement, where consumers are encouraged to know more about where their food comes from. Over the last 20 years, publications on ethical omnivorism have multiplied. They focus on just about every aspect of food production, from critiques of industrial food systems to sustainable crop and animal production recommendations (George 1990; Pollan 2006). Additionally, these publications often provide dietary advice, such as "nose to tail" recipes and food label recommendations, etc. (Dalrymple and Hilliard 2020).

This variety of topics highlights the complexity of living an ethical omnivore lifestyle. Publications include dietary recommendations, but these recommendations are often guided by deeply held ethical beliefs concerning agriculture. It is telling that one of the founders of the website the "ethical omnivore movement" writes that she "had been a locavore, sustainable-agricultural advocate and environmentalist, as well as being a holistic health and functional fitness professional for 3 decades already" (Salant 2023, n.p.). These paths led her to embrace regenerative agriculture as the actualization of food sovereignty. Environmental concerns, sustainable agriculture practices, ethical crop production, and animal husbandry all come to the forefront as factors that influence what is on an ethical omnivore's plate. It's about more than food as fuel, as what we eat has far reaching social and environmental consequences. In this way, ethical omnivorism shifts our focus from fad diets to responsible agriculture.

The aim of *The Ethical Omnivore Diet: Better Eating for Everyone* is to provide an overview of the ethical omnivore diet and the deeply held commitments guiding it. In short, it is an attempt to help eaters understand the complexity of eating with an eye towards production. As you can see from our discussion thus far, eaters spend a lot of time thinking about their food choices and the many factors that influence what's on our plates. The ethical omnivore diet presents us with a unique and refreshing perspective in a saturated field, as it stresses the importance of maintaining high ethical standards on the farm and reducing environmental impacts. However, ethical omnivorism is often ignored in the wider literature, as other diets take the spotlight. When it is discussed, scholars tend to focus on meat eating, as the primary difference between it and other diets (Cuneo 2015; Rothgerber 2015). Though as we can see from even the brief treatment above, ethical omnivores are worried about more than farm animal welfare. It is a diet growing from far richer ethical soil, so to speak. The section below provides a brief overview of each chapter, to show the wide-ranging and well-grounded normative commitments guiding the ethical omnivore diet. As we will see, each obligation and responsibility fit together into a unified whole, capturing a cornucopia of food related issues within a single diet. I'm personally looking forward to exploring the many ways that we can change the world, one meal at a time. Let us pick up our theoretical shovels and unearth the bountiful history of the ethical omnivore diet together.

## Overview of Chapters

The second chapter discusses the historical reasons why ethical omnivores take production seriously and are deeply concerned with wider social and environmental impacts. In fact, books and articles on this subject often connect dietary choices to regenerative types of agriculture. This interplay between consumption and production, between the field and the fork, is because the birth of ethical omnivorism can be traced back to The Organic Movement. As soon as industrial agricultural practices were widely adopted, this movement was created to promote sustainable farming worldwide. While global communities historically practiced sustainable agriculture, The Organic Movement can be understood as a response to the development of industrial agriculture. Important advances in biochemistry and technology during the 20th century ushered in a period of rapid change for agriculture. Affordable nitrogen fertilizers, new pesticides (such as DDT), and advances in mechanization transformed daily operations on the farm. Along with these technological innovations, changing priorities in agricultural policy also greatly impacted farming, as increasing efficiency and food production tended to be prioritized over long-term sustainability (Berry 1977). These changes heralded in an age where a single farmer could feed over 100 people and food availability in many countries increased. However, increases in efficiency often come with large environmental and social price-tags.

There are many connections between The Organic Movement and the ethical omnivore diet, as both are worried about the harms of industrial agriculture. Both early and late organicists agree that alternative models of farming need to be nurtured to help promote diverse visions of what food production can look like. Chapter 2 ends by arguing that the ethical omnivore diet is the other side of the organic coin, so to speak. It is a diet that asks eaters, in addition to farmers, to be mindful about how their food is produced and to think deeply about the consequences of decisions made on the farm. When grappling with the question "what should I eat?," they embrace a diet where products can be: (a) traced back to an organic farm and (b) that are sustainably and ethically raised and harvested. While the organic movement desires to change production systems, the ethical omnivore movement galvanizes eaters to care and to support this change with their wallets and their plates.

Chapter 3 builds on this historical foundation, as it describes the robust food ethic guiding the ethical omnivore diet. Rather than focusing on a single normative concern, this diet asks eaters to engage in a heuristic or practice "an ethic of seeing," where we learn more about how our food choices impact other communities. This leads us to the pillars of ethical eating that make up the ethical foundations of the omnivore diet. These include the following: Impacts to society, individuals, the environment, and animal liberty and welfare. First, social impacts are important for ethical omnivores, as how food is produced and distributed often brings up issues of justice. Additionally, many eaters are worried about how agricultural practices and choices, such as the use of specific pesticides or herbicides, are impacting their health and that of the environment. These twin concerns came up again and again when I worked at MSU's Student Organic Farm, as visitors were worried about the quality of their food and whether conventionally grown vegetables were safe to feed to their families. Discussions concerning diet, labeling, and food safety all fall under impacts to individuals. Finally, animal welfare considerations are important, as how we treat our farm animals matters. This chapter ends by using avocados to illustrate how each of these lenses highlight unique concerns that eaters should pay attention to.

Chapter 4 more deeply explores the environmental commitments guiding the ethical omnivore diet. These eaters place great importance on producing food through sustainable and environmentally friendly methods. Typically, ethical omnivore recommendations stress food quality and mindful eating, prioritizing locally, ethically, and organically produced meats, dairy, eggs, and fruits and vegetables (Salant 2023). Organic and regenerative farming seem to do a lot of the heavy lifting in this diet. However, what does it mean to produce food in this way? Why do ethical omnivores buy organic? And, what is regenerative agriculture? This chapter unpacks these terms, as it explores ethical omnivores' environmental ethic more deeply. As we will discuss, ethical omnivores are committed to making sure that food that isn't harmful to the land, soils, animals, and humans, alike. One worry is that agricultural pesticides, herbicides, and other inputs will be harmful when consumed. Another worry is that these inputs, and agricultural methods more generally, will harm the environment. By embracing a diet grounded in environmental ethics, these eaters are committed to living more in balance with the environments that produce our food.

Chapter 5 discusses the many ways that ethical omnivores embrace buying "local" or the local food movement. The ethical omnivore diet is built on eating food that is produced in ethically and environmentally friendly ways. This includes supporting organic and regenerative production methods, as well as pasture raised and free-range animal agriculture. Additionally, popular websites and books often recommend that omnivores buy locally produced foods, as well. Why is this? It is true that, from a general perspective, buying local means purchasing products grown close to home, but it also means so much more. Buying that local tomato or pint of strawberries is a way for eaters to support community agriculture projects, farmers who care about the environment, and producers who prioritize animal welfare. This is especially the case when you can talk to the farmer or visit the farm itself. These and other interactions provide eaters with opportunities to learn about how their food is produced and agriculture, more generally. Engaging with local producers deepens our understanding food systems and how our food choices impact the environment, animals, and other communities.

In this overview, we discuss the many reasons why ethical omnivores embrace local food. To do this, it defines what local food is and explores the reasons why eaters are embracing locavorism. It should be no surprise to readers that these projects can take on many forms. In fact, the local food movement is not static, but should be understood as a diverse initiative that includes several distinct types of food projects. It then discusses the many connections between ethical omnivorism and local food movements. In a way, the ethical omnivore diet and locavorism share the same roots in The Organic Agriculture Movement. As such, both are simultaneously a food ethic and a social initiative aimed at bringing about structural changes to agriculture, or how we produce food. They are also deeply intertwined, as we will see, helping to bolster each other. The chapter ends with a discussion of local food as a heuristic (Thompson 2023) and how increasing personal knowledge and developing habits are important for eaters.

Chapter 6 deepens our analysis of ethical omnivorism even further by placing justice considerations on the plate. Having access to safe and nutritious foods is important, but it's also important to recognize that the pursuit of "public goods" informs both diets and agricultural policy. For instance, eaters who buy local often do so for environmental and community reasons. They want their food to be produced in ecologically friendly ways, their food dollars to go towards supporting local farmers who embrace these methods, etc. On the policy side, The U.S. Farm Bill, a package of legislation passed every 5 years, has a tremendous impact on how food is grown, what kinds are grown, and farming livelihood (Elliot and Raziano 2012). It funds programs aimed at increasing access to nutritious foodstuffs, but there are also programs devoted to conservation, rural development, farm worker safety, crop insurance, etc. These "public goods" programs address concerns well beyond consumer access to agricultural products. Many of these duties can be distilled down to the idea that we should treat others fairly, and are thus built on social justice commitments, as well as ethical commitments. Ethical omnivores' engagement with community focused local food projects highlights the important role that food and environmental justice play for these eaters.

In addition to the pursuit of "public goods," maintaining the food sovereignty of communities is another justice issue that guides eaters and food movements, alike. At the most basic level, food sovereignty simply means that communities exercise greater control over where and how they obtain food. Lots of food projects embrace food sovereignty, as an ideal, guiding action on the ground. These could include neighborhood gardens, community supported agricultural projects, farmers markets, and other initiatives where communities exercise greater control over their food system. Local food projects like these are typically called "community focused" initiatives (Noll and Werkheiser 2017). A commitment to food sovereignty is one way they are distinct from both individual and policy focused projects. Where individual focused projects are an overlap of local food with lifestyle politics, community focused initiatives are an overlap of local food with community-based food justice movements. Given this commitment to fairness and equity, local food projects are important because they help communities exercise meaningful control over their food practices in ways that strengthen and preserve their community and individual identities. Food acts as a powerful touchstone, translating abstract ideals and principles into practice in real life.

This chapter uses community-centered food projects to explore how ethical omnivorism is built on social justice commitments. It begins by defining food justice and food sovereignty. Then, it draws connections between important components of ethical omnivorism and justice-oriented food movements. When we recognize that ethical omnivorism is deeply connected to the local food movement, several normative commitments discussed earlier in the book make more sense. This connection at least partially explains why ethical omnivores are committed to ensuring that food products support small-scale sustainable farming methods. Additionally, the flexibility concerning what products can be eaten is compatible with food sovereignty. Respecting food traditions is an important part of food justice initiatives, as foodways are deeply connected to cultural identity. Thus, respecting diverse foodways is a part of enabling the autonomy of individuals and groups. Both food justice and food sovereignty overlap with ethical omnivorism in interesting ways, as we will see.

Chapter 7 deals with the cow in the room, so to speak, when we talk about eating ethically. We first go over the ethical omnivore recommendations concerning meat eating. As we just discussed, ethical omnivores embrace organic and regenerative organic agricultural standards. When many think of organic, they tend to think of vegetables and fruits. However, the USDA National Organic Standard, created in 2000, also includes strict requirements for meat, dairy, and egg production (USDA 2020. For example, animals must be fed and managed organically, allowed year-round access to pasture or the outdoors, as appropriate for the species, raised on certified organic land and pasture, and cared for following the animal welfare standards. They also need to be raised in a manner that is sensitive to environmental conservation and biodiversity. The USDA is quite strict and performs yearly farm inspections to ensure that the farmer's organic plan and their management plans align.

In addition to practical recommendations, this chapter also provides a detailed overview of ethical arguments supporting meat eating. The first is that people should be allowed to eat meat, if certain conditions are met. In fact, in some situations, eating meat may be the best course of action, otherwise food would go to waste. For example, there are cases where animals need to be culled for health or ecological reasons. Here, the argument is relatively straightforward. Ecological health and/or animal welfare demands that we cull certain animals, and the byproducts of these conservation actions should not be wasted. Second, ethical omnivores often espouse a more philosophical argument supporting meat eating, known as the "new omnivorism" position in the literature. Theorists such as Andy Lamey (2007) and especially Josh Milburn and Christopher Bobier (2022) argue that omnivorism should be taken seriously as a food ethic. They argue that eaters who embrace this diet typically observe that: (a) animals suffer in industrialized plant-based agriculture and (b) that there are relatively harm-free methods of raising animals for food. Land clearing, field traps, pesticides, and mechanical harvesting all harm a wide range of animals. Some of the harms are intentional (e.g., removing pests), while other harms are unintentional (e.g., accidently destroying a field mouse nest while tilling). Some omnivores argue that, paradoxically, allowing for some meat eating could reduce the suffering of sentient animals, when producing food. They recommend a diet of mostly plants and some animal protein, from sustainable farms, to minimize harm to animals in food production, while also maintaining high yields.

This chapter goes on to place ethical omnivore's justifications for meat eating in conversation with the wider animal welfare literature and the animal rights movement. It highlights key synergies, as well as conflicts between the different positions. Readers will find that ethical omnivores embrace an animal welfare ethic, and a rather stringent one at that, as they do not endorse factory farming. For these eaters, it is ethical to eat meat, but not all meat is the same. Eating animals raised in a sustainable manner, with high animal welfare standards fits the bill. For many eaters, this means eating less meat and far more vegetables than is typical in industrial countries. Raising animals in farms with high standards means that farms will raise fewer animals and thus meat products will cost more. It ends with the argument that the moral overlap between vegetarians and ethical omnivores is substantial, but they disagree when it matters. They are united in their critique of industrial agriculture, however, and are worried about its environmental impacts.

Chapter 8 discusses how ethical omnivores largely support hunting and fishing within certain parameters. The analysis presented in this chapter utilizes the environmental ethicist Gary Varner's (2002) distinction between three types of hunting: Therapeutic, subsistence, and sport hunting. It argues that each are important for understanding ethical omnivores' position on hunting and fishing, as they involve distinct focal practices and are justified by different ethical arguments. We will find that, unsurprisingly, ethical omnivores support therapeutic and subsistence hunting for both animal welfare and environmental reasons. As they are critical of industrial agriculture, both subsistence and therapeutic hunting provides an alternative way to obtain meat products. The latter can be justified on both environmental and animal welfare grounds, if we target mandatory management species. The chapter ends with a discussion of care ethics, as ethical omnivores gain important knowledge about food systems by interacting with nature and these insights bolster personal ethical growth.

The final chapter discusses what agriculture should look in the future. We live in an age where many events impact the resilience of ecosystems and agricultural production. However, if we want to continue growing food, we need to ensure that ecosystem services also continue. Climate change reinforces the tension between the goals of increasing yields and ensuring sustainable harvests. Agricultural lands are already stressed, and population pressures are increasing demand for foodstuffs, bringing this conflict to the forefront (Malhi et al. 2021; FAO 2009). Considering climate pressures, it's easy to argue that we should prioritize food security, potentially sacrificing other goals at the altar of increased yields. However, if farms are simply production zones, then embracing technological innovation to improve crop yields makes sense. From this perspective, the ethical omnivore diet, with its focus on regenerative organic agriculture, is quint. It's reflective of an earlier era of agriculture, where farmers had the luxury to care about biodiversity and animal welfare. We must push our farmland to brink, eking out every ounce of productivity they can muster.

Depending on how we define food security, improving efficiency could be the main value guiding food production. However, greater consolidation means that fewer people will have the opportunity to produce their own food and that local production systems could further fall into the hands of powerful conglomerates. As fields become larger, technologies could be employed to maximize commodity production. Alternatively, the nurturer argues that we should embrace a standard of care and prioritize the health and carrying capacity of the land. Rather than giving in to an extractive mentality, this chapter argues that the ethical omnivore diet is firmly grounded in maintaining ecological resilience. This goal isn't in conflict with food security but is necessary to maintain food production now and in the future. In short, we should eat for a healthy planet and resiliency is what's for dinner.

## Conclusion

After each chapter explores a unique facet of the ethical omnivore diet, the book ends with a call to action. Ethical omnivores embrace the idea that agricultural zones are valuable, and they think about the environmental costs of the food on their plates. Industrial agriculture might, at one point, have been able to feed the world. However, today food and agricultural systems face unprecedented stressors. As food system failures loom, consumers no longer have the luxury of ignoring the true costs of present-day consumption. The modern world demands a morality that prompts eaters to realize the true cost of today's consumption. By pushing eaters to think more critically about how their food is produced, the ethical omnivore diet is one strategy that we can use to reconnect with the wider realities of food production. It's not a perfect fix and doesn't replace the contextual expertise of farmers, but it is a first step—A step that can hopefully push eaters to think beyond habits and preferences and embrace an agrarian ethic of seeing. Understanding how and where we grow, raise, and harvest our food is the foundation of the ethical omnivore diet. These eaters have taken up the call to influence the way that we produce food and, thus what is on our plates. Beyond the plate, our decisions can change agricultural systems and even ecosystems. So, what should agriculture and our food systems look like going forward? As you practice an ethic of seeing, that is up to you. It is my hope that you find your personal vision of eating in the pages ahead. Take these pieces of advice with you, as you decide what's for dinner.

## References

Berry, Wendell. 1977. *The Unsettling of America: Culture & Agriculture*. Sierra Club Books.

Cuneo, Terence. 2015. "Conscientious Omnivorism." In *Philosophy Comes to Dinner*, edited by Andrew Chignell, Terence Cuneo, and Matthew Halteman, 22–38. New York, NY: Routledge.

Dalrymple, Laura, and Grant Hilliard. 2020. *The Ethical Omnivore: A Practical Guide and 60 Nose-to-Tail Recipes for Sustainable Meat Eating*. Sydney: Murdoch Books.

DeLind, Laura B. 2011. "Are Local Food and the Local Food Movement Taking Us Where We Want to Go? Or Are We Hitching Our Wagons to the Wrong Stars?" *Agriculture and Human Values* 28 (2): 273–83.

Donati, Kelly. 2005. "The Pleasure of Diversity in Slow Food's Ethics of Taste." *Food, Culture, and Society* 8 (2): 227–42.

Elliot, Patricia, and Amanda Raziano. 2012. *The Farm Bill and Public Health: A Primer for Public Health Professionals*. American Public Health Association. www.apha. org/-/media/files/pdf/factsheets/farm_bill_and_public_health.pdf.

FAO. 2009. *Coping with a Changing Climate: Considerations for Adaptation and Mitigation in Agriculture*. Rome, Italy: FAO.

George, Kathryn Paxton. 172AD. "So Animal a Human..., Or the Moral Relevance of Being an Omnivore." *Journal of Agricultural and Environmental Ethics* 3 (2): 1990.

Gruen, Lori, and Robert Jones. 2016. "Veganism and Aspiration." In *The Moral Complexities of Eating Meat*. Oxford: Oxford University Press.

Hargreaves, Shila, Antonio Raposo, Ariana Saraiva, and Renata Zandonadi. 2021. "Vegetarian Diet: An Overview through the Perspective of Quality of Life Domains." *International Journal of Environmental Research and Public Health* 18 (8): 4067.

Hirschman, Charles, and Elizabeth Mogford. 2009. "Immigration and the American Industrial Revolution From 1880 to 1920." *Social Science Research* 38 (4): 897–920.

Holler, Sophie, Holger Cramer, Daniela Liebscher, Michael Jeitler, Dania Schumann, Vijayendra Murthy, Andreas Michalsen, and Christian Kessler. 2021. "Differences Between Omnivores and Vegetarians in Personality Profiles, Values, and Empathy: A Systematic Review." *Frontiers in Psychology*, Oct 7 (12): 1–22.

Lamey, Andy. 2007. "Duty and the Beast." *Journal of Social Philosophy* 38 (2): 331–48.

Malhi, Gurdeep, Manpreet Kaur, and Prashant Kaushik. 2021. "Impact of Climate Change on Agriculture and Its Mitigation Strategies: A Review." *Sustainability* 13 (3): 1–17.

Milburn, Josh, and Christopher Bobier. 2022. "New Omnivorism: A Novel Approach to Food and Animal Ethics." *Food Ethics* 7 (5): 1–17.

Mozaffarian, Dariush, Irwin Rosenberg, and Ricardo Uauy. 2018. "History of Modern Nutrition Science- Implications for Current Research, Dietary Guidelines, and Food Policy." *Science and Politics of Nutrition* 2392:361.

Noll, Samantha, and Brittany Davis. 2020. "The Invasive Species Diet: The Ethics of Eating Lionfish as a Wildlife Management Strategy." *Ethics, Policy, and Environment* 23 (3): 320–35.

Noll, Samantha, and Ian Werkheiser. 2017. "Local Food Movements: Differing Conceptions of Food, People, and Change." In *Oxford Handbook of Food Ethics.*, 112–39. Oxford: Oxford University Press.

Paull, John. 2010. "From France to the World: The International Federation of Organic Agriculture Movements (IFOAM)." *Journal of Social Research & Policy* 1 (2): 93–102.

Pierre, Michelle. 2023. "Canada's Farms Are Adjusting the Ways They Sell Their Products to Consumers." Statistics Canada. www150.statcan.gc.ca/n1/pub/96-325-x/2021001/article/00014-eng.htm.

Pollan, Michael. 2006. *The Omnivore's Dilemma: A Natural History of Four Meals.* Penguin.

Rodale Institute. 2021. "The Leaders Who Founded the Organic Movement." Nonprofit Organization. *Why Organic?* (blog). 2021. https://rodaleinstitute.org/blog/leaders-organic-movement/.

Rothgerber, Hank. 2015. "Can You Have Your Meat and Eat It Too? Conscientious Omnivores, Vegetarians, and Adherence to Diet." *Appetite* 84:196–203.

Salant, Lana Joe. 2023. "#SorryNotSorry: A Message from Our Founder to Our Detractors." Ethical Omnivore Movement. www.ethicalomnivore.org/about-eom/.

Schanbacher, William D. 2010. *The Politics of Food: The Global Conflict Between Food Security and Food Sovereignty.* Santa Barbara, CA: ABC-CLIO.

Thompson, Paul. 2023. *From Silo to Spoon: Local and Global Food Ethics.* Oxford: University of Oxford.

USDA. 2020. *Organic: A Thriving Agriculture Segment.* United States Department of Agriculture. www.usda.gov/media/blog/2020/10/28/organic-thriving-agriculture-segment#:~:text=According%20to%20the%20recently%20released,there%20are%20more%20than%2016%2C500.

USDA Agricultural Marketing Service. 2013. *Organic Livestock Requirements.* U.S. Department of Agriculture. www.ams.usda.gov/sites/default/files/media/Organic%20Livestock%20Requirements.pdf.

Varner, Gary. 2002. "Can Animal Rights Activists Be Environmentalists?" In *Environmental Ethics: An Anthology*, edited by Andrew Light and Holmes Rolston III, 94–113. New York, NY: Blackwell Publishing.

Vecchio, Riccardo. 2009. "European and United States Farmers' Markets: Similarities, Differences and Potential Developments." *Presentation at the 113th EAAE Seminar "A resilient European food industry and food chain in a challenging world"*, Chania, Crete, Greece. https://core.ac.uk/download/pdf/6689734.pdf.

Voakes, Greg. 2011. "America's Obsession with Losing Weight Fast: Analyzing Google Search Data." *Business Insider*. www.businessinsider.com/americas-obsess ion-with-losing-weight-fast-analyzing-google-search-data-2011-12.

Wright, Laura. 2021. "Framing Vegan Studies." In *The Routledge Handbook of Vegan Studies*, edited by Laura Wright, 1–12. New York, NY: Routledge.

Young, Charles. 1985. "Aristotle on Temperance." *The Society for Ancient Greek Philosophy Newsletter* 125.

Zwart, Hub. 2000. "A Short History of Food Ethics." *Journal of Agricultural and Environmental Ethics* 12 (2): 113–26.

# 2

# HISTORICAL ROOTS

## A Diet Grounded in Organic Agriculture

I spent the last spring of my grandfather's life planting potatoes. With his health failing, Pop Pop (as we affectionately called him) sat in his lawn chair, supervising the family as they placed the tiny seed potatoes into the earth. It was a promise of food for the upcoming winter—one he would never live to see. But agriculture is as much about renewal, about rebirth, as it is about death. The soil connects lives. It provides sustenance and is the final destination of us all. The potatoes would feed his family, even when he could not. In many ways, the life of a modern farmer is a tragic tale. The push to increase productivity led many farming families to embrace ever more expensive technology—tractors became bigger, and farms expanded, eating their smaller neighbors. Families lost their way of life and their way. My grandfather's own father lost his farm, as the big city bankers drove into the country, with their auctioneers in tow. This man, my great grandfather, died of a broken heart—Literally, of a heart attack. My Pop Pop, still heartbroken himself by that loss, fed his family from the few acres behind the family home, until his strength gave out and he could no longer tend to his garden.

This pattern of bankruptcy and consolidation is common in the farm-belt surrounding Philadelphia (where I'm from) and in most rural communities in the United States and beyond. Writing in 1977, Wendell Berry warned of the increasing human costs of industrialization. He argued that new industrial agricultural practices of his day determined that farmers were easily replaceable parts of the system, a change made in the name of greater efficiency. Berry (1977) lamented the hyper focus on productivity, rather than long-term sustainability. Better two bushels now then one bushel for the foreseeable future, especially when one bushel can be sent overseas as aid or sold for corporate profit. Over-industrialization is leading to the

DOI: 10.4324/9781003215189-2

loss of balanced farming methods guided by other goals, such as increasing sustainability, supporting biodiversity levels, improving drought resistance, and protecting farmers from economic failure. Berry (1977) predicted that we would see a loss of skills necessary for renewal—for ensuring a truly sustainable agricultural practice. With the agriculture landscape changing so dramatically, he feared that without an informed and engaged urban population, sustainable agriculture would be unattainable in the future. As agricultural machines grow bigger, there was an absence of moral restraint. Diets are about more than choice. They are connected to the way that we grow our food.

Ethical omnivores have taken up the call to influence the way that we produce food and, thus what is on our plates. Today, thoughtful eaters are embracing Berry's (1977) call to learn about and change agricultural systems. The twin commitments: (a) to know what's happening on farms and (b) to demand that food be produced in an environmentally friendly and equitable manner are the cornerstones of the ethical omnivore diet. In many ways, both the local food movement, made up of eaters committed to supporting local farmers by buying regionally produced goods, and the ethical omnivore movement, are reactions to changes in the way modern farming is done. While the agricultural policies that Berry critiqued galvanized farmers to grow more food than ever before, these same policies also produced troubling social and environmental impacts—impacts that include the loss of family farms, the degradation of soils, the overcrowding of domesticated animals into ever smaller enclosures, and an increased use of pesticides, herbicides, and fertilizers. One of the key goals of ethical omnivorism as a movement, is to galvanize urban, suburban, and rural communities to help transform agriculture in positive ways, beyond merely increasing production. Their major concerns echo Berry's, as they recognize that the people who grow our food are not replaceable and how we grow our food matters. But to understand why ethical omnivores call for change, we need to first place the movement in historical context.

## A Brief History of Industrial Agriculture

Agriculture underwent tremendous transformation during the 20th century (Dimitri et al 2005). Earlier agricultural methods were labor-intensive and took place on many small farms in rural areas, though some food was produced in urban areas, mainly using greenhouses. In the United States, these small farms employed over half the total workforce, and housed approximately 22 million working animals. Despite their small size, farms were also highly diversified and produced several different types of commodities, such as vegetables, fruit, tree nuts, as well as field crops, dairy, and meat products. Rural areas were dotted with several thriving family farms that, in turn, supported bustling small towns, which offered various services to farmers. However, during the 21st century, these compact, diversified farms gave way to a small number of large, specialized farms, which employ a tiny fraction of the labor force. For example, today the average size of an U.S. farm is 446 acres and direct on-farm employment accounts for roughly 1.3% of U.S. employment (USDA 2022). These larger farms typically focus on producing a handful of crops, such as corn, soybeans, wheat, dairy products, meat, etc. In many parts of the United States, it's common to drive through rural areas and be surrounded by monocrop fields of wheat or corn, as far as the eye can see.

Wendell Berry (1977) was writing at the tail end of this transformation, when a handful of workers armed with a fleet of over 5 million tractors replaced the massive number of humans, horses, and mules needed to tend farms. Due to this transformation, agriculture became increasingly efficient and fruitful. From a production standpoint, new farming innovations were a resounding success. In the 1800s, farmers grew enough food to feed approximately three to five people (Dimitri et al. 2005). Today, farmers produce enough food and fiber for between 150 and 168 people, depending on which source you look at (American Farm Bureau 2023). This increase is incredible. It frees a large share of the population from farm work, allowing them to contribute to the economy in other ways. In addition, consumers spend a much smaller portion of their income on food, helping feed families and increase food security. This sector is also a major contributor to the economy, as agriculture and food related industries contributed $1.264 trillion (or 5.4%) to U.S. gross domestic product in 2021 (USDA 2023). So much food is produced that agricultural exports reached a record $177 billion in 2021, as excess soybeans, corn, beef, and other products were sold overseas (Good 2022). The agriculture sector has become a cash cow, so to speak, for the handful of producers and companies at the top. However, these profits are not equally distributed among farming communities. Paradoxically, greater efficiency in agriculture has come at a time when farm and ranch families are facing a great extinction (Semuels 2019) and when rural communities face unprecedented food insecurity.

Thus, there are also downsides to increasing farming efficiency, as well. While we produce more food than ever before, around 34 million people (10.2%) are food insecure, with another 53 million people turning to food banks and community programs to put food on the table (NIHCM 2023). In the United States, rural communities make up 87% of counties with the highest rates of food insecurity (Feeding America 2023; Pointak and Schulman 2014). It Is surprising that hunger is a problem in areas producing more food than at any other time in history. What is also surprising is that changes in agriculture production and policy contributed to food insecurity in rural areas. Consumer access to foodstuffs is largely mediated through market-based mechanisms, rather than through production. What this means is that when people lose their jobs or have little cash, they often do not have the resources needed to purchase food through the market. The economist Amartya Sen (1981) argues that most famines occur when communities can't access commodity bundles (i.e., foodstuffs) through market-based mechanisms (Devereux 2001). In short, hunger is often not caused by a lack of food, as we produce massive amounts, but rather by barriers to accessing this food. A great example of this happened during the Dust Bowl of the 1930s, a period where removing prairie grasses in the Great Plains region led to severe dust storms, ecological devastation, and agricultural collapse (Lee and Gill 2015). Low crop prices combined with high machinery costs caused farmers to abandon soil conservation practices to stay afloat. However, as the market corrected due to an overabundance of commodities on the market, farmers eventually went out of business. In a time of exploding production rates, these farmers and their families simply didn't have the money to purchase food, or the commodity bundles necessary to live. People starved to death, as crops rotted in granaries. Environmental devastation followed shortly after.

However, when you live in a farm producing a diverse array of commodities, food is available even if you are cash poor. For example, when over 20% of the population was unemployed during the Great Depression from 1929 to 1939 (Margo 1993), many farming families weathered food insecurity better than others, simply because they produce their own foodstuffs. My own grandparents spun tales about the ingenuity of family members during this time, as they made do with what could be gleaned from the land. Luckily, sustainable agriculture practices are a cornerstone of Pennsylvania Dutch farming methods (Paoletti 1989), and thus saved us from ecological catastrophe, such as discussed above. In addition, many farms hadn't fully transitioned into monocrop operations yet, so they produced several different types of commodities. This diversity provided a much-needed safety net for farmers, as they could fall back on eating their own crops, rather than relying on market mechanisms to access primary goods, or those needed to survive. Producing one crop might be efficient but it also places farmers in a position where they are at the mercy of economic forces beyond their control. In addition, larger tractors and other farming technologies might be necessary to increase production, but hefty bank loans could spell disaster in lean times. In this way, smaller, more diversified farms were more resilient, or better able to weather harsh economic cycles. As my grandfather would say, while tending his garden, "you can't eat feed corn." Thus, while these farming communities were cash poor, they were food rich.

But agriculture was changing across the United States. Consolidation of farms continued unabated after World War II (1939–1945) until today, where many farmers are no longer on their land. My own family lost three farms during this time-period, and we were lucky to survive into the 1990s. Many others weren't so lucky. Wendell Berry (1977) was very worried that the agricultural landscape was changing in ways harmful to rural communities. Most notably, he was highly critical of Earl Butz, the Secretary of Agriculture from 1971 to 1976 under Presidents Richard Nixon and Gerald Ford. Butz made major changes to federal agricultural policy, revising many New Deal farm support programs. For instance, farmers were paid to not plant crops on all their acres to prevent a national oversupply of commodities and thus falling market prices (Imhoff 2007). In a drastic reversal of this policy, Butz urged farmers to plant commodity crops "from fencerow to fencerow," and pushed greater mechanization in the agricultural sector. He famously stated that farmers should "get big or get out," in response to the plight of small-scale producers due to these changes (Wurtz 2023, 1). These policy responses were a result of rising food prices in the United States and increasing global demands for food products and humanitarian aid (Pollan 2006). The changes during Butz' tenure led to increased agricultural production and falling food prices. However, family farms paid the ultimate price for cheap food, as their financial stability declined, and their numbers fell rapidly. According to Berry, the intentional dismantling of price controls and economic protections for farmers allowed large farms to flood the market with cheap commodities, driving small farms out of business (Wurtz 2023). Governmental priorities were loud and clear, as protecting family farms gave way to increasing productivity. This shift also (intentionally or not) coincided with the rise of agribusiness companies taking advantage of the farming boom of the 1970s.

The amount of family farms lost since World War II is hard to conceptualize, due to the sheer numbers involved. Agricultural employment declined by 2 million people in the 1960s (Daly 1981). Losses slowed over the years, but the farming sector continued to shrink, especially with producers growing old and not being replaced by younger farmers. (The average age of a farmer was 57 years old in 2021.) There are several reasons, beyond policy changes, that led to the loss of family farms. First, as already discussed, farming technologies became bigger and more expensive, causing many family farms to go bankrupt when they couldn't pay back loans needed to upgrade. In addition, others simply fell-off the agricultural "technology treadmill," as they waited to adopt new technologies that increased yield, efficiency, etc. This term describes how advances that improve productivity also results in increased supply, falling prices, and economic harm for farmers slow to embrace agricultural innovations (Ward 1993). Profit margins are tight in farming and even small drops in prices could spell disaster for farming families.

Second, the shift from diversified farms to monocrop farming is another potential pitfall. On the surface, specializing is great for efficiency and seems like it would be beneficial. However, while focusing on growing a few crops increases efficiency, this also increases risk for farmers. When you're growing a diverse array of commodities and a crop fails, you have other products to fall back on. But when margins are tight and you're producing a single commodity, a failed harvest or even a small decrease in yield could spell disaster for a family farm. Greater efficiency garnered through consolidation of farmlands and crops translates to greater risk being placed on the shoulders of producers. Risk is compounded, as agriculture relies on fickle weather patterns. As farms are lost, rural towns are also lost. With smaller farms being subsumed into larger ones, there are fewer citizens to support rural towns, leaving many to wither and die. The current rural landscape is dotted with dying towns, monuments to farm efficiency.

While the transformation of agriculture is seen as a win for national economies, it was also harmful for many families like mine, as well as the environment. Wendell Berry (1977) argues that these negative impacts can at least partially be attributed to a shift in identity for farmers. He claims that modern agriculture is like strip-mining, where agricultural "operators" have forsaken the role of nurturer and instead have taken up the mantel of exploiter. Efficiency is modern agriculture's siren call, and the goal of many farmers, and especially agri-business, is money and profit. Speaking to this point, Berry argues that "the exploiter asks of a piece of land only how much and how quickly it can be made to produce… [and] wishes to earn as much as possible by as little work as possible" (7). These words might sound overly critical, but farms are getting bigger, becoming more highly specialized, and are organized to increase efficiency and productivity. In contrast, the old-fashioned farming ideal was that of steward of the land, or nurturer, so that both humans and nature thrived. In this vision, if the soil, plants, and animals are healthy, then they will produce more. Thus, it is a win–win for the farmer and the farm. My grandfather always said that if you take care of the land, then the land will take care of you. The nurturer recognizes that families only thrive when the land thrives. As family farms are generational affairs, this means taking care of the farm with an eye towards long-term sustainability, as future generations depend on the environmental health and productivity of the farm. The philosopher Bernie Rollin (1995) echoed this sentiment, when he argued that a historical ethic built on self-interest permeated the social ethos. Historically, a large percentage of populations engaged in food production, anchoring their very lives to the ground they worked and called home. In an inverse of what my grandfather said, Rollin stresses the harsh realities of farming. If you treat your farm badly, your animals will sicken, and you'll go hungry. All agriculture relies on ecosystem services. If these are disrupted, then food crops will fail.

## Environmental and Human Health Impacts

These worries set the tone for many discussions concerning current agriculture practices. As farming changed and began to embrace the mantra of efficiency, critics became increasingly concerned about mounting environmental harms.

According to the United Nations Environment Programme (2023), "the low retail cost of industrialized food can obscure its very high environmental price tag" (1). It's not the bargain it seems. When we buy that conventionally grown apple at the store, few of us think about the externalized costs that were not considered when pricing that item. According to some estimates, industrialized farming pollutes water and air, destroys wildlife, and produces greenhouse gas emissions. These environmental costs are the equivalent of approximately $3 trillion dollars yearly. As they are externalized costs, or costs which are unaccounted for by the industry, taxpayers, and local communities are often left to pick up the tab, so to speak. In addition, new research shows that certain pesticides, herbicides, and other agricultural compounds used in crop production could cause intergenerational harms, or harms suffered by future generations (Korolenko et al. 2023). In other words, choices made on the farm today could damage genetic material, and your children's children might be less healthy going forward. That's quite the externalized cost.

Production choices are incredibly important and have far-reaching consequences. A recent article published in *Science* looked at nearly 40,000 farms and 1600 processers and packaging companies (Poore and Nemecek 2018). The authors found that where and how we produce food can drastically influence the overall environmental impacts of the 40 major food products that they analyzed. In this vein, Joseph Poore says:

> two things that look the same in the shops can have extremely different impacts on the planet. We currently don't know this when we make choices about what to eat. Further, this variability isn't fully reflected in strategies and policy aimed at reducing the impacts of farmers.
>
> *(Oxford News 2018, 1)*

You might think that apples are all the same, for example, but production practices and geographic location matter. One could be produced using high concentrations of pesticides or in areas where irrigation is needed, while another could be produced in an area with enough rainfall to make irrigation unnecessary. A common rule of thumb to live a more environmentally friendly life is to eat less beef, as cows produce a lot of $CO_2$, a greenhouse gas that contributes to climate change. High-impact beef producers (or those using methods with a large ecological footprint) use more land and create 12–50 times more $CO_2$ than low-impact producers, for example (Poore and Nemecek 2018). There is a strong case that beans, peas, and other plant-based protein sources are more environmentally friendly, as they create very little $CO_2$ and use less land to produce. But being careful to only buy products produced using low-impact methods is also important. Even how we produce low-impact crops could make a big difference in the long run, as every little bit helps. For all the beer lovers reading this, one pint of beer could use four times more land and create three times more emissions, depending on how it is produced. Thus, it's not enough to simply purchase products that may have a lower environmental impact, as it's very difficult for eaters to determine what those impacts are. In short, buying specific products doesn't guarantee that you're supporting sustainable or environmentally healthy practices. The production side of things matter and greatly impacts whether you're actually reducing ecological harm or eating for a small planet.

Ethical omnivores are concerned about the environmental impacts of agriculture. This commitment is clearly expressed by those who embrace this diet. It is not uncommon for them to state that they "stand for a way of living that's kind, healthy, and sustainable" (Salant 2023). According to Lana Joe Salant (2023), the founder of ethicalomnivore.org, "the ethical omnivore movement is a fast grown group of people all around the world who believe that the most natural, ethical, and healthy lifestyle should include local, organic, and humanely reared food" (n.p.). If we want to eat with an eye towards improving human health, animal welfare, and environmental sustainability, then we should be very concerned about agriculture. They advocate for eating products that are local, organically produced, and sourced in sustainable ways. The next chapter provides an in-depth overview of the normative foundations of this movement, but it is important to note here that an ecological orientation is built into the diet. They want us to think long and hard about how our food is produced and only consume foodstuffs produced in sustainable ways. This call to be mindful reminds me of Berry's argument that we should push back against agricultural systems where farmers take on the role of an exploiter. Instead, we need to return to the ideal of the farmer as nurturer, where human and ecological health are more important than increasing overall yield.

For Berry (1977), the farmer as nurturer is worried about carrying capacity of the land. This is an ecological orientation that pushes us to ask what is the number of people, crops, and other living organisms that can be supported without environmental degradation. Carrying capacity is foundational in conservation science, and natural resource management. For example, Gifford Pinchot (1865–1946), the first head of the United States Forestry Service, established our modern definition of conservation, where wise land-use involves "using the earth and its resources for the lasting good of men" (Clayton 2019). In other words, we should use land sustainably, so that future generations can enjoy its fruits. Poor land-use occurs when you exploit the land, allowing any benefits to degrade or be lost for future generations. But, as farmers often say, sustainability should also include farmer livelihood. Good stewards of the land shouldn't be forced from it, in an effort to improve overall efficiency. Understanding the ecological rhythms of place demands that people spend time on the farm. Standardizing farming so that uniform methods can be applied no matter the context may increase productivity, but it also reduces situated ecological knowledge. Earl Butz' policies (and the removal of New Deal productions for family farms) had the effect, intentional or not, of removing stewards from the land. Thus, Berry's nurturer ideal cares about earning a living while farming, as this ensures that their family keeps their farm, but they also serve their community, land, and place.

What we have here are two competing visions of what the ideal farmer should be and what values should guide food production: The nurturer or exploiter. Modern agricultural policy is underscored by a zealous commitment to consumer culture and to increasing U.S. power abroad, through food aid and capturing a larger market share. Wurtz (2023) stated this well, when he argued the following: "For Butz, the depopulation of the countryside meant increased efficiency in production and less farmers to pay" (n.p.). He saw lowering food prices as a way for middle-class United States to save money and enjoy previously unachievable levels of affluence. The livelihoods of farming families were an acceptable price to pay for citizens to have "built-in maid service" and multiple television sets. As the statistics concerning hunger in the U.S. attest, this age of opulence never came. Yet, rural United States is dying, as the nation lost another 100,000 farms between 2011 and 2018. This great extinction prompted some of the few farmers left standing to argue that they are "trying to wipe us off the map" (Semuels 2019, n.p.). In contrast to increasing productivity, ethical omnivores ask us to step back and think about the larger social and environmental consequences of how we farm. They ask us to think about how we can balance food security and cheap food prices with other goals, such as paying local farmers fair wages and improving long-term environmental sustainability. They want us to think deeply about the environmental costs of increasing productivity and how current practices could impact our ability to feed future generations. Ethical omnivores embrace the nurturer ideal and have built an entire diet around it.

## A Diet Grounded in Organic Agriculture

Ethical omnivores are committed to pushing back against exploitative types of agriculture, while supporting sustainable, healthy, and thoughtful food production. The interplay between consumption and production, between the field and the fork, can be traced back to the historical roots of the diet. In particular, it has deep roots in The Organic Movement, which promotes sustainable and healthy agricultural production methods. As industrial agricultural practices began to be widely adopted, critics provided a counterpoint to the changes discussed previously, with the creation of this movement (Conford 2001). The Rodale Institute (2023) captures its ethos well, when they state in their mission that natural, organic agricultural methods were the norm for as long as people have been farming, but the rise of chemical-based industrial agriculture fundamentally altered the way that we produce food (n.p). Mechanization, and increasingly corporatized conventional farms make ample use of artificial pesticides, herbicides, and fertilizers specifically designed to reduce labor, while increasing crop yields. These changes are leading to a food and agricultural crisis. In their words:

> we have failed to recognize the unintended consequences of conventional, chemical-based farming practices. Soil health degradation, loss of organic matter and erosion, as well as water pollution, toxic residues in our food supply, and lack of biodiversity — to name a few. We have also failed to recognize what is at stake. If we continue on this path, there will soon come a time when our soil gives out and we will be unable to feed our children and grandchildren
>
> *(Rodale Institute 2023, n.p.)*

Thankfully, though, there are many ways to produce food and we can embrace more responsible ways of farming, centered on ecological sustainability and human health. The Rodale Institute is only one of the several voices trying to bring about positive and transformative change. Connectedly, their mission statement highlights how The Organic Movement is a response to changes in agriculture after World War II, as well as the wholesale adoption of large-scale production methods. Important advances in biochemistry and agricultural technology during the beginning of the 20th century ushered in a period of rapid change for farming. As we discussed, affordable nitrogen fertilizers, new pesticides (such as DDT), and abundant and large advances in mechanization transformed daily operations on the farm. These innovations heralded in an age where a single farmer can now feed over 150 people (American Farm Bureau 2023).

The Organic Movement was historically made up of figures dedicated to preserving alternative agricultural methods, grounded in holistic visions of food production (Conford 2001). At the beginning of the 20th century, a small group of farmers worldwide were concerned about negative consequences to the land, soils, animal populations, and human communities. Key figures in this movement included George Washington Carver, Lady Eve Balfour, and Sir Albert Howard (Rodale Institute 2021). Later leaders crystalized themes and lessons from these early figures into powerful critiques of late 20th-century farming methods. For example, the Indian scholar and environmental activist Vandana Shiva is highly critical of industrial agriculture, as practiced in her country. Shiva (1988) states the following: For industrial methods "nature is unproductive; organic agriculture based on nature's cycles of renewability spells poverty... because it is assumed that 'production' takes place only when mediated by technologies for commodity production, even when such technologies destroy" (2). Shiva's critique harkens back to Berry's concerns, especially his juxtaposition of efficiency with care. For both thinkers, efficiency ultimately feeds the goal of profit and money, while care involves ensuring the health of the land, community, and self. Thus, any benefits that industrial agriculture produces should be weighed against the environmental, community, and health costs of increasing efficiency.

Shiva and Berry were writing about farming nearly 100 years after The Organic Movement was founded, but their analyses encapsulate key themes driving alternative production today. Both early and late organicists agree that alternative models need to be nurtured to help promote diverse visions of what food production can look like. To help promote these alternatives, concerned farmers worldwide formed associations during the mid-20th century, such as the Australian Organic Farming and Gardening Society, the Soil Association of the United Kingdom, as well as the Rodale Institute. In 1972, the International Federation of Organic Agriculture Movements was created (Paull 2010). Today, this umbrella organization represents approximately 800 affiliate organizations in 117 countries. Many passionate individuals, groups, and communities laid the groundwork for a holistic vision of agricultural production—a vision that was meant to challenge and provide alternatives for industrial models.

Before we dive into what this vision entails, it is important to remember that traditional agricultural practices from around the world are examples of organic production. Many of these methods are still used today and greatly inform current regenerative farming priorities and techniques. In the United States, Indigenous populations embraced holistic land management, that often relied on crop rotation, companion crop planting, terracing, and other sustainable methods. A common illustration of holistic farming is the Three Sisters Garden, which is practiced by several tribes across North America (Eames-Sheavly 1993). Corn is planted with beans to provide support for the climbing vines. Squash is also planted to provide shade, act as a living mulch, and deter pests. Using a similar strategy, Mayan agricultural methods are also being used today throughout Central America (Ford and Nigh 2010). Like the Three Sisters, "Milpa" forest agriculture is a companion crop growing method, where a variety of plants are cultivated together. It is sustainable, self-sustaining, and designed to produce large yields of foodstuffs in harmony with surrounding ecosystems. In India, farmers developed a food production system called Vedic agriculture, where soil health plays a central role. In this system, integrating plant and livestock cultivation improves the quality and health of the soil yearly (Rodale Institute 2021). A key lesson to take from these examples is that The Organic Movement utilizes knowledge developed over thousands of years and is clearly indebted to traditional agricultural systems used around the world. As The Rodale Institute (2021) so eloquently stated: "Today, regenerative organic agriculture seeks to bring that balance to the forefront once more, renewing agriculture under a philosophy built on thousands of years of ancestral knowledge from all over the world" (n.p.).

This debt is clearly visible when we recognize the connection between early founders of The Organic Movement and long practiced regenerative systems.

Sir Albert Howard's career highlights The Organic Movement's indebtedness to traditional practices. Howard was a well-respected English botanist who worked in India as an agricultural advisor (Conford 2001). Working alongside the botanist Gabrielle Matthaei, he was originally tasked with improving food production methods in Indore. During the many years he spent working with local farmers, Howard realized that local rather than Western techniques provided substantial benefits, such as the improvement of plant health and an increase in crop resilience to drought, pests, and disease. One important take-away from his observations was that there are connections between healthy communities, soil, livestock, and crops. He argued that there is a connection between healthy soil and healthy populations. Medical professionals and health-conscious eaters ignore agriculture at their peril. In 1943, he published the book *An Agricultural Testament*, which provided part of the foundation for the early Organic Movement.

Other founders followed Howard's lead, spending years and entire careers collecting scientific evidence to support organic farming. For example, in 1939, the English farmer Lady Eve Balfour became interested in alternatives to chemical agriculture and put her theories to the test (Conford 2001). With the experienced farm manager Alice Debenham, she purchased and modernized Walnut Tree farm, an 80-acre farm that was a victim of the depression. Balfour was familiar with compost-based farming and launched the first long-term, side-by-side scientific comparison of organic and chemical-based farming. The study was called The Haughley Experiment. It involved dividing 216 acres into three sections, each using a unique combination of inorganic and organic fertilizers. In 1943, Balfour published the results in *The Living Soil*, which explained the experiment and echoed the claim that there are links between healthy soil and human health. In this work, she argues that "we cannot safely separate human health from the health of farm produce whether animal or vegetable. All have their origin in a fertile soil" (quoted in Rodale Institute 2021, n.p.). The Haughley Experiment was an inspiration for Rodale Institute's comparisons of conventional and organic farming methods, which began in 1981 and continues to this day.

This research helped to cement organic agriculture as a major force in agricultural science communities. Prior to the 1970s, few scientists would even consider doing serious research out of fear of ridicule and damage to their careers (Kuepper 2010). The research above, along with the 1980 USDA evaluation of organic farming, helped to improve organic's reputation. This report included interviews of farmers in the United States and Europe, and supported the claim that organic farming provides environmental benefits. The Organic Foods Production Act passed in 1990 and today organic labels are commonly found in grocery stores across the country. According to the

USDA, there are at least 3.6 million acres of certified organic cropland, and retail sales of organic produce reached 52 billion in 2021 (USDA 2023). This is good news for farmers. Studies have shown that organic farmers are likely to be younger and of diverse backgrounds. There are substantial retail price premiums for these products, which helps producers stay economically viable, even when the market for conventional crops is tight. Also, a large percentage of small-scale farms have opted into organic production and tend to embrace environmentally sustainable practices more readily than large farms (Liebert et al. 2022). As smaller operations tend to produce products for local consumption, they have outsized impacts on local communities. According to the economist Luanne Lohr (2002), organic farms "contribute more to local economies through total sales, net revenue, farm value, taxes paid, and purchases" and "give more support to rural development with higher percentages of full-time farmers, greater direct to consumer sales, more workers hired, and higher worker pay" (1). Farming is hard at the best of times, but The Organic Movement is creating alternative paths for farmers, beyond the "get big or get out" mentality of mainstream agriculture.

### The Ethical Omnivore: A Diet Is Born

In important ways, Wendell Berry is getting what he yearned for in the 1970s. We are living in an age with a more informed urban constituency that is worried about agricultural impacts to human health, local communities, and the environment. These worries are reflected in the literature on why people buy organic. Studies have shown that "healthfulness" is the main reason why eaters buy these products (Howie 2004; Dimitri and Nessa 2000). However, healthfulness can and does mean many things when we're discussing agriculture. More specifically, consumers are increasingly confident that organic foodstuffs are healthier and more environmentally friendly. They're also concerned that there are higher environmental and personal health risks associated with what is now called the "conventional" food system (Van Huy et al. 2019). Echoing the founders of The Organic Movement, consumers believe that eating healthy food is key for maintaining healthy people and communities. According to the horticulturalist George Kuepper (2010), "since most food originates with the soil, they naturally promoted a method of growing that was based on soil health and vibrancy... They believed that soils thus managed would yield more nutritious food" (4).

However, it should be briefly noted that the nutritional superiority of organic produce is a controversial claim, where experts are clearly divided on the issue. In the article *Nutritional Quality of Organic Foods: A Systematic Review* (Dangour 2009), the authors argue that there is no nutritional difference between conventional and organic foods. In contrast, other research shows that organic foods contain more antioxidants (Benbrook 2009). While still other studies show that customers who eat organic foodstuffs have lower exposure to pesticides, potentially causing less harm to the human body, though health benefits are contested (Mesnage et al. 2020). The claim isn't surprising, as organic production systems avoid the use of synthetic chemicals, though other inputs are used. In contrast, environmental benefits are more widely accepted. Modern organic production is understood as "an ecological production management system that promotes and enhances biodiversity, biological cycles, and soil biological activity. It is based on minimal use of off-farm inputs and on management practices that restore, maintain, and enhance ecological harmony" (Winter and Davis 2006). With this definition in mind, it is again not surprising that environmentally conscious eaters are opting to eat organic foodstuffs.

When placed in this larger context, the ethical omnivore movement is the other side of the organic coin, so to speak. It is a movement that asks *eaters* (rather than producers) to be mindful about how their food is produced and to think deeply about the consequences of decisions made on the farm. When grappling with the question "what should I eat?" they embrace a diet where products can be: (a) traced back to an organic farm and that (b) are sustainably and ethically raised and harvested. While The Organic Movement desires to change production systems, the ethical omnivore movement galvanizes eaters to care and to support this change with their wallets and their plates. There are three commitments that ethical omnivores have inherited from The Organic Movement—commitments that form the ethical foundation of both. If you've made it to this point in the chapter, you probably already know what these are. Food should be produced in ways aimed at improving human, environmental, and community health. This is what's at stake when ethical omnivores pronounce that they're embracing a diet where products should be traced back to an organic farm and that are ethically produced. At its root, these normative concerns are all about reducing harm. We need to be mindful that agriculture has far reaching consequences and we should reduce harms, when possible, at the level of the individual, community, and environment. The English philosopher John Stuart Mill famously argued that the actions of individuals should only be limited when these actions harm others. This is known as the "harm principle." Ethical omnivores have taken this principle to heart, embracing the commitment to reduce harm, when possible, in food systems.

## Conclusion

This chapter provided an overview of ethical omnivorism's historical roots. As we've seen, placing the movement in context is important for understanding why it developed and what supporters care about. Both the ethical omnivore and organic movement are critical of industrial agriculture and their commitments reflect specific concerns with how food is produced. Ethical omnivore's dietary obligations align with The Organic Movements' alternative vision of agriculture. For ethical omnivores, it matters whether farmers are exploiting the land or trying to live up to the ideal of the nurturer. It matters whether we are causing ecological damage and impacting our ability to feed future generations. It matters whether family farms and rural communities are paying the price for cheap food. Food ethicists rarely engage with ethical omnivorism, and when they do, they tend to focus on one of these three commitments, while ignoring others. This is a mistake. For example, the philosophers Terence Cuneo (2015), as well as Josh Milburn and Christopher Bobier (2022) drill down into the diet's commitment to eating animal products, if humanely produced. In contrast, Kathryn Paxton George (1990), digs into human health concerns, arguing that omnivore diets are ethically acceptable, when they align with improving the health and wellbeing of eaters. Other accounts focus on environmental commitments that guide both the diet and movement. These writers each fail to fully realize the scope of ethical concerns associated with agriculture and thus miss important aspects of the diet. My grandfather would appreciate the fact that consumers are beginning to care about the plight of farmers. I certainly do. As Wendell Berry (1977) argued all those years ago, "sane and healthy agriculture requires an informed urban constituency" (xi). Only by placing ethical omnivorism into context can we truly understand what is at stake, when making food choices. The next chapter will explore the normative commitments of the ethical omnivore movement more deeply, to better understand its ethical implications.

## References

American Farm Bureau Federation. 2023. *Fast Facts About Agriculture & Food*. www.fb.org/newsroom/fast-facts.

Benbrook, C. 2009. *Organic Center Response to the FSA Study*. The Organic Center. www.organiccenter.org/science.nutri.php?action= view&report_id=157.

Berry, Wendell. 1977. *The Unsettling of America: Culture & Agriculture*. Sierra Club Books.

Clayton, John. 2019. *Natural Rivals: John Muir, Gifford Pinchot, and the Creation of America's Public Lands*. New York, NY: Pegasus Books.

Conford, Philip. 2001. *The Origins of the Organic Movement*. Glasgow: Floris Books.

Cuneo, Terence. 2015. "Conscientious Omnivorism." In *Philosophy Comes to Dinner*, edited by Andrew Chignell, Terence Cuneo, and Matthew Halteman, 22–38. New York, NY: Routledge.

Daly, Patricia. 1981. "Agricultural Employment: Has the Decline Ended?" *Monthly Labor Review*, 11–17.

Dangour, A.D., Sakhi Dodhia, Arabella Hayter, Elizabeth Allen, Karen Lock, and Ricardo Uauy. 2009. "Nutritional Quality of Organic Foods: A Systematic Review." *The American Journal of Clinical Nutrition* 90 (3): 68–685.

Devereux, Stephen. 2001. "Sen's Entitlement Approach: Critiques and Counter-Critiques." *Oxford Development Studies* 29 (3): 245–63.

Dimitri, Carolyn, Anne Effland, and Neilson Conklin. 2005. *The 20th Century Transformation of U.S. Agriculture and Farm Policy*. United States Department of Agriculture: Economic Research Services. www.ers.usda.gov/webdocs/publicati ons/44197/13566_eib3_1_.pdf.

Dimitri, Carolyn, and Nessa Richman. 2000. "Organic Food Markets in Transition." *Policy Studies Report No. 14*.

Eames-Sheavly, Marcia. 1993. *The Three Sisters: Exploring an Iroquois Garden*. Ithaca, NY: The Cornell Cooperative Extension Publication.

Feeding America. 2023. *Hunger in Rural Communities*. Feeding America. www.fee dingamerica.org/hunger-in-america/rural-hunger-facts.

Ford, Anabel, and Ronald Nigh. 2010. "The Milpa Cycle and the Making of the Maya Forest Garden." *Research Reports in Belizean Archaeology* 7: 183–90.

George, Kathyrn Paxton. 1990. "So Animal a Human..., Or the Moral Relevance of Being an Omnivore." *Journal of Agricultural and Environmental Ethics* 3 (2): 172–86..

Good, Keith. 2022. *2021 U.S. Ag Exports Highest on Record, Corn the Primary Contributor*. University of Illinois. https://farmpolicynews.illinois.edu/2022/04/ 2021-u-s-ag-exports-highest-on-record-corn-the-primary-contributor/.

Howie, Michael. 2004. *Industry Study on Why Millions of Americans Are Buying Organic Foods*. Organic Consumers Association. www.organic- consumers.org/ organic/millions033004.cfm?>.

Imhoff, Daniel. 2007. *Food Fight: The Citizens Guide to a Food and Farm Bill*. Healdsburg, CA: Watershed Media.

Korolenko, Alexandra, Samantha Noll, and Michael Skinner. 2023. "Epigenetic Inheritance and Transgenerational Environmental Justice." *Yale Journal of Biology and Medicine* 96: 241–50.

Kuepper, George. 2010. "A Brief Overview of the History and Philosophy of Organic Agriculture." *Kerr Center for Sustainable Agriculture*, 1–23.

Lee, Jeffrey, and Thomas Gill. 2015. "Multiple Causes of Wind Erosion in the Dust Bowl." *Aeolian Research* 19: 15–36.

Liebert, Jeffrey, Rebecca Benner, Rachel Kerr, Thomas Bjorkman, Kathryn De Master, Sasha Gennet, Miguel Gomez, Abigail Hart, Alison Power, and Matthew Ryan. 2022. "Farm Size Affects the Use of Agroecological Practices on Organic Farms in the United States." *Nature Plants* 8: 897–905.

Lohr, Luanne. 2002. "Benefits of U.S. Organic Agriculture." *MPRA* 24327: 1–18.

Margo, Robert. 1993. "Employment and Unemployment in the 1930s." *Journal of Economic Perspectives* 7 (2): 41–59.

Mesnage, Robin, Ioannis Tsakiris, and Michael Antoniou. 2020. "Limitations in the Evidential Basis Supporting Health Benefits from a Decreased Exposure to Pesticides Through Organic Food Consumption." *Current Opinion in Toxicology* 19: 50–55.

Milburn, Josh, and Christopher Bobier. 2022. "New Omnivorism: A Novel Approach to Food and Animal Ethics." *Food Ethics* 7 (5): 1–17.

NIHCM Foundation. 2023. *Hunger in America*. NIHCM Foundation. https://nihcm. org/publications/hunger-in-america.

Oxford News and Events. 2018. *New Estimates of the Environmental Cost of Food*. University of Oxford. www.ox.ac.uk/news/2018-06-01-new-estimates-enviro nmental-cost-food.

Paoletti, Maurizio. 1989. "In Search of Traditional Farm Wisdom for a More Sustainable Agriculture: A Study of Amish Farming and Society." *Agriculture, Ecosystems & Environment* 27: 77–90.

Paull, John. 2010. "From France to the World: The International Federation of Organic Agriculture Movements (IFOAM)." *Journal of Social Research & Policy* 1 (2): 93–102.

Piontak, Joy, and Michael Schulman. 2014. "Food Insecurity in Rural America." *Contexts* 13 (3): 75–77. https://doi.org/10.1177/1536504214545766.

Pollan, Michael. 2006. *The Omnivore's Dilemma: A Natural History of Four Meals*. Penguin.

Poore, J, and T Nemecek. 2018. "Reducing Food's Environmental Impacts Through Producers and Consumers." *Science* 360 (6392): 987–92.

Rodale Institute. 2021. "The Leaders Who Founded the Organic Movement." Nonprofit Organization. Why Organic? (blog). 2021. https://rodaleinstitute.org/blog/leaders-organic-movement/.

Rodale Institute. 2023. *Our Story*. Rodale Institute. https://rodaleinstitute.org/about/our-story/.

Rollin, Bernard. 1995. *Farm Animal Welfare: Social, Bioethical, and Research Issues*. Ames, IA: Iowa State Press.

Salant, Lana Joe. 2023. *About the Ethical Omnivore Movement*. Ethical Omnivore Movement. www.ethicalomnivore.org/about-eom/.

Semuels, Alana. 2019. *'They're Trying to Wipe Us Off the Map.' Small American Farmers Are Nearing Extinction*. Time Magazine. https://time.com/5736789/small-american-farmers-debt-crisis-extinction/.

Sen, Amartya. 1981. "Ingredients of Famine Analysis: Availability and Entitlements." *Quarterly Journal of Economics* 96 (3): 433–64.

UN Environment Programme. 2023. *10 Things You Should Know About Industrial Farming*. UN Environment Programme. www.unep.org/news-and-stories/story/10-things-you-should-know-about-industrial-farming.

USDA, Economic Research Service. 2023a. *Organic Agriculture: Overview*. United States Department of Agriculture. www.ers.usda.gov/topics/natural-resources-envi ronment/organic-agriculture.aspx.

USDA, Economic Research Service. 2023b. *What Is Agriculture's Share of the Overall U.S. Economy?* www.ers.usda.gov/data-products/chart-gallery/gallery/chart-detail/?chartId=58270#:~:text=Agriculture%2C%20food%2C%20and%20related%20 industries,%2C%20a%205.4%2Dpercent%20share.

USDA and National Agricultural Statistics Service. 2022. *Farms and Land in Farms: 2021 Summary*. United States Department of Agriculture. www.nass.usda. gov/Publications/Todays_Reports/reports/fnlo0222.pdf?>.

Vandana, Shiva. 1988. *Staying Alive: Women, Ecology, and Development*. New York, NY: North Atlantic Books.

Van Huy, Le, Mai Thi Thao Chi, Antonio Lobo, Ninh Nguyen, and Phan Hoang Long. 2019. "Effective Segmentation of Organic Food Consumers in Vietnam Using Food-Related Lifestyles." *Sustainability* 11 (5): 1–16.

Ward, Neil. 1993. "The Agricultural Treadmill and the Rural Environment in the Post-Productivist Era." *Sociologia Ruralis* XXXIII (3/4): 348–64.

Winter, C.K., and S.F. Davis. 2006. "Orgnaic Foods." *Journal of Food Science*, no. 71, 117–24.

Wurtz, Noah. 2023. *Butz's Law of Economics*. Nonprofit Organization. *Agrarian Trust* (blog). 2023. www.agrariantrust.org/blog/butzs-law-of-economics/.

# 3

# ETHICAL OMNIVORISM AS A PHILOSOPHY OF FOOD

As a girl, I loved visiting my father who lived in a small apartment in Philadelphia. My parents divorced when I was one, but my father was a constant fixture in my life. I spent weekends with him and one of the ways that he showed his love was by sharing different types of foods with me. As a butcher, and later a fishmonger, in a well-known Italian market, my father loved everything about food. On weekends, he would whip-up creamy pasta with langostino, or squat lobster, and thinly slice beef tenderloin for carpaccio, drizzling it with lemon juice and olive oil, then sprinkling it with capers. He'd call me "mon bijou" (my jewel) as he whipped-up Italian butter cookies, echoing Julia Child's view that you can never add too much butter. We'd watch cooking shows and often walk to the Reading Terminal Market, one of the oldest farmers markets in the country, tasting every cuisine that Philadelphia had to offer. There, you can enjoy everything from Amish crumb cake and shoefly pie, to dim sum and oysters on the half shell, the latter a favorite since colonial times. (It's sometimes said in jest that New York city was built on a midden of oyster shells.) The quality of food matters as much as how it's prepared, and everything is enjoyed at its peak in the market. One of his favorite dishes, that he often made at home, involved cutting avocados in half, filling them with cheese and chilies and roasting them in the oven. For my father, food was a joyous affair, something that is beautiful, sensual, and meant to be shared with those you love.

## Food Connects People to Each Other

Food is life and it connects us in interesting ways. My father taught me this, but this insight also guides the ethical omnivore to be mindful of their food

DOI: 10.4324/9781003215189-3

choices. Here, I want to take a moment to discuss the history and connections of a staple ingredient that we will then use as a touchstone for our discussion of food ethics going forward. In food systems, these interconnections run deep and are global in scale. Take the seemingly simple avocado, for example. Americans are obsessed with this tough shelled superfood, and put it on everything from cheesecakes to pancakes, let alone toast. In 2023, before the pandemic, the nation consumed an estimated 250 million pounds of it during the Super Bowl (Burfield 2023). However, this beloved fruit has been at the center of some notable cultural and political controversies over the last century (Gilbert 2017). The United States had a contentious relationship with avocados from the beginning. Before the 20th century, they were a part of Latin American cuisines and archeologists estimate that people have been consuming them for nearly 10,000 years. However, they didn't catch on in the United States until the 1950s. For one thing, the Spanish name for avocados is "aquacate," which is hard to pronounce for some and stems from the word for "testicle" (Silva and Ledesma 2014). California farmers came up with the name "avocado," as part of a marketing strategy aimed at increasing consumption of the fruit and, as we see, it worked (Gilbert 2017). They were touted as a luxury item and the "aristocrat of salad fruits," featured frequently in restaurant dishes and cookbooks. In the 1980s, the anti-fat movement, led by nutritionists spreading the message that eating fatty foods leads to obesity and heart disease, spelled doom for avocado popularity. It was during this time that my father introduced me to avocados, filling them with chilies and cheese, before placing them under the broiler. For him, this was a decadent treat to share with his daughter.

Fast forward to 2014, and the avocado once again became popular, as restaurant chefs started to spread mashed avocado on toast, sometimes adding a slice of tomato, fried egg, and microgreens. Couple this trend with the rise of social media and Instagram and avocado toast became an Internet obsession (Orenstein 2016). This trend was promptly followed by a backlash, with avocado toast becoming a cultural touchstone for clueless millennials. This pushback continues, with *The Guardian* asking if enthusiasts "could stomach the unpalatable truth" about avocados (Gilbert 2017). Vast quantities of avocados are being consumed and this consumption has been linked to environmental degradation, illegal deforestation, drought (avocado trees use copious amounts of water), exploitation of migrant workers, and fund drug cartels, as they take over orchards. Avocados have a surprising political history, as well. The importation of avocados from Mexico was banned in 1914, but American growers were worried that this ban would be overturned with the ratification of the North American Free Trade Agreement in the 1990s. By 1997, the ban was overturned in 19 states, with California being a notable exception (Luscombe 2022). Fast forward to 2017, and this fruit once again made headlines, as they were subject to a 20% tariff leveled at Mexican imports. By 2022, they were again subject to a temporary import ban, due to cartel violence.

So, you're probably wondering what do avocados have to do with ethical omnivorism? They could fit into the diet, if they are organically produced, but so can many other foodstuffs. As we will see, this fruit is an excellent touchstone to explore what it means to be an "ethical" eater, and being mindful of the impacts of food systems is a key part of the ethical omnivore diet. What we eat says a lot about us. Food choices reflect personal values, or issues that we care deeply about. Since the development of industrial agriculture, the public has been grappling with larger implications concerning food production and choice. For example, how does our dinner impact personal health, animals, and the environment? What about the hard-working people who produce our food, both globally and locally? Today, it is common for eaters to "vote with their dollars," or use their purchasing power to support practices they value, while not supporting others. For those eaters committed to supporting local communities, the farmers' market may be a great place to shop, even if it is less convenient. Choosing to eat (or not to eat) that avocado shipped from Mexico may have consequences for the environment where it was produced, the climate, the farmers who produced it, grocers and shipping companies, and even international trade agreements. The history of this fruit is a great example of how foodstuffs are connected to environments, communities, technology, and even political systems. The food ethicist Roger King (2007) argues that understanding how our food choices impact others is the first step to eating ethically. Echoing King, this chapter has two goals: First, it introduces readers to the diverse array of ethical issues concerning food and second, it discusses which issues are important for ethical omnivores and why they're important.

## What Does It Mean to Eat Ethically?

As the name implies, ethical omnivores embrace thoughtful eating. The field called food ethics can help us to better understand what it means to eat ethically. Ethics can roughly be defined as the systemization of standards and values that we use to guide decisions regarding human conduct (Thompson and Noll 2015). Unpacking this, ethicists embrace two seemingly simple activities. They study how ethical norms: (a) can be discovered using reason and (b) guide cultural practices and standards. Scholars interested in values and norms see them as an accessible part of the world that can be discovered. In fact, when values guide personal choice and social practices, they're often codified in standards, or an agreed level of qualities and quality. For example, "ugly" apples that are small or blemished will often be discarded, as they don't meet grocery store standards for apples, which are typically big and round without blemishes. Similarly, the USDA's Organic Standard is made up of requirements that must be met for food to be certified organic, which includes many environmentally friendly practices. These standards were created because people care about eating quality food and they ensure that this food was produced using environmentally friendly methods. People have standards, too. As my mother always says, we should all have high standards, especially concerning the company that we keep. But joking aside, grocery stores adopted fruit-focused standards because consumers prefer unblemished fruit. The USDA's organic standard came about because citizens wanted to be able to purchase organically grown produce with confidence.

Our culinary choices are excellent examples of how values and standards inform everyday practices. Take grocery store purchases, for example. I love watching people when they're making food decisions. You often see them pick-up products. They read the labels and nutritional information and compare them to similar products. They'll bring fruit and vegetables up to their noses, smell deeply, tap the sides of melons, and use various ways to determine quality and ripeness. How many of you squeezed an avocado or breathed in the aroma of a tomato? Or even checked your eggs to make sure they're not broken or cracked? Every time we do this, we have needs and standards in mind and we're determining whether the product will fulfill this need and if it meets specific standards. Food advice on the Internet is rife with discussions concerning values, as well. If you care about eating healthy foods, then some recommend drinking milk, while others say that dairy products are problematic. Some swear that eating lean meat is good for you, while others argue that a vegetarian diet is both healthier and more ethical, as no animals were harmed in the production of that veggie burger. There are even videos out there critical of fruit, due to the sugar content. I'm sure many readers have looked for eating advice online or taken the time to read labels and compared similar products. There are lots of reasons why eaters decide to purchase one brand, rather than another brand. Sure, there's the desire to buy quality products, but as we see, values also come into play when people are making food decisions. People often buy products that align with what they care about (Williams et al. 2022), but these values can be muddied or in the background. This is where the field of food ethics can help, as it highlights how specific values influence food choice.

Food scholars interested in ethics try to develop general principles to help eaters separate "right" actions from "wrong" actions and thus explain why some choices are better than others. All food advice is descriptive, as it describes a specific diet, but advice also includes reasons for why one diet is better than others. When a person argues that you should eat more fruit, or that you shouldn't drink milk, for example, they are also making a normative claim. Here, "normative" just means that a claim is related to or derived from a standard or norm. When Michael Pollan was asked what we should eat, he responded that we should "Eat food. Not too much. Mostly plants"

(Pollan 2009, 2). This response is both descriptive, as it briefly describes a diet, and it's normative, as it communicates what we *should* eat. While eating advice can be quite simple at face value, such as Pollan's recommendation, the normative reasons for why one diet is better than another diet can be quite complex. For example, the reasons why Pollan argues that we should follow his simple advice are actually quite nuanced. When he states that we "should eat food," he's making the claim that most of the products available at modern grocery stores are actually not food products. They are food-like substances that are overly processed and contain very little nutrients. So, when you're looking for food, he goes on to argue that you should shop around the edges of the grocery store, where they typically sell fresh fruits, vegetables, meats, and other whole foods, or foods that are minimally processed. Here, Pollan is using a standard to determine what is (and is not) food, and his food recommendations are derived from this standard. The next part of the recommendation that we shouldn't eat too much is similarly grounded in the view that we should value our health, and eating too much food could be harmful to our health. Similarly, the claim that we should eat mostly plants is also derived from a nutritional standard, as eating fruits and vegetables is an important part of a balanced diet. We've spent a lot of time breaking down Pollan's simple dietary rules of thumb, but this is to highlight how (often unspoken or assumed) standards, norms, and values greatly influence diets, food choice, and recommendations. Ethical issues concerning food are often complicated, as food systems impact people, places, and animals. These themes will play a major role in the exploration of food ethics presented in this chapter.

However, before we more deeply explore ethical issues concerning food, it is important to discuss the things ethical omnivores care about. For the ethical omnivore, normative issues concerning food are deeply tied to environmental health, agricultural production methods, and the fate of the family farm. As the previous chapter discussed, agriculture is one of the oldest of human activities, with many environmental and social impacts. Innovation concerning food production has been continuous for at least the last 10,000 years, as humans learned to domesticate animals, cultivate crops, and build systems of irrigation (Thompson, 2015). According to the USDA, agriculture is an umbrella term that also includes the cultivation, harvesting, processing, storage, and distribution of commodities produced. For ethical omnivores, it is imperative that we place food decisions in this wider context— a context well beyond the grocery store and nutritional labeling. As the ethicist Roger King (2007) argues, modern food ethics grapples with questions that arise during all stages of production and processing, and this clearly includes what happens on the farm. This focus on agriculture is what separates modern food ethics from historical approaches. The organic and ethical omnivore movement each grapple with questions concerning agriculture. Indeed, both are critical of conventional agriculture practices, and they worry how food is produced today. While many eaters are rightly concerned about the freshness and quality of foodstuffs, ethical omnivores take a broader view, recognizing that foodstuffs are connected to environments, communities, technology, and political systems. Each of these intersections bring up important normative concerns. As it is both a social movement and a diet, ethical omnivorism is guided by twin comments to change what we eat and the systems of production that produce food products. But the transformative power of the movement hinges on normative commitments. Drawing from the field of food ethics, we'll be exploring how ethical, justice, and social/political considerations inform this diet.

## The Four Pillars of Ethical Eating

Food ethics is complex and multifaceted, as it encompasses a range of issues related to the production, distribution, and consumption of foodstuffs. For food scholars and eaters alike, there are important areas of concern that bring up ethical questions. These areas or pillars of ethical eating are the following: Impacts to (1) society, (2) individuals, (3) the environment, and (4) animal liberty and welfare. First, there is a large body of literature on social impacts. These are particularly important for ethical omnivores. As we've discussed, they care about how food choices impact farmers and rural communities. It also matters if the way we're producing food impacts our ability to feed future generations. More generally, cultural sensitivity is another important social topic, as communities increasingly demand that traditional food practices and diets are respected (Schanbacher 2010). Second, many eaters are worried about how agricultural practices and choices, such as the use of specific pesticides or herbicides, could impact their health. In fact, one of the first ethical issues that eaters usually grapple with is the worry that their food is contaminated or produced in a way that poses a risk to human health (Singer and Mason 2007). This concern came up again and again when I worked at MSU's student organic farm, as visitors were worried about the quality of their food and whether conventionally grown vegetables were safe to feed to their families. The farm, as a teaching center, helped eaters grapple with these pressing concerns. Discussions concerning diet, labeling, and food safety all fall under impacts to individuals.

However, it is important to recognize that it is difficult to separate individualistic concerns from wider social and environmental concerns. It's hard to make nutritious choices if you live in a food desert, for example, or an area that lacks access to grocery stores, farmers markets, and other types of distribution centers. Decisions made on the farm greatly impact the quality of foodstuffs produced. For example, research led by Sam Myers, the Director of the Planetary Health Alliance at Harvard, found that rising $CO_2$

levels causes staple crops (like wheat, rice, corn, and soy) to lose up to 5% of their iron, 10% of their zinc, and 8% of their protein content (Medek et al. 2017; Sweeney 2024). These nutrients are essential for people's health and the lowering quality of food represents a major risk to populations around the globe. This leads us to the third area that brings up ethical concerns— environmental impacts. Agriculture relies on ecosystem services and environmental conditions impact plant and animal health and food quality. Thus, environmental impacts are important considerations that carry ethical weight. Improving sustainability, maintaining biodiversity levels, protecting native species, and mitigating climate change impacts are all topics that fall under the environmental impacts category. Animal welfare is another area of concern for many, when choosing what to eat. This topic has been a public issue since at least the mid-1800s, with the rise of the anti-vivisectionist movements and the founding of the American Society for the Prevention of Cruelty to Animals (ASPCA) (Freeberg 2020). So far, we've defined food ethics and discussed how normative concerns impact food choices and recommendations. I'd now like to explore the areas of concern that bring up ethical questions in more detail, highlighting why each is important for ethical omnivores.

### Food Ethics: Impacts to Society

People have been discussing social impacts of food systems for a very long time. For example, this topic featured prominently in 18th-century literature on food (Thompson and Noll 2015).

The economists Adam Smith (1723–1790) and Thomas Malthus (1766–1834) famously framed hunger as a social issue, and their work is still being talked about today. Just this morning, the *Wallstreet Journal* ran a story on Adam Smith and hunger, and the popular podcast *Freakonomics Radio* has several shows dedicated to Smith and his ideas. Not to be outdone, Malthus' work is also important for current discussions in food ethics, as he was the first thinker to argue that there's a connection between agriculture technology and population growth. As agricultural technology develops, crop yields increase. When crop yields increase, population numbers also increase. However, population growth tends to outstrip agricultural production gains, leading to famine, war, or disease. This is known as the Malthusian theory, and it's still used to explain the delicate balance that needs to be struck between agricultural production and sustainable population levels. The discussion of hunger continues today, with Amartya Sen, Jeffery Sachs, and other prominent scholars engaging robustly with the topic. These thinkers push the discussion beyond Malthusian concerns about growth and "carrying capacity" to make room for ethical concerns about duties. They want us to consider what ethical duties (if any) we have to food insecure communities. For example, Peter

Singer (1972) attempts to answer this question, arguing that we have a duty to help those in need, irrespective of distance, and this is especially the case during times of famine. He wrote his famous essay outlining this position during the East Bengal famine that occurred in the early 1970s. The famine made the front page of newspapers in Australia, his home, but no one was sending aid. People were literally dying in the streets. He argued that the root of this indifference is the failure to recognize that we have a basic duty to help others, no matter where they live. We are all citizens of the world and, in our global society, the well-being of communities around the world are intertwined. This view is known in the literature as an egalitarian ethic, meaning that it stems from the belief that all people deserve equal rights and opportunities. It's also cosmopolitan, or grounded in the belief that humans deserve respect, no matter where they live. We're all part of a global community. These ideals play a prominent role in food ethics, as they are often used to support the claim that we should provide food and other types of aid. With this being said, Singer's work sparked a passionate debate, with several thinkers criticizing his view. The economist Garrett Hardin (1915–2003) is highly critical of cosmopolitan views. He stresses Malthus' concern that population growth will outstrip agricultural productivity (1968), bringing classic arguments into conversation with newer work. In his view, nations have a duty to provide their citizens access to basic needs (such as food), and this does not extend to other nations. Ensuring the health of their citizens is their responsibility. For Hardin, we shouldn't harm our ability to feed our citizens and future generations to help feed the world today. Other well-known thinkers have also criticized these views.

## Cosmopolitanism: Ethics in a World of Strangers

This debate between cosmopolitan and nationalist ideals concerning aide is a great example of how ethics influences food-related decisions. At the root, the conflict is about fairness. Is it fair or just to prioritize the needs of one community over another community? Should fair distribution of foodstuffs be based on the amount of work that you do, or what ethicists call "desert." Or should distribution be based on need, or what is equitable? With global populations doubling roughly every 25 years and agricultural land being finite, these questions matter. How we answer them will have large impacts on our agricultural systems, as we attempt to provide for citizens and distribute food aide, when needed. This is one example of how justice issues crop-up in food conversations. Egalitarians, such as Singer, believe that equality is central to justice. If all people deserve to be treated equally, then laws and policies should be designed to ensure that this happens. This is because each society has economic, political, and social systems (realized through laws, institutions, and policies) that influence how benefits and burdens are distributed. Rather than focusing on individual conduct, philosophers such as John Rawls (2001) argue that the appropriate place to bring about change is at the level of policy and the social institution. Anytime we talk about how the benefits and harms of farm policy and food systems are distributed, we're firmly in the realm of justice. When lawmakers argue about food subsidies and aide programs in the Farm Bill, they're making policy that greatly effects people's lives on the ground. Similarly, consumers who shop at farmers markets because they want to support local farmers and communities often justify their choice citing justice concerns, as they feel that it's more equitable than supporting "big" agriculture.

Justice can be defined broadly as the ethical idea that people should be treated fairly and impartially. An important justice issue for food producers involves deciding if laws are justified in limiting the personal liberty of citizens (Gaus et al. 2018). For instance, the USDA's decision to ban a specific pesticide is a justice one for two reasons. First, if the pesticide is harmful, then the United States has a duty to regulate its use to protect citizens, as harms shouldn't be borne by the few, while others enjoy benefits. But this ban would also limit the farmer's liberty by constraining the choices available. Here, regulators and policy-makers must weigh the benefits and harms of agricultural practices, with an eye towards protecting citizen health and liberty. Distributive justice frameworks are very important when making food choices. Here, distributive justice refers to the idea that resources should be fairly allocated, and communities shouldn't have to bear the burden of harms, while not enjoying appropriate benefits (Figueroa 2017). For example, fire fighters agree to place themselves in harm's way, but they're compensated for this activity, or are at least able to opt in or out of the profession. Many people think that serving your community is worth the increased risk, but these risks shouldn't be involuntarily imposed. Let's look at a farming example. Costa Rica's heavy pesticide and fungicide use in rural areas has been linked to an increased cancer risk (Bruhl et al. 2023). A biometric study of the past 10 years on cancer and occupational exposure found that certain pesticides, herbicides, and fungicides play a role in the development of cancers, such as multiple myeloma and bladder, prostate, and breast cancers. One could argue that farmers opt into this kind of work and thus have agreed to accept an increased risk of developing cancers, though there are many reasons why this defense fails. Additionally, there are others who live in the area that have not agreed to shoulder these harms. Agricultural inputs do not stay on the farm. Drainage and run-off from farmland can contaminate rivers and impair water quality, impacting entire communities. Years ago, I spent the summer farming in Costa Rica and visited communities, next to banana plantations, that needed to have water trucked in weekly due to agricultural contamination. Cancer rates for these communities were skyrocketing and the local government had to step in to provide clean drinking water. This is a stark example of a distributive justice issue, where large agri-business' enjoy the benefits of fruit production, while harms are distributed to workers and rural communities. The local government is often left to clean up the mess.

Justice claims such as this example permeate social discussions concerning food. For instance, Singer's statement that we have a duty to help famine victims, irrespective of distance, can also be considered a justice argument. In fact, food security programs are often guided by egalitarian conceptions of justice, or the idea that individuals have what is called a "positive right" to food, or an entitlement strong enough to compel others to act on their behalf (Noll & Murdock 2020). At its most fundamental level, egalitarianism begins with the basic claim that individuals should be treated as equals, as we discussed. But, it also includes a commitment that goods necessary for life should be distributed fairly. The famous political theorist John Rawls (2001) argues that we should adopt the "difference principle," or that inequalities of the distribution of basic goods and services are only permissible if unequal distribution benefits the least well-off, as this will ultimately create an equal distribution of goods. This is just one example of a normative ethic that helps us to figure out what is fair, especially when we're talking about distributing important goods, such as foodstuffs. As agriculture uses and creates resources, it is not surprising that concerns over what constitutes just distribution (of risks and benefits) is an important topic. Egalitarian frameworks are often used to justify claims that maintaining social goods should be prioritized (Thompson 1996; Noll 2017) or that resources should be distributed throughout society in a particular way (Rawls 2001; Shrader-Frachette 2002). The United Nations Universal Declaration of Human Rights makes the strong claim that all people have a basic right to access to food (United Nations 1948). Non-governmental Organizations providing hunger relief, such as Action Against Hunger and Feeding America, also use this language as part of their mission statements. If people have a right to healthy food, then this means that others have a duty to provide this food. This could be fulfilled through charitable giving or by creating public programs and policy to help ensure that basic needs are met. In this way, justice acts as a spotlight, illuminating how the lives of individuals and social systems are deeply connected. In the same way that drivers can't escape traffic laws, eaters cannot escape the wider economic, social, political, and agricultural systems that put food in grocery stores.

In recent years, the idea that people have a right to food was expanded by international farmers groups to include other rights claims—claims that highlight the need to recognize larger social impacts of food production. Critiques of international food security programs, which only focus on addressing hunger, sparked the development of an alternative model called food sovereignty (Morales 2011; Schanbacher 2010). While this is an unusual term, chances are that you've engaged with a food initiative that embraces food sovereignty. Local food groups, such as community gardens and neighborhood markets, often use this language in their mission statements. Providing food to neighborhoods, planting school and church gardens, and doing other activities to ensure that citizens have access to healthy products are ways for neighborhoods to exercise some control over local food systems. Food sovereignty supporters embrace the idea that communities should not only have access to foodstuffs but also have greater control over food systems. They demand that communities should have a place at the table when agricultural policy is made, and that local consumption and community health should be prioritized over global concerns. They also demand that farm workers should be protected from harm, including protection from violence and occupational hazards, such as exposure to cancer causing agents. For initiatives that embrace food sovereignty, food is more than just a commodity that we are entitled to—food is intertwined with political action, culture, identity, and place. Thus, supporters of food sovereignty embrace more holistic models of justice. Using this framework, farmers groups around the globe are attempting to change food systems, one neighborhood at a time.

So far, we've explored two types of societal impacts concerning food. We've discussed individual focused questions, such as whether people have a right to food. And we've talked about wider agricultural concerns, such as determining how benefits and harms of food production should be distributed in a fair manner. Ethical omnivores embrace the idea that eaters should have access to safe and healthy foodstuffs. They are also very worried about what happens on the farm and demand that food be produced in an equitable manner. For these eaters, eating ethically goes well beyond buying products at the grocery store or farmers' market. It also involves supporting sustainable and organic agricultural practices, by helping to make a market for these products. Farmers, rural communities, and eaters are all impacted by decisions made on the farm and in the grocery isle. It's no surprise that many of the norms and ideals that we've just discussed are also used by eaters embracing an ethical omnivore diet. For the organic and ethical omnivore movements, the social costs of modern agriculture are high. These need to be discussed and play a more prominent role in food decision-making.

## Human and Environmental Health

In addition to social concerns, worries about human and environmental health drive eaters to embrace the ethical omnivore diet. For example, Lana Joe Salant, founder of ethicalomnivore.org explicitly embraces these commitments in the following statement:

> Everyone knows that the food and consumer products we choose to buy can have a big impact on our health and on the environment. The way the

food and other products we consume are produced is the most important issue facing us as a species.

*(2023, n.p.)*

These are the very first sentences Salant uses to describe what ethical omnivores care about. They are worried that most of the food being sold in the grocery store, typically produced using conventional agricultural methods, is not healthy to eat and is harming the environment. These worries are at least partially guided by ethical claims and based on a basic desire to eat better and to live well. Humans have been on the quest to identify better dietary choices since the birth of agriculture, itself (Zwart 2000). The Ancient Greeks thought that mindful eating was a key part of living a good life. For some Greek philosophers, morality involves developing virtues or "habits" that help us perform well, no matter the circumstances. When faced with a problem, we could act excessively, deficiently, or just right. A wise person finds the "golden mean," or the middle path between the two. This middle path is a virtue. Take the virtue of temperance, for example, or acting in moderation. Eating is a wonderful opportunity to develop this virtue, as each food choice helps us to identify the perfect diet to maintain personal health. Some days, we may eat that fast-food burger and other days we might forget to eat, but gradually training our habits helps us to eat well overall. Dietetics, or the branch of knowledge concerned with diet and its effect on health, reigned supreme in early food ethics debates.

Today, eaters are still obsessed with finding the perfect diet that fits with their lifestyle and values. Social media is filled with influencers who provide advice on what to eat, or not to eat. Nutritionists have written many books on ideal diets, and they'll write many more. Ethical omnivores are increasingly worried about health impacts associated with industrial agricultural practices. As we discussed earlier, both the organic farming and ethical omnivore movement are grounded in concerns about how food systems impact human health (Delind 2011). For example, common justifications for buying organic products include claims that the food is healthier, free from contaminants, or produced in a way that does not pose a disease risk (Thompson 2015). In this way, food ethics is still very much worried about dietetics. This brings up an important ethical consideration that often comes up in medical and health-related discussions: respect for persons, or the principle of autonomy (Beauchamp and Childress 2001). This is the idea that we have an ethical duty to respect other people and their decisions. In medical contexts, this means that patients have the right to decide what treatment options are best for them and can even refuse treatment. Concerning food, people should have the ability to make food choices that align with their values and these choices should be respected. Here, food labeling becomes an ethical issue, as consumers need information to make informed choices that align with their values. If they're not provided this information, then this is a violation of autonomy, as it doesn't respect the eater's desire to make their own choices.

But, food choices don't simply impact the individual who is eating. We make food choices for others all time, especially when you're preparing food for your family. Children depend on their parents to provide healthy and safe foodstuffs and visitors assume that any food provided will not be harmful. Imagine, if this wasn't the case and it was a coin toss whether you were going to be sick at a party. It would sure make things interesting. But all joking aside, two other ethical principles often guide treatment of others. Grounded in respect for persons, the ethical principle of "beneficence" mandates that we do actions that benefit others, and the ethical principle non-maleficence requires that we do not harm others, as a general rule. When providing food to others, this means that we should think about the health and safety of those we're feeding. Additionally, we have special duties to our family, friends, and members of the community, based upon the bonds that we share (Schneewind 1982). This view is steeped in the communitarian normative tradition, or the idea that social ties matter when thinking about ethics. As the philosopher Daniel Bell (2024) explains:

> we live most of our lives in communities, similar to lions who live in social groups rather than individualistic tigers who live alone most of the time. Those communities shape, and ought to shape, our moral and political judgments and we have a strong obligation to support and nourish the communities that provide meaning for our lives, without which we'd be disoriented, deeply lonely, and incapable of informed moral and political judgment.
>
> *(n.p.)*

Many people nourish families and wider communities through food. Sharing food and breaking bread is an important way that we reinforce social ties. Think of all the times a cherished family member made a special dish for you, or when neighbors bring over food as a welcome to the neighborhood. Social events often include food, and the best ones are those where people can share dishes with each other. Food is often given as a gift, too, cementing relationships. For example, matsutake mushrooms are prized for their unique flavor and often given as gifts in Japanese culture. Even the word "love" comes from the middle English word for breaking bread, because we share food with people we care about it. This is one of the reasons why the food ethicists Lisa Heldke and Raymond D. Boisvert (2016) argue that hospitality is an important virtue in food ethics. At its heart, hospitality honors the relationship between a guest and a host, and mandates that the host receive the guest with goodwill, food, and sometimes entertainment. It's an important virtue around the world. In many religious traditions from Buddhism to Christianity, for example, offering hospitality to guests is a virtuous deed and says a lot about who we are. Flipping the coin, how guests act towards hosts also reflects on their character, as well. I have a family member who ate food that she knew she was mildly allergic to because she didn't want to refuse hospitality offered to her. I don't recommend this, but it struck me how important honoring this virtue was to her, so much so that she sacrificed her health to do so.

Ethical omnivores are aware of the connections between food and community, which is reflected in their commitment to purchase healthy food for friends and family. This commitment permeates conversations at farmers markets and community agriculture projects. Eaters buying locally produced foodstuffs often argue that quality matters and they want to provide their families with healthy products that are nutritious and free of potentially harmful agricultural inputs. Other common reasons that consumers give for buying local produce align with the third category of concern, namely environmental impacts. These concerns were first discussed by the founders of the organic movement in the early 20th century, but the publication of Rachel Carson's *Silent Spring* in 1962 galvanized the public with her dire portrait of environmental devastation brought about by dichlorodiphenyltrichloroethane (or DDT), a common pesticide of her day. She wanted us to imagine walking by a lake that is silent, because the birds died due to DDT exposure and its impact on reproductive systems. Her prose captures health and environmental concerns poetically. She asks us why we should tolerate a diet of weak poisons and stresses that they concern us all, humans and non-humans alike. For Carson, "if we are going to live so intimately with these chemicals eating and drinking them, taking them into the very marrow of our bones – we had better know something about their nature and their power." A public outcry and congressional hearings were the result of *Silent Spring*'s portrayal of how pesticides harm farm workers and wildlife. After reading excerpts, then President John F. Kennedy asked his Science Advisory Committee (PSAC) to investigate her claims. In 1963, PSAC released its report, which supported many of the claims in the book. It silenced most industry critics, who vehemently argued that DDT is safe, some even drinking the pesticide to prove their point (Stoll 2020). The United States banned the use of DDT in 1972, but the debate concerning pesticides continues, as inputs may be harmful when improperly stored, handled, or applied.

These and other ecological issues continue to play an important role in ethical discussions concerning food production. People are worried that the way we're farming could be harming themselves and their children, as the DDT case illustrates. But, they're also worried that environmental damage could harm our ability to feed future generations. Farming is dependent on ecological services, such as water filtration, pollination, erosion control, and other necessary activities. Leaders in environmental ethics expanded egalitarian ethical frameworks, built on the idea that everyone deserves to be treated fairly, to the environment. For example, Aldo Leopold (1968) and many later philosophers, argued that ethical consideration should be expanded to include ecosystems, biotic communities, and non-human animals (Noll 2017). We should see the land as a community to which we belong, rather than a commodity that is owned. We have a duty to be a good citizen in this community, as our lives depend on mutual flourishing. He famously argued that "there are two spiritual dangers in not owning a farm. One is the danger of supposing that breakfast comes from the grocery, and the other that heat comes from the furnace." When we go the market, with all the packaged goods and pretty advertising, it's easy to forget that we depend on farmers and the environment for everything that we need to survive. Recognizing the connection between human and ecological flourishing is an important part of the ethical omnivore diet and food ethics, more generally.

One of the criticisms of this view is that it is anthropocentric. For example, much of the work in environmental ethics from the 1970s to the 1990s emphases the view that the natural world does not exist solely for the use of humans, but rather it has intrinsic value. In 1973, the famous Australian environmental philosopher Richard Sylvan kicked off this trend. He asked a crowded room to imagine that the entire human race had gone extinct, except for one man (Brennan and Lo 2024). When this person dies, there will be no more humans walking this earth. Now, imagine that this person spends the rest of their life eliminating as many species as possible. If no one is there to enjoy the forests and beaches, why shouldn't they also go extinct with humankind? His goal is to exterminate every animal, plant, and microbe, as painlessly as possible before he dies. I ask this question to people sometimes, and I get some very odd looks. Most people think that the last human going around killing things is doing something wrong. It seems like animals, plants, and other living beings are valuable, even if there's no human left to enjoy them. The point Sylvan is trying to make here is simple. In his view, traditional Western ethics are built on the idea that people can do what they want, if they don't harm anyone, or themselves. They're anthropocentric, or human-centric. However, even when we remove people from the earth, it seems like there are good reasons to value the environment, beyond human interests. This is called intrinsic value, or the idea that something can have value in and of itself. If it is wrong to harm nature, then we need to include these harms in our ethical decisions. For Aldo Leopold (1968), we abuse the land because we regard it as a commodity that we own, rather than a community. We use the land to extract as many resources as possible, without thinking of the land as something that is intrinsically valuable. In contrast, environmental ethicists ask us to enlarge "the boundaries of the community to include, soils, waters, plants and animals, or collectively the land" (Leopold 1968, 110). Ethical omnivores' commitment to environmentally friendly farming is grounded in this commitment. While farming by definition produces products, it can be done in many ways. Embracing the "nurturer" role, to borrow from Wendell Berry, rather than that of the exploiter, is built on Leopold's idea that we are a part of an ecological community. Just as the birds, muskrats, and other animals have the right to thrive, so do we. Thus, practicing an ecological ethic doesn't mean that humans reduce their ecological footprint to the point where we drive ourselves to extinction. It means that we learn to work with ecological communities, using the most environmentally friendly methods possible, when producing necessary goods, such as food and fiber.

## Animal Welfare and Liberty

Another important area in food ethics focuses on animal use and welfare. The legal and ethical protection of animals has a long history in both the United States and Europe. Public concern rose steadily for the well-being of farm animals. According to the legal scholars David Favre and Vivien Tsang (1993):

> the legal system began the century viewing animals as items of personal property not much different than a shovel or plow. During the first half of the century, lawmakers began to recognize that an animal's potential for pain and suffering was real and deserving of protection against its unnecessary infliction.
>
> *(1)*

In New York, Henry Bergh successfully lobbied and helped pass the nation's first anti-cruelty laws, which became the foundation on which contemporary laws were built. During his lifetime, he witnessed horrific cases of animal cruelty on the streets of New York, where horses were used for transportation and livestock was slaughtered in the city. Bergh not only raised awareness of animal cruelty but also founded the ASPCA. Views have continued to transform and today, we have both state and national laws that regulate the treatment of animals in research and agricultural settings. Interestingly, newspapers across the country lauded the passing of the Animal Welfare Act in 1966, the same year social security was amended with little public attention.

So far, we've been focusing on the U.S. context, but UK set the stage for animal ethics to capture public attention (Favre and Tsang 1993). Some of the first calls to recognize the moral status of animals appeared in British writing. For example, Jeremy Bentham, the English lawyer and philosopher also advocated for better treatment. In his *Introduction to the Principles of Morals and Legislation* published in 1781, Bentham argued that animals should be accorded protection under the law. In particular, he argued that animals, "on account of their interests having been neglected by the insensibility of the ancient jurists, stand degraded into the class of *things,*" but the capacity for suffering is the primary characteristic that gives a being the right to ethical and legal consideration. Today, the debate concerning animal use has become quite heated, with parties on both sides taking firm positions. Few food ethicists would deny that we have a responsibility to assure the well-being of animals under our care, including food animals.

Many farmers historically embraced a personal stewardship ethic, where animal health and well-being are thought to correspond closely with a producer's interest in farm efficiency (Rollin 1995). Bernard Rollin argues that this ethic was enforced at least partially by self-interest. Farmers who treated their animals badly would lose them to sickness and injury and this could be disastrous, as they depend on their animals for labor and foodstuffs. But, this connection between producer self-interest and animal welfare breaks down when one of three conditions occurs (Thompson and Noll 2015). First, food products, such as veal, require production methods that could harm animal well-being. A great example is foie gras, a delicacy in French cuisine, made from the liver of a duck or goose. To produce foie gras, workers insert pipes down the throats of ducks, force feeding them to intentionally cause their livers to swell in size. There is a fierce ethical controversy over this product. Second, high animal welfare standards may be realizable only under ideal conditions seldom realized in production contexts. Third, in some large operations, the management costs of taking care of the needs of a few individual animals might not be matched by returns based on aggregated sales of animal products. Each of these points prompted sharp criticism from animal protection organizations.

These criticisms galvanized the public to call for improved animal welfare standards and/or abolition of animal use in agriculture. The debate also shows that there is some confusion concerning the terms "animal welfare" and "animal rights." For some eaters, the term "animal rights" denotes an extreme reformist position, while "animal welfare" is taken to imply an attitude favoring moderate reform in animal agriculture. However, popular use of animal rights assumes that individual animals' interests deserve consideration. More formal uses of these terms have been introduced into the literature by Tom Regan and Peter Singer, two influential voices in the animal liberation movement. For example, Peter Singer's (2015) view is utilitarian, meaning that the right action is the one that brings about the best consequences for all those involved. It allows for situations where human interests should be favored over animals', and even where animal pain could be justified. However, Singer also argues that animals in industrial agriculture suffer to a degree that makes it impossible to justify human consumption of animal products. For this reason, he is commonly associated with animal rights groups and their abolitionist positions. The tension concerning animal welfare and animal rights definitions reflects a wider tension in food ethics concerning animal use.

## Practicing an Ethic of Seeing

Social impacts, human and environmental health, and animal welfare discussions will continue to play a major role in food ethics discussions going forward. Depending on their personal values, ethical omnivores are mindful of the areas of concern that we just discussed. Popular books and articles abound on this topic, as people look for ways to improve their well-being and the well-being of the planet. As I read through popular pieces on the subject, several themes emerge. First, some writers focus on environmental impacts of dietary choices. For example, the nutritionist Adrienne Seitz (2024) focuses on both health and environmental concerns in an article on how to be an ethical omnivore. Before diving into nutrition, she writes that "food production creates an inevitable strain on the environment [and] your daily food choices can greatly affect the overall sustainability of your diet" (n.p.). She goes on to argue that the demand for energy, food, and water will continue to rise, as the world's population increases, and this will put increased stress on our planet and agricultural lands. As half of the world's inhabited land is being used for some form of food production, how we use this land matters for the environment (Ellis et al. 2010). Other ethical omnivores urge eaters to buy local, as eating highly perishable food that is produced close to home could reduce carbon emissions and provide eaters with more information on how foodstuffs are produced. Still other supporters, such as Laura Dalrymple and Grant Hilliard, cite animal welfare as a major area of concern. In their book *The Ethical Omnivore*, they state that meat is the most controversial ingredient in our kitchens today. They see ethical omnivorism as a way to move forward with good intent. Their solution is "living with a conscience; asking the right questions of whomever sells you meat or of the labels you read; and learning how to respect the animal..." (cover). They go on to argue that people want to do the right thing, but agriculture is opaque and confusing. An important part of following an ethical omnivore diet is coming to understand which food production systems you want to support. This sometimes involves getting to know the people who produce your food and asking them questions. It also involves supporting the farmers who have high ethical standards in place. As we can see even from this small sampling of books and articles, ethical omnivores are worried about each of the five areas in food ethics, from impacts to individuals and society, to environmental and animal health. When it comes to eating ethically, knowledge is power. The more you know, the more opportunities you have to purchase products that align with your values. Let's return to avocado, as an example of this.

### Applying the Four Pillars of Food Ethics

Many eaters purchase avocados because they're delicious, but also because they're packed with nutrition, as they are rich in fiber, folate, and heart healthy fats. But, there are ethical concerns that also influence whether someone purchases that avocado toast. The popularity of avocados was questioned by *The Guardian* when readers were asked if they could stomach the dark side of this fruit (Dehghan 2019). Made in 2019, this critique largely focused on environmental concerns, as avocado production is linked to environmental degradation, illegal deforestation, and drought. One avocado takes roughly 50 gallons of water to produce, and this is a big deal in areas like California, that have been facing water shortages for years, if not decades. Overconsumption of water harms local wildlife, as ecosystems dry up, while those avocados, almonds, alfalfa, and other crops hog it for themselves. Fast forward to 2019, and this newspaper tentatively labeled avocados a blood or conflict commodity, up there with blood diamonds from Sierra Leone and conflict minerals from the Democratic Republic of Congo. Mexico produces more avocados than any other country, as they're worth billions every year. Avocados have been called "green gold," Mexico brought in $2.4bn of profit in 2018, alone. Drug cartels are fighting for dominance over this market. The analytics group Verisk Maplecroft is concerned that ethical costs are increasing, due to the growing involvement of cartels, rising violence and deaths, and the use of forced and child labor on the farms. Environmental costs are also being exacerbated due to cartel involvement, as deforestation and clearing of protected forests goes unchecked.

So, what does it mean to eat ethically? If we look at the above overview, then several red flags concerning avocados should stand out. Let's apply the four pillars of food ethics here. We have impacts to: (1) society, (2) individuals, (3) the environment, and (4) animal liberty and welfare. Right off the bat, animal welfare isn't an issue, unless we're worried about impacts to wildlife, though these are typically placed under the umbrella of environmental concerns. Speaking of environmental impacts, as we can see, there are several ecological harms associated with avocado production, especially in some areas of Mexico. Individual impacts to human health are generally good, if avocados are eaten as part of a balanced diet. However, depending on where they're grown, farmer lives could be threatened by violence and forced labor. Societal harms are also a concern if cartels are taking over production is certain areas. This doesn't mean that we should stop eating avocados, though. The ethical omnivore would argue that not all avocados are grown equally. The harms make sourcing the fruit very important, to ensure that they are being produced in an ethical manner. They need to be grown in a way that is environmentally healthy and sustainable, and where farmers, farm workers, and communities are treated with dignity.

Here is one example of how the four pillars of food ethics can act as a heuristic to think through the ethical costs of foodstuffs. This is practicing an ethic of seeing, which is important for the ethical omnivore diet. These eaters don't focus on one ethical issue but try to better understand how the food on their plate is interconnected with the communities and world around them. In a complex and global food system, it's hard to make good decisions. That strawberry or bunch of bananas grown in Costa Rica and shipped to your country, to be trucked to a distribution center and then transported to your store, touches so many different communities. Ethical omnivores embrace this complexity. The best we can do is educate ourselves to make better decisions, one purchase and one meal at a time. So, what is ethical eating for an omnivore? It's thoughtful eating. One meal at time. Everyday.

## References

Appiah, Kwame Anthony, and Henry Louis Gates. 2006. *Cosmopolitanism: Ethics in a World of Strangers*. New York, NY: W.W. Norton.

Beauchamp, Tom L., and James F. Childress. 2001. *Principles of Biomedical Ethics*. Oxford University Press.

Bell, Daniel. 2024. "Communitarianism." In *The Stanford Encyclopedia of Philosophy*, edited by Edward Zalta and Uri Nodelman, n.p. Stanford, CA: Stanford University. https://plato.stanford.edu/archives/sum2024/entries/communitarianism/.

Bentham, Jeremy. 1781. *An Introduction to the Principles of Morals and Legislation*. Oxford: Clarendon Press.

Boisvert, Raymond D., and Lisa Heldke. 2016. *Philosophers at Table: On Food and Being Human*. Chicago, IL: Reaktion Books.

Brennan, Andrew, and Y.S. Lo. 2024. *Environmental Ethics*. n.p. Stanford, CA: Stanford University. https://plato.stanford.edu/archives/sum2024/entries/ethics-environmental/.

Bruhl, Carsten, Maria Andres, Silvia Echeverria-Saenz, Mirco Bundschuh, Anja Knabel, Freylan Mena, Lara Petschick, Clemens Ruepert, and Sebastian Stehle. 2023. "Pesticide Use in Banana Plantations in Costa Rica – A Review of Environmental and Human Exposure, Effects and Potential Risks." *Environmental International* 174:1–13.

Burfield, Tom. 2023. *Avocado Suppliers and Retailers Kick off Super Bowl Plans*. The Packer. www.thepacker.com/news/retail/avocado-suppliers-and-retailers-kick-super-bowl-plans.

Carson, Rachel. 1962. *Silent Spring*. Houghton Mifflin Harcourt Trade & Reference Publishers.

Coleman, Sydney. 1924. *Humane Society Leaders in America*. Albany, NY: The American Humane Association.

Dalrymple, Laura, and Grant Hilliard. 2020. *The Ethical Omnivore: A Practical Guide and 60 Nose-to-Tail Recipes for Sustainable Meat Eating*. London: Murdoch Books.

Dehghan, Saeed. 2019. *Are Mexican Avocados the World's New Conflict Commodity?* The Guardian. www.theguardian.com/global-development/2019/dec/30/are-mexican-avocados-the-worlds-new-conflict-commodity.

DeLind, Laura B. 2011. "Are Local Food and the Local Food Movement Taking Us Where We Want to Go? Or Are We Hitching Our Wagons to the Wrong Stars?" *Agriculture and Human Values* 28 (2): 273–83.

Ellis, Erle, Kees Klein Goldewijk, Stefan Siebert, Deborah Lighman, and Navin Ramankutty. 2010. "Anthropogenic Transformation of the Biomes, 1700 to 2000." *Global Ecology and Biogeography* 19 (5): 589–606.

Favre, David, and Vivien Tsang. 1993. "The Development of the Anti-Cruelty Laws During the 1800's." *Detroit College of Law Review* 1:1–36.

Figueroa, Robert. 2017. "Bivalent Environmental Justice and the Culture of Poverty." *Rutgers University Journal of Law and Urban Policy* 1 (1): 27–42.

Freeberg, Ernest. 2020. *A Traitor to His Species: Henry Bergh and the Birth of the Animal Rights Movement.* New York, NY: Basic Books.

Gaus, Gerald, Shane D. Courtland, and David Schmidtz. 2018. "Liberalism." In *The Stanford Encyclopedia of Philosophy*, edited by Edward N. Zalta, Spring 2018. Metaphysics Research Lab, Stanford University. https://plato.stanford.edu/archives/spr2018/entries/liberalism/.

Gilbert, Sophie. 2017. *The Political Saga of Avocados.* The Atlantic. www.theatlantic.com/entertainment/archive/2017/02/a-brief-history-of-avocado-controversy/514748/.

Hardin, Garrett. 1968. "The Tragedy of the Commons." *Science, New Series* 162 (3859): 1243–48.

King, Roger. 2007. "Eating Well: Thinking Ethically about Food." In *Food and Philosophy*, by Fritz Allhoff and David Monroe, 177–91. New York, NY: Blackwell Publishing.

Leopold, Aldo. 1968. *A Sand County Almanac: With Other Essays on Conservation from Round River.* Ballantine Books.

Luscombe, Richard. 2022. *US Halts Avocado Imports from Mexico after Threat to American Inspector.* The Guardian. www.theguardian.com/world/2022/feb/14/us-avocado-imports-mexico-threats.

Medek, Danielle, Joel Schwartz, and Samuel Myers. 2017. "Estimated Effects of Future Atmospheric $CO_2$ Concentrations on Protein Intake and the Risk of Protein Deficiency by Country and Region." *Environmental and Health Perspectives* 125 (8): 087002-1-087002–8.

Milburn, Josh, and Christopher Bobier. 2022. "New Omnivorism: A Novel Approach to Food and Animal Ethics." *Food Ethics* 7 (5): 1–17.

Morales, Alfonso. 2011. "Growing Food and Justice: Dismantling Racism Through Sustainable Food Systems." In *Cultivating Food Justice" Race. Class, and Sustainability*, 149–76. Cambridge, MA: MIT Press.

Noll, Samantha. 2017. "Climate Induced Migration: A Pragmatic Strategy for Wildlife Conservation on Farmland." *Pragmatism Today* 8 (2): 17.

Noll, Samantha, and Esme Murdock. 2020. "Whose Justice Is It Anyway? Mitigating the Tensions Between Food Security and Food Sovereignty." *Journal of Agricultural and Environmental Ethics* 33:1–14. https://doi.org/10.1007/s10806-019-09809-9.

Orenstein, Jayne. 2016. *How the Internet Became Ridiculously Obsessed with Avocado Toast.* The Washington Post. www.washingtonpost.com/news/wonk/wp/2016/05/06/how-the-internet-became-ridiculously-obsessed-with-avocado-toast/.

Pollan, Michael. 2009. *In Defense of Food: An Eater's Manifesto.* New York, NY: Penguin USA.

Rawls, John. 2001. *Justice as Fairness: A Restatement*. Harvard University Press.

Rollin, Bernard. 1995. *Farm Animal Welfare: Social, Bioethical, and Research Issues*. Ames, IA: Iowa State Press.

Salant, Lana Joe. 2023. *About the Ethical Omnivore Movement*. Ethical Omnivore Movement. www.ethicalomnivore.org/about-eom/.

Schanbacher, William D. 2010. *The Politics of Food: The Global Conflict between Food Security and Food Sovereignty*. Santa Barbara, CA: ABC-CLIO.

Schneewind, J.B. 1982. "Virtue, Narrative, and Community: MacIntyre and Morality." *The Journal of Philosophy* 79 (11): 653–63.

Seitz, Adrienne. 2024. *How to Be an Ethical Omnivore*. Healthline. www.healthline.com/health-news/raw-milk-health-risks#Takeaway.

Shrader-Frechette, Kristin. 2002. *Environmental Justice: Creating Equality, Reclaiming Democracy*. Oxford University Press.

Silva, Tomas Ayala, and Noris Ledesma. 2014. "Avocado History, Biodiversity and Production." In *Sustainable Horticultural Systems*, edited by Dilip Nandwani, 157–205. New York, NY: Springer.

Singer, Peter. 1972. "Famine, Affluence, and Morality." *Philosophy and Public Affairs* 1 (3): 229–43.

Singer, Peter. 2015. *Animal Liberation: The Definitive Classic of the Animal Movement*. Open Road Media.

Singer, Peter, and Jim Mason. 2007. *The Ethics of What We Eat: Why Our Food Choices Matter*. Potter/Ten Speed/Harmony/Rodale.

Stoll, Mark. 2020. *The US Federal Government Responds*. Environment & Society Portal. www.environmentandsociety.org/exhibitions/rachel-carsons-silent-spring/us-federal-government-responds.

Sweeney, Chris. 2024. *As Carbon Dioxide Levels Climb, Millions at Risk of Nutritional Deficiencies*. Harvard T.H. Chan School of Public Health. www.hsph.harvard.edu/news/press-releases/climate-change-less-nutritious-food/.

Thompson, Paul B. 1996. "Pragmatism and Policy: The Case of Water." In *Environmental Pragmatism*, edited by E Katz and Andrew Light, 187–209. New York, NY: Routledge.

Thompson, Paul B. 2015. *From Field to Fork: Food Ethics for Everyone*. Oxford University Press.

Thompson, Paul B., and Samantha Noll. 2015. "Agriculture Ethics." In *Ethics, Science, Technology, and Engineering: An International Resource*, 2nd ed., 35–42. Independence: Cengage Press.

United Nations. 1948. "Universal Declaration of Human Rights." United Nations. 1948. www.un.org/en/universal-declaration-human-rights/.

Weber, Christopher, and H. Scott Matthews. 2008. "Food-Miles and the Relative Climate Impacts of Food Choices in the United States." *Environmental Science & Technology* 42 (10): 3508–13.

Williams, Patti, Jennifer Escalas, and Andrew Morningstar. 2022. "Conceptualizing Brand Purpose and Considering Its Implications for Consumer Eudaimonic Well-Being." *Journal of Consumer Psychology* 32:699–723.

Zwart, Hub. 2000. "A Short History of Food Ethics." *Journal of Agricultural and Environmental Ethics* 12 (2): 113–26.

# 4

# ETHICAL OMNIVORE'S ENVIRONMENTAL ETHIC

## How to Eat the World

During summers and weekends, I used to live with my grandparents near Kutztown, Pennsylvania. On chill mornings, I would run along the county roads winding around fields, dew glistening in the grass. Rabbits would nibble on wild mint along the roads, while the birds harkened in the day with their songs. Each farm had its own character. Most fields grew a single crop, be that corn, wheat, or soybeans. Corn is a staple in my State and very popular among farmers. Soy, the small squat legumes, were also popular, as they add nitrogen to the soil. As anyone who's ever grown corn knows, it's a greedy plant and depletes soil nutrients quickly. There is also a demand for soy, as more than 90% grown in the United States is used for animal feed, and it helps bolster corn production, by fixing nitrogen. It's easy to spot the corn fields that are nitrogen depleted, as the plants are a pale sickly yellow with spindly stalks. They're certainly too small to play in, which was an important criterion for my cousins. We particularly liked when healthy corn was grown, as we'd play hide and seek among the stalks, running along rows with vaulted ceilings of corn leaves overhead. Our uncles never minded, as we knew better than to harm the crop. Pastures broke up the landscape, as well, cows running to the fence line, while I passed. I'd always take a few sugar cubes from my grandmother's kitchen as a treat, and they knew it.

Coming around a bend, I remember how the landscape changed, as I got closer to Rodale's property. This leader of organic farming is headquartered on a 386-acre certified organic farm in Kutztown. Rodale has done a lot for farmers in the area, helping them to transition from conventional agriculture to organic, as well as leading soil health initiatives. I, personally, learned so much attending their seminars and farm tours, as a young person. Running along those back roads, it felt like the agricultural landscape shifted when

DOI: 10.4324/9781003215189-4

I got close to their property. Numbers of wild animals increased, birdsong intensifying, rather than crops. Their property looks like other farms and yet is quite different. They have field tests going, demonstration gardens, a pastured hog facility, and even a honeybee conservancy. I remember how they incorporated wildlife corridors into their landscape, careful to maintain biodiversity levels while still obtaining high yields. My favorite part of their operation is the pastured pigs, however, as they wiggle their bodies in joy, enjoying the beautiful landscape with hoof and snout. Watching the land from year to year and as seasons changed, land-use patterns also changed in the winding foothills of Kutztown. I didn't realize it at the time, but this picture of what farming could be stayed with me, even many years later. Organic and regenerative agriculture provides an environmentally friendly alternative to conventional farming that is better for the land, wildlife, and people. This chapter discusses the ecological realities of farming and how we can practice an environmental ethic rooted in the fields.

Perfecting organic and regenerative production methods is one of the missions of the Rodale Institute, a leader in organic farming. Ethical omnivores place great importance on producing food through sustainable and environmentally friendly methods. However, what does it mean to produce food in this way? Why do ethical omnivores buy organic? And what is regenerative agriculture? This chapter unpacks some of these terms. It explores ethical omnivores' environmental ethic more deeply. As we discussed, this diet centers on making sure that food that isn't harmful to the land, soils, animals, and humans, alike. One worry is that agricultural pesticides, herbicides, and other inputs will be harmful when consumed. Another worry is that these inputs, and agricultural methods more generally, will harm the environment.

## Ethical Omnivore Recommendation Snapshot

As we discussed, environmental critiques fueled the birth of The Organic Movement in the 19th and 20th centuries and the ethical omnivore diet grew out of this movement. Early figures were worried that new farming techniques of their day would negatively impact the land, soils, farm animals, wildlife, and human communities (Rodale Institute 2024; Conford 2001). Founding voices, such as Sir Albert Howard, Lady Eve Balfour, and J.I. Rodale spent their lives developing alternative methods of production that prioritized environmental health and sustainability (Noll 2024). Later, leaders crystalized lessons learned from these early figures into powerful critiques of late 20th-century farming methods. For instance, the Indian scholar and activist Vandana Shiva is highly critical of industrial farming systems. Shiva expresses her views in this powerful statement: For industrial agriculture "nature is unproductive; organic agriculture based on nature's cycles of renewability spells poverty… because it is assumed that 'production' takes place only when mediated by technologies for commodity production, even when such technologies destroy" (1988, 4). Similarly, the Rodale Institute (2024), a leader in The Organic Movement asks eaters to recognize the environmental harms caused by conventional, chemical-based farming. These include "soil health degradation, loss of organic matter and erosion, as well as water pollution, toxic residues in our food supply, and lack of biodiversity— to name a few" (n.p.). In this vein, Wendell Berry (1977) juxtaposes efficiency with care, arguing that efficiency ultimately feeds the goal of profit and money, whereas care involves ensuring the health of the land, your family, community, and self. He asks farmers to grapple with the type of person they want to be, a nurturer or exploiter. For Shiva, The Rodale Institute, and Berry, any benefits that conventional agriculture produces should be weighed against environmental, community, and health costs. And, the "externalities," or costs not included in the price to grow food, can be staggering. United Nations Environment Programme (2023) has gone so far as to argue that "the low retail cost of industrialized food can obscure its very high environmental price tag" (1). It's not the bargain it seems.

### Omnivores Eat Plants Too but They Better Be Organic

*The Ethical Omnivore Diet in a Nutshell: Grow or source your food locally. Eat organic produce and environmentally sustainable & ethically raised meats, poultry, fish, dairy, and eggs. Enjoy.*

The above thinkers recognize agricultural zones as areas of value and push eaters to think about the environmental costs of the food on their plates. Ethical omnivores, practicing an ethic of seeing, have answered this call. Most of the academic literature on this diet focuses on new omnivorism or conscientious carnivorism, stressing that omnivores embrace a diet where meat eating is acceptable, if the animals were raised in a farm with high animal welfare standards (Rothgerber 2015; Milburn and Bobier 2022). This is an important part of the ethical omnivore diet, but as the term omnivore suggests, plants are also on the menu and people care about how they're produced. As Dalrymple and Hilliard (2020) plainly state, ethical omnivores grapple with which food production systems they want to support. Sustainable animal production is only achievable as part of a larger environmentally friendly farming system. Animals provide much needed nitrogen, as they graze in the fields, while plants thrive in a system decoupled from petroleum fertilizers and inputs. Such a context may be hard to imagine, especially for eaters without the experience that comes from working on a farm or who are from a rural area. Farms are very different places when they're managed using sustainable and environmentally friendly methods. This wholistic view, that puts the plants back in the ethical omnivore diet, is important for understanding the environmental ethic at its heart. This diet includes eating grass-raised meat, butter and dairy products, wild-caught fish and game, but it also stresses the need to support regenerative and organic farming methods. When looked at wholistically, how and where we grow, raise, and harvest our food is the foundation of the ethical omnivore diet. Environments matter. What we eat and how we grow our food has a large impact on nature. Nature, in turn, impacts the quality and nutritional content of our food.

Typically, ethical omnivore recommendations stress food quality and mindful eating, prioritizing locally, ethically, and organically produced meats, dairy, eggs, and fruits and vegetables (Salant 2023). Organic and regenerative farming seem to do a lot of heavy lifting in this diet. But what is "organic" and "regenerative" farming? To get a handle on these terms, let's turn to the Rodale Institute and the USDA National Organic Standard. Agricultural activism after the 1950s led to the passing of the Organic Foods Production Act of the 1990 Farm Bill, which mandated that the USDA develop national organic standards for products and production (USDA 2021). The National Organic Program, that enforces national standards, was created in 2000. This program recognizes and rewards farmers for adopting more environmentally friendly farming methods (Noll 2024). Today, consumers rely on the USDA Organic label to ensure that they are buying food produced without synthetic fertilizers, pesticides, herbicides, and that is GMO-free (USDA 2023). The process for certification is quite expensive and time-consuming. Producers need to develop an organic system plan; implement the plan with the help of a certifying agent; be inspected by USDA representatives, who will then compare how the farmer's actual operation compares to their organic system plan; and only then will they obtain certification. And, this process doesn't end there. To ensure compliance, farmers need to repeat the inspection process yearly. In addition, land must be free of all prohibited substances for at least 3 years before farmers can grow organically certified crops. And, the standard requires that farmers use practices that conserve biodiversity, cycle resources, and preserve ecological balance. With these strict environmental and animal welfare standards in mind, it is no wonder that ethical omnivores have embraced organic agriculture. The creation of the USDA Organic Program was a huge win for eaters worried about the environmental impact of those tomatoes or lettuce in their salads.

But all organic agriculture is not the same. Producers embrace various production methods for their farms, which could differ widely. Large organic production still embraces many practices common in industrial farming, such as conventional tillage and monocrop planting. This led Robert Rodale, of the Rodale Institute, to coin the term "regenerative organic" to distinguish a kind of food production that goes beyond the organic label. This type of agriculture takes the organic standard as a starting point but pushes producers to go beyond it in their management practices, looking for even better ways to improve biodiversity levels, soil health, animal welfare, and the flourishing of farm systems. The three pillars of regenerative organic farming include soil health, animal welfare, and social fairness (Rodale Institute 2024). The USDA Certified Organic seal is a rigorous standard but there are several gaps, especially concerning soil health and animal welfare. It is also blind to ethical treatment of farm workers and farmers, alike. Soil is the lifeblood of the farm. It ensures the health of crops, increases their nutritional value, and guards against droughts. Regenerative farming uses practices like crop rotation, cover crops, and conservation tillage to build organic matter and promote biodiversity in soils. Their animal welfare standards incorporate the "Five Freedoms" that are important for ethical omnivores, and mandate that all animals be grass-fed and pasture raised. No CAFOS (concentrated animal feeding operations) are allowed. Finally, they also incorporate social fairness into the standard, to ensure that farm workers are paid living wages and work in safe conditions. Regenerative Organic Certified is a new standard, created by the Regenerative Organic Alliance (2024), including the Rodale Institute, Dr. Bronner's, and Patagonia, the popular outfitter. With topsoil levels dwindling globally, a more environmentally rigorous standard is needed.

Now, you may be wondering why companies dedicated to environmentalism would be supporting agriculture. The next sections of this chapter will answer this question in two ways: First, we'll briefly explore just how much land is under agricultural production and thus why we need to take farming seriously, as part of environmental protection. Then, we will discuss how agriculture and environmental protection are not separate issues but are, in fact, intertwined. At the most fundamental level, ethical omnivores embrace the idea that agriculture should feature prominently in environmental discussions, beyond those concerning hazards. And, indeed, it does in other disciplines. Ecologists, geographers, and other scholars tackling environmental problems often begin by looking at human impacts on water and land. This quickly brings them to agriculture (Thompson 2010). This is not surprising, as agriculture dominates the world's total landmass. For example, according to the Food and Agriculture Association of the United Nations, approximately 5 billion hectares, or 38%, of the world's total landmass is used for agriculture (FAO 2020). In the UK, land-use for farming is around 40%, whereas agricultural lands take up approximately 50% of the United States. To put this in perspective, we often think that public lands and parks are vast in the United States. However, only 20% of U.S. lands are set aside for conservation, including swamps, deserts, and remote mountain ranges. These percentages are staggering. The sheer amount of land used for agricultural production led Paul B. Thompson (2010) to argue that agriculture plays a major role in the way humans impact the environment. Thompson's point is driven home when you look at water-use numbers. In 2017 alone, 42% of U.S. water withdraws were used for crop irrigation (USDA 2022). Thus, "a very large portion of what we take to *be* the environment—nonurban land and water—is caught up in agriculture" (Thompson 2010, 19). With these numbers in mind, it's easier to see why the Rodale Institute, Dr. Bronner's, and Patagonia are worried. Not including agriculture in environmental protection plans is a grave mistake. We need to embrace the idea that agricultural lands are environments of value, beyond the products that they produce. Aldo Leopold, writing on his farm in Sand County was an early voice for a new environmentalism practiced down on the farm. But what kind of environmental ethic can be practiced on tilled and managed land?

## The Farm and Nature: Tensions

Before we explore this question, we first need to discuss how agriculture and environmental protection are intertwined. Farms are environments, for sure, but when we typically think of environments that need protecting, most people don't picture a farm. I asked several people around my town to describe their thoughts about environmental protection. I received some interesting answers. One person discussed the importance of maintaining public lands and habitats for wild animals. Others mentioned parks and mountains and how those should be protected. Still, others discussed historical figures that these parks are often named for, such as John Muir and Gifford Pinchot. Wilderness areas seemed to loom as large as Mt. Rainer in their understanding of environmentalism. They all seemed to be saying that wild areas are important and need protecting, but these environments are out there, away from the town. They're the mountain ranges, the still blue lakes, and forests that many Pacific Northwesterners have come to love. We go into nature to recharge and return home to where we work, live, and grow our food. And, when nature comes to town, in the form of a young bull moose or a cougar, we call the Department of Fish and Wildlife and help them find their way back to their natural habitats—back to nature. These are just a few replies from citizens in a small town, but I suspect many people share this vision of environments and environmentalism. These responses beg the question, though. What does farming have to do with protecting nature?

In one sense, you could argue that agriculture has very little to do with protecting nature, beyond the fact that agriculture is dependent on ecosystem services. To grow food, we need clean air and water, the pollination of crops, and other positive ecosystem benefits. All of these services are provided by the abstract processes that make up mother nature and not from human labor. Thus, this view frames farming as an extractive endeavor, gleaning necessary resources from the environment. It does not embrace the idea that farms *are* environments, beyond highly controlled ones. It focuses on the benefits that farms get from nature, rather seeing farms as a part of ecosystems. This idea that agricultural zones are somehow separate from nature has deep roots. In fact, the historical idea that farms are production zones, carved out of natural areas, is quite accurate. Wendell Berry (1977) and other agrarian writers have gone so far as to highlight the violence involved in wrestling back wilderness to "tame" land for human use. Pastures and farms didn't appear fully formed from the head of Zeus, but rather they are the product of blood, sweat, and tears. This history and juxtaposition between pasture/farm and wilderness impacts the ways that we manage land today. It's also the vision of farming that pioneers in The Organic Movement and ethical omnivores push back on, as we will see.

To understand just how unique The Organic Movement's declaration that "farms are ecosystems" is in today's agricultural context, we need only turn again to Wendell Berry. As he so eloquently illustrates, the idea that farms are separate from nature is old and grounded in sometimes brutal land use practices. Buried deep in the middle of Berry's (1968) essay "A Native Hill," there is an excerpt from the Collins' *History of Kentucky* published in 1878, describing when European settlers were first making inroads into its vast forests. Collins' quote an earlier text called "The Battle of the Fire-Brands" published in "The autobiography of Rev. Jacob Young, a Methodist minister." I won't republish the entire passage here, but Young described events that occurred while opening a new road from Newcastle to the mouth of the Kentucky River. It involved 100 men and one captain dressed in hunting shirts, buckskin pantaloons, leather belts, and hats. By day, the men jovially worked, clearing the forest for the road. At night, as it would get cold, they set large bonfires ablaze and rest beside them. One night, after much singing and drinking, the men divided themselves into two camps and waged a mock war. It was in good fun, at first, but turned ugly quickly. The men fought with fire-brands and some were severely wounded and the blood flowed freely into the soil of the newly cleared road. Berry quotes this passage to help readers understand the "heritage" that we inherited from the past. The significance of this snippet of history is its extreme violence. The work of clearing the forest to build a road is itself violent. And from the orderly violence of that labor, disorderly violence bloomed. I often think about this passage, when new areas are opened up for farming or pasture. First comes the road, then bit by bit the forest is beaten back, trees cut down, and fields expand out. Before long, the forest has been turned into productive farmland. Then, farmers spend years removing rocks to make the fences protecting their fields. People see farms and they think of bucolic nature, when in fact, farmland is the distinct absence of nature. Agriculture areas are carved out of natural landscapes, as unwanted plants and animals are removed through labor, pesticides, herbicides, and violence.

Protecting lands that have been carved out for human uses is what comes after the initial transformation. Indeed, the extirpation of competing species is part of farming. When a farmer sprays glyphosate (better known as roundup) on their fields, for example, every other plant dies except for the desired crop. This increases yield because those pesky weeds, like milkweed which monarch butterflies need, are no longer competing for limited amounts of nitrogen and other resources. You don't want your fields to be filled with unproductive plants (aka "weeds") or other species (aka "pests") that could harm the crop. In this vein, every year The USDA Wildlife Services posts data on wildlife management actions taken on farms. The 2022 report begins by stating that wildlife is a public resource and held in trust to be managed for future generations. But then, it notes that "predators cause an estimated $232 million in losses to livestock producers annually and bird damage to crops exceeds $150 million each year" (2022, n.p.). In the span of 1 year, the report estimates that approximately 21.5 million animals caused damage to farming operations, and nearly 20 million were removed unharmed from rural, urban, and other settings. This number is staggering, as are the efforts to safely remove animals. Additionally, though, 1.85 million animals were lethally removed, which included 1,175,244 European starlings, 136,791 feral swine, 450 bears, and various other species. They also tracked 463,000 coyotes over the last 5 years of (2014–2018) in state-regulated fur harvests. To limit waste, the USDA donated 150 tons of deer, goose, and other meat for animal consumption at rehab centers and other facilities, as well. Most of the lethal removals involved invasive species and were done to protect areas from damage. And, these are just the reported numbers, when wildlife management services are requested. Farmers remove many an animal from their land without the help of the USDA.

My point here is that agricultural environments are highly managed and protecting crops and livestock from competing species is common practice. Anyone who has ever tilled a field or raised chickens knows this well. Thus, modern farms are production zones, to pull from the agricultural philosopher Paul Thompson. They are tended and designed to produce specific agricultural products as efficiently as possible, in a controlled setting. This is the heritage that Berry was writing about all those years ago—The extirpation of competing species from our production zones and subsequent management to ensure that we get the lion share of resources.

From this view, agriculture may have very little to with protecting nature, indeed. And, these numbers should cause ethical vegetarians to pause and, perhaps, rethink those industrially produced vegetables. But all agriculture is not the same. Both ethical omnivores and environmental ethicists, such as Paul Thompson, Bernard Rollin, and I understand that agricultural lands are very important for environmental protection. To find examples, we just need to turn to the history of environmental thought in the United States. For instance, as discussed in an earlier chapter, the father of ecology, Aldo Leopold (2013) wrote at length about agriculture throughout his career and in his tour de force *Sand County Almanac*. In several of his published works and letters,

Leopold stressed the important role that farmers can play as conservationists (Meine 1989). After all, this book describes the many years that Leopold spent rehabilitating a mismanaged farm. This rehabilitation was driven by his land ethic, which sees humans as a part of an ecological community, or citizen, rather than exploiters. Similarly, Rachel Carson's (1962) *Silent Spring* discussed more than the perils of DDT. She spent several chapters discussing agriculture, where she was clearly concerned about harmful pesticide impacts to farm workers and nature, alike. Her work, published in the 1960s, shared some of Wendell Berry's concerns. Carson's work included scathing critiques of practices that were commonplace in her day. This work set the tone for environmentalist's critiques of agricultural land use for years to come. An important takeaway from these publications is that agricultural land use decisions have impacts beyond the farm. Like other species, pesticides and pollutants do not recognize property boundaries.

## Agriculture Lands: From Production Zones to Ecosystems

In this way, environmental ethics, as a field, typically treated farms, at best, as areas of environmental hazards and, at worst, examples of the technological arrogance of humans who think they can control nature (Noll 2024). Like urban areas, farms were typically written off as sacrifice zones (barring Aldo Leopold, Paul Thompson, and a handful of other thinkers) and thus not worthy of rehabilitation and thoughtful inspection. However, wilderness areas and those outside human control, were seen as worthy of attention. This was due to the fact wilderness has intrinsic value, or value in and of itself, irrespective of any instrumental gain we could glean from the harvest of natural goods (Piccolo 2017). We walk into a forest and entire communities of species live their lives without the need for human intervention. In John Muir's words, "the clearest way into the Universe is through a forest wilderness" (Quoted in Wolfe 1979, 313). Wilderness areas are places where we can go to learn truths about ourselves and the world around us, ones that escape us in human dominated environments. They teach us valuable lessons and are themselves valuable. And, they help us to develop virtues, as we interact with the world around us (Cafaro 2004). As Richard Sylvan later argued, we intuitively know that nature is valuable and precious, even if there are no humans there to enjoy it.

Yet, this focus on intrinsic value blinded early environmental ethicists to the reality that production zones, too, are environments worthy of consideration. Unsurprisingly, environmental philosophers have been debating valuation for years (Thompson 2008). Many philosophers embrace the view that value is derived from use, or how either humans or other entities use nature, and the impact of ecosystem processes. Another school of thought centers on preferences, or evaluative dispositions and attitudes of humans concerning their economic behavior or other measurements. These values inform justifications for preserving environmental "goods" and protecting them from consumption or destructive use, especially when costs or burdens to society are deemed too high. Intrinsic value plays a role here, as some environmental philosophers and activists believe that non-human entities (such as sentient creatures, ecosystems, landscapes, species, etc.) are valuable irrespective of their usefulness to humans. Thus, they need to be protected irrespective of any benefits we could glean from them. Paul B. Thompson argues that the term is typically used to signify values not associated with environmental use and it implies "that these intrinsic values override the uses that humans might make of the environment" (Thompson 2008, 535). Thus, intrinsic value arguments are used to constrain land use. For example, in 1965, the Sierra Club criticized Disney's plan to create a resort in Mineral King Valley on the grounds that the mountain was a natural treasure and should be preserved (Selmi 2022). After a lengthy court battle, ultimately, the courts sided with the Sierra Club and the mountain was made into a National Park. Mineral King was lauded as a success for environmentalists. Here, intrinsic values played an important role in framing objections to the use of this area for a ski resort, as Disney desired. But what happens when human development is not constrained? From this perspective, farms and cities, are the result of a failure to protect environments. I'm sure many readers are familiar with pictures of declining rainforests in Brazil, as agriculture lands expand, and natural habitat is cut down. The environmentalist does not advocate for the farm but decries the loss of the forest.

However, farms may be more greatly marked by the hands of humans, but they are still ecosystems. Humans are a part of nature as *Homo sapien sapiens*, after all. We change habitats more thoroughly, perhaps, but like the termite or ant this isn't something done outside of nature. This bias concerning human controlled environments is also found in Muir's work, when he so eloquently wrote that "I'm losing the precious days. I am degenerating into a machine for making money. I am learning nothing in this trivial world of men. I must break away and get out into the mountains to learn the news" (Quoted in Young 1915, 216). Here, the "world of men" and nature is juxtaposed as opposites, with our factories and towns characterized as distinct from the natural environment, and of lesser value, at that. Statements like these (along with the criticism that he can't do environmental ethics in New York City by his peers) prompted Andrew Light (2001) to write his influential article "The Urban Blindspot in Environmental Ethics." In it, he argues that the field suffers from an anti-urban bias. Light's critique was extended to agricultural lands, as well, as they are also production zones (Thompson 2010; Noll 2024). Thus, environmental protection is alive and well, but only for some areas. Others are placed outside of the scope of concern, destined to be sacrificed to fulfill the needs and desires of humans.

And, here we are. Environmentalists focus on protecting dwindling natural reserves, while agricultural zones get sprayed with glyphosate several times a year, not to mention our lawns.

The environmental ethicist Gene Hargrove's (1992) research provides an origin story, of sorts, for how this production zone bias came to be. Building off the above discussion of intrinsic value, Hargrove and later Light (2001) blame environmentalists' historical dissatisfaction with: (a) instrumental and (b) anthropocentric-based environmental ethics. Roughly, instrumental ethics are those that prioritize management strategies aimed at providing goods or services, and anthropocentric ethics are those that benefit humans, or prioritize human values. These types of justifications are popular in the literature. For example, Muir is often depicted as one of the first thinkers to champion the view that environments are intrinsically valuable. However, there has been some pushback, as reading from "the book of nature" is itself an extractive activity. Muir stated just above that we can glean truths from the natural world, which is a type of epistemic (or knowledge based) use. Though, outside of the anthropocentric/ecocentric debate, Muir is also refreshingly pragmatic, stressing the idea that human beings are part of a larger system and the need for harmonious living. As for resources, his contemporary Gifford Pinchot, the first head of the U.S. Forestry Service, recommended we adopt a utilitarian approach to forest management, but with an eye towards future generations. Finally, contemporary arguments that ecosystems should be protected, so that we can continue to enjoy the services they provide is also instrumental. Later, environmental thinkers argued that stressing human use and benefits is part of the problem, exacerbating the harmful treatment of wilderness (Callicott and Nelson 1998). In fact, there is a rather lively debate between those who argue for preservation and those who instead recommend wise use of wilderness. Beyond the forest, the emphasis on wild nature led to the anti-urban and anti-agricultural biases that we have today.

These concerns about anthropocentrically and instrumentally valuing nature are understandable, as we should be protecting wilderness. Wildlife habitat around the world is dwindling and if we are committed to living in balance with nature, then this destruction needs to stop. It seems like skeptical environmental ethicists are worried that embracing instrumental and human-centered land use practices could create a slippery slope, where all lands become potentially open to human use. If farms and cities are natural environments, albeit ones where humans dominate the landscape, then what's the difference between these and wilderness areas? Why not simply allow humans to move into protected habitat? After all, humans are species, like any other, and if our land use is "natural," then the distinction between field/pasture and wilderness is an illusion. We should simply follow Gifford Pinchot's lead and manage all public lands like our forests, so that the needs of current and future human generations are met. This is a serious critique and one that could easily be applied to The Organic Movement's challenge that farms are areas worthy of discussion and of environmental value. After all, aren't human needs and desires prioritized on agricultural lands, even if we use environmentally friendly practices? An environmentalist critical of anthropocentric instrumental land use practices would be skeptical of this challenge, at best, and hostile, at worst. Intrinsic values, as a constraint to use, is built on the ontological demarcation of artificial and natural entities.

In reply, I argue that the slippery slope criticism creates a false dilemma fallacy, where we only have two options when it comes to land use: The protectionist (or hands-off) approach or the extractive (or the strip mining) approach. In our desire to provide a pristine defense of wilderness, urban and agricultural areas are indeed sacrificial zones, both in practice and in much of the environmental ethics literature. Many contemporary environmental ethicists, several of which we already discussed, are vehemently opposed to framing land use in this way. One way to address the slippery slope criticism is to point to the diverse ways agricultural lands *are* valued. The Organic Movement and ethical omnivores do not accept the view that farms are simply production zones. They are valued in complicated ways, that are both intrinsic and instrumental. For example, small-scale sustainable farming operations produce a wide array of agricultural products. When you visit a farmstand, you might find honey, corn, beans, tomatoes, wool, yarn, sheepskin, meat products, and plethora of other goods for sale. Yet, the ways that they produce these goods are also driven by ecological commitments. You can produce products and also maintain biodiversity levels, increase soil health, promote flourishing on the farm etc., especially when you use the most environmentally friendly methods possible and work within the constraints of ecological systems and with other species. This is what it means when Wendell Berry (1977) urges producers to embrace the role of "nurturer" rather than that of exploiter. It is also what Aldo Leopold (2013) means when he urges us to manage farms like we are a member of the ecological community. Being a part of an ecological community means that your needs are important, but you should always be sensitive to the needs of the land— the water, soils, and other species that make up your farm. All species require sustenance, after all, humans included.

Hargrove (1992) provides a useful taxonomy to better understand how production zones are valued, that is sensitive to both anthropocentric and intrinsic values (Noll 2024).

These can be placed into the following categories: "(1) non-anthropocentric instrumental value, (2) anthropocentric instrumental value, (3) non-anthropocentric intrinsic value, and (4) anthropocentric intrinsic value" (186). Let's start at the beginning to unpack this list, as the jargon is strong in philosophy. Non-anthropocentric instrumental valuations, are found throughout nature, as flora and fauna have instrumental relationships, where they benefit or harm each other. These values are often converted into factual claims and are typically not discussed in ethical ways. For example, a lion may rely on hunting gazelles to obtain food. Here, the lion is benefiting from the gazelle, and this has nothing to do with humans. We also typically don't fault the lion and say that they are unethical because they hunted the gazelle. Similarly, anthropocentric instrumental value claims are common and uncontroversial, as humans can benefit or are harmed by plants and animals. Willow bark (which contains acetylsalicylic acid) can benefit or harm us, independent of how we feel about willow trees. The same argument can be made for nightshade, or any other plant. Hargrove finds non-anthropocentric intrinsic value uncontroversial, as well. The recognition that beings have goods of their own, irrespective of human values, is not problematic. Here, he draws from the work of Holmes Rolston III and Paul Taylor, arguing that animals can be "centers of purpose" in the Aristotelian sense of that term (187). This simply means that species often rely on their own natures to fulfill their needs. Anyone who walks in the woods knows this well. Other species, from the aardvark to the zebra finch, go about their business, doing what they need to do to survive. For Hargrove, anthropocentric intrinsic value judgements are the only valuations that rely on human judgement. His overall point is that the ways humans value environments are complex. When we take anthropocentric or human-centered values off the table, we're losing an important part of the picture, so to speak. This is similarly the case when we reject instrumental or use-based values.

How we value agricultural land is quite complex, for a single farmer, let alone as a society. First, we do value farmland instrumently, regardless of the type of production methods used (Noll 2024). Barring foraged foodstuffs, most of our food is obtained through agriculture, after all. Rural communities and local farmers are also economically supported by these activities and farming often bolsters local food security. My own family ate quite well during the Great Depression, as they were fortunate enough to live on a farm. In addition to anthropocentric instrumental value, farms are environments where non-anthropocentric instrumental and intrinsic values abound, as flora and fauna attempt to thrive and interact with each other. Wheat and canola are not going to complain about optimal growing conditions. In *The Botany of Desire*, Michael Pollan (2001) has gone so far as to argue that certain plants may have tricked us into tending to them, so that they thrive. The endless acres of corn in the Midwest tended by a small army of farmers lend credence to this view. Domesticated crops are doing very well, it seems, in the grand scheme of things. Additionally, anthropocentric intrinsic values play a key role in how we appreciate farming areas. A farmer lovingly tending to the barn built by her great-great grandfather, for example, is an example of someone valuing a farm, irrespective of the crops currently being stored in the building or the money that she will make selling them.

Agricultural land can be valued simultaneously as an intergenerational family home (Thompson 2010; Wender 2011), a center of conservation (Leopold 2013), a wildlife corridor (Noll 2017), and a place of cultural and educational significance (Delind and Bingen 2008), etc.

One of the things that I appreciate about Hargrove's (1992) work is his nuanced understanding of how humans value environments. There are human-centered ways that we create and cherish landscapes, other species, each other, and things. Pushing back against the myopic view that anthropocentric values are problematic, Hargrove instead argues that "anthropocentric intrinsic value judgments, rather than being in competition with nonanthropocentric intrinsic values, are absolutely essential if humans are to muster any environmental concern about nonhuman living centers of purpose... objectively existing out in the world" (187). Here, he single-handedly dismantles the critique that human-centered ethics are problematic for environmental protection. We can't help but engage with the world in these ways. Similarly, instrumentally using the environment is not always problematic, but necessary for life. All species rely on the environment to obtain basic necessities. Agricultural regions are excellent examples of the myriad ways that humans and nonhumans alike depend on ecosystems and each other to thrive. This doesn't mean that we should open wilderness areas for development. Rather, it shows how we value different environments in unique ways and these contextual factors matter for determining what ethical use looks like. Thus, farms can act as a looking glass to better see how we value environments and what that means on the ground, concerning use.

Drawing from Hargrove (1992), one of the strengths of the ethical omnivore diet is that it pushes eaters to better understand how human's intrinsically value farming environments. Farms are not simply large of tracts of land that are used to produce our food. They could be a family farm, a legacy, educational center, a seed bank, wildlife habitat, migration corridor, photographer's paradise, and a myriad other things beyond a production zone. This deeper conceptualization of farms is essential for bolstering environmental concern for agricultural lands. This makes sense, as a necessary condition for passing agricultural and conservation policy often includes human recognition of intrinsic value claims. These insights are incredibly important for understanding the environmental ethic at the heart of The Organic Movement and the ethical omnivore diet.

### The Ethical Omnivore Environmental Ethic

So, we return full circle, back to the ethical omnivore diet and its commitment to organic and regenerative farming. On the surface, the recommendations are quite simple. (1) Grow or source your food locally, (2) eat organic produce, and (3) source environmentally sustainable & ethically raised meats, poultry, fish, dairy, and eggs. However, when we unpack these recommendations, by looking at organic and regenerative farming standards, we find that the diet is grounded in a robust environmental ethic. Gene Hargrove's (1992) work helps to illustrate how it is connected to other environmental ethics but is also unique. For one thing, this environmental ethic is unapologetically instrumental, meaning that ethical omnivores demand that farms should embrace the idea that they are places of anthropocentric and non-anthropocentric instrumental value. They are environments where food is grown for humans to enjoy and they are areas of production, where individuals earn a living selling this food. But, they are also areas where other species find sustenance, live, and even pass through, in the case of migratory species. This also includes the recognition of intrinsic values for both humans and non-humans alike, as humans and domesticated animals attempt to live full lives. When we uncover its roots, the ethical omnivore diet is built on a robust ethic that is about more than supporting high welfare standards on the farm. It is about recognizing the realities that humans and non-humans alike need food and habitat, but also deserve to live a good life. It mandates that we strive for balance between the four cardinal values of Hargrove's taxonomy.

For example, let's return to environmental ethicists concern with anthropocentric and instrumental environmental ethics. Here, the historical emphasis on nature's value in and of itself, irrespective of humans, created blind spots in environmental ethics (Light 2001). Questioning human goals and desires is understandable, as wildlife habitat around the world is dwindling. But ironically, ethical omnivores largely agree with the sentiment that led to the agricultural blind-spot, just not in the conclusion that cities and farms should be treated as sacrifice zones.

For example, they agree that: (1) it is bad when human values are the primary ones allowed to influence land use and (2) that treating an environment as only a means to obtaining some resource is ethically problematic. Large-scale industrial agriculture and systems that prioritize efficiency and yield over all other goals, at face value, are guilty of unchecked anthropocentric instrumentalism. All other values in Hargrove's taxonomy are sacrificed at the altar of productivity. The ethical omnivore environmental ethic does not condone this type of farming. Rather, it pushes us to find balance when producing food, so that other things of value can be protected and nurtured, such as biodiversity, wildlife habitat, and animal welfare for today and for generations to come.

### An Ethic Grounded in Agrarian Pragmatism

In addition, the environmental ethic is grounded in agrarian pragmatism. Both agrarianism and pragmatism, as schools of thought, have long and varied histories, though Thompson (2008) is careful to point out that pragmatism is heir to much older agrarian ideas. Indeed, many of the thinkers we've discussed in this book can be considered agrarians or agrarian pragmatists, such as Wendell Berry, Andrew Light, Paul Thompson, and even Aldo Leopold. Agrarian thinkers stress the role of practice when forming values, norms, and social institutions (Thompson 2008). In particular, they are interested in the ways that these features of life emerge from human's interaction with nature "in the form of material subsistence practices such as obtaining food, clothing, and shelter" (528). For this tradition, values are products of human–environment interactions. Environmental differences, such as climate, soil type, and other landscape features, will lead to different production practices, which in turn influence the norms and values of communities. In this way, the environment "selects" for culture. If one farmer adopts a production method that successfully produces a crop, other farmers will follow suit, or they will go out of business. Norms that are passed from one generation to another, or from season to season, are selected by the environment due to their ability to feed people. From this perspective, farming practices (such as the use of irrigation, conventional tillage, slash and burn, intercropping, etc.) are the product of nature and culture, and change from year to year in response to the natural and social environment. Because of this dynamic process, agrarian thinkers often talk about ethical strengths and failings as a feature of personal character. Wendell Berry's distinction between "good farming" and "exploitation" is a nice example of this tendency.

Agrarian theories are environmental ethics because they are grounded in human–environment interconnections and emphasize the role that nature plays within the farmer's consciousness (Thompson 2008). As Henry David Thoreau believed, practical interactions with the environment like planting potatoes, building a home, fishing, and walking your fence line influence the development of human character. Here, environments are not wilderness but whatever context we find ourselves in. Rather than myopically focusing on maximizing positive benefits of land use, these thinkers see production as a type of three-way co-production. As Thompson so eloquently states, "the farmer produces crops and livestock, to be sure, but in doing so adapts to soil and climate in producing the farm" (541). This co-production creates the context for moral evaluation. Agrarian pragmatist approaches build off this dynamic understanding of how farming methods, norms/virtues, and society dynamically influence one another. From an agrarian pragmatist perspective, human beings are part of a larger system "that has a formative role in their activities and practices, and subsequently in what is valuable or important for them" (Thompson 2008, p. 11). Ethics then should concern itself with the relationships between humans and this larger whole, and in seeking harmony between us, nature, and other species.

## The Ecological Eater

Ethical omnivores embrace this call for harmony. They push back against this idea that we should fully optimize land-use for our benefit. The farmer has an important role as steward, producing crops and livestock, while ensuring soil health and thriving within the farming environment. From this perspective, they also have a duty to work within the larger ecological whole, seeking balance. It is precisely industrial agriculture's impact, decoupling agricultural production from ecological carrying capacity, that Wendell Berry critiqued in *The Unsettling of America*. We should live in balance with nature, ensuring sustainable food production for years to come, rather than mining topsoil to profit in the short-term, while removing biodiversity from agricultural areas. With habitat dwindling and extinctions on the rise, these management strategies are short-sighted. Looking back at the Organic Standard, the recommendations make better sense when placed in this context. We should grow produce and grains using natural fertilizers, eco-friendly pest control methods, and protect soil and water from pollution. We have a duty to farm animals, to ensure that they can roam freely outdoors, have a high welfare, and not use pharmaceuticals that could harm their development. We should prioritize soil health, build wildlife corridors, and promote biodiversity on the farm. Not all species are in competition with us, after all. Farmers and farm workers should make a living wage, so that management strategies aren't wholly dictated by economics. Both organic and regenerative organic standards provide an alternative to industrial farming systems. This may be what Salant (2023) meant when she stated that ethical omnivores are committed to eating in line with Mother Nature. These eaters may not all be farmers but, by supporting farmers who embrace this vision, they are trying to bring about change, one meal at a time.

## References

Berry, Wendell. 1968. "A Native Hill." *The Hudson Review* 21 (4): 601–34.

Berry, Wendell. 1977. *The Unsettling of America: Culture & Agriculture*. Sierra Club Books.

Cafaro, Philip. 2004. *Thoreau's Living Ethics: Walden and the Pursuit of Virtue*. Athens, GA: University of Georgia Press.

Callicott, J. Baird, and Michael Nelson, eds. 1998. *The Great Wilderness Debate*. Athens, GA: University of Georgia Press.

Carson, Rachel. 1962. *Silent Spring*. Houghton Mifflin Harcourt Trade & Reference Publishers.

Conford, Phillip. 2001. *The Origins of the Organic Movement*. Glasgow: Floris Books.

Dalrymple, Laura, and Grant Hilliard. 2020. *The Ethical Omnivore: A Practical Guide and 60 Nose-to-Tail Recipes for Sustainable Meat Eating*. Sydney: Murdoch Books.

Delind, Laura B., and Jim Bingen*. 2008. "Place and Civic Culture: Re-Thinking the Context for Local Agriculture." *Journal of Agricultural and Environmental Ethics* 21 (2): 127–51. https://doi.org/10.1007/s10806-007-9066-5.

Food and Agriculture Organization of the United Nations. 2020. *Sustainable Food and Agriculture: Land Use in Agriculture by the Numbers.* 2020. www.fao.org/sustain ability/news/detail/en/c/1274219/.

Hargrove, Eugene. 1992. "Weak Anthropocentric Intrinsic Value." *Monist* 75 (2): 183–208.

Leopold, Aldo. 2013. *A Sand County Almanac & Other Writings on Ecology and Conservation.* Edited by Curt Meine. Library of America.

Light, Andrew. 2001. "The Urban Blind Spot in Environmental Ethics." *Environmental Politics* 10 (1): 7–35. https://doi.org/10.1080/714000511.

Meine, Curt. 1989. "The Farmer as Conservationist: Aldo Leopold on Agriculture." *Journal of Soil and Water Conservation* 42 (3): 144–49.

Milburn, Josh, and Christopher Bobier. 2022. "New Omnivorism: A Novel Approach to Food and Animal Ethics." *Food Ethics* 7 (1): 2–17.

Noll, Samantha. 2017. "Climate Induced Migration: A Pragmatic Strategy for Wildlife Conservation on Farmland." *Pragmatism Today* 8 (2): 17.

Noll, Samantha. 2024. "Environmental Ethics Down on the Farm." *Environmental Ethics* 46 (3): 247-254.

Piccolo, John. 2017. "Intrinsic Values in Nature: Objective Good or Simply Half of an Unhelpful Dichotomy?" *Journal for Nature Conservation* 37:8–11.

Pollan, Michael. 2001. *The Botany of Desire: A Plant's-Eye View of the World.* New York, NY: Random House.

Regenerative Organic Alliance. 2024. "Why Regenerative Organic?" *Regenerative Organic Alliance.* https://regenorganic.org/why-regenerative-organic/.

"Rethinking Wilderness: The Need for a New Idea of Wilderness." n.d.

Rodale Institute. 2024a. *Leaders Who Founded the Organic Movement.* Nonprofit Organization. Rodale Institute. 2024. https://rodaleinstitute.org/blog/leaders-orga nic-movement/.

Rodale Institute. 2024b. *Regenerative Organic Certified.* Rodale Institute. https://roda leinstitute.org/regenerative-organic-certification/.

Rothgerber, Hank. 2015. "Can You Have Your Meat and Eat It Too? Conscientious Omnivores, Vegetarians, and Adherence to Diet." *Appetite* 84:196–203.

Salant, Lana Joe. 2023. *About the Ethical Omnivore Movement.* Ethical Omnivore Movement. www.ethicalomnivore.org/about-eom/.

Selmi, Daniel. 2022. *Dawn at Mineral King Valley: The Sierra Club, the Disney Company, and the Rise of Environmental Law.* Chicago, IL: University of Chicago Press.

Shiva, Vandana. 1988. *Staying Alive: Women, Ecology, and Development.* New York, NY: North Atlantic Books.

Thompson, Paul B. 2008. "Agrarian Philosophy and Ecological Ethics." *Science and Engineering Ethics* 14:527–44.

Thompson, Paul B. 2010. *The Agrarian Vision: Sustainability and Environmental Ethics.* University Press of Kentucky.

United Nations Environment Programme. 2023. *Ten Ways You Can Help Fight the Climate Crisis.* United Nations. www.unep.org/news-and-stories/story/10-ways-you-can-help-fight-climate-crisis.

U.S. Department of Agriculture. 2021. *U.S. Department of Agriculture: National Agricultural Library.* Governmental Website. Organic Production/Organic

Food: Information Access Tools. 2021. www.nal.usda.gov/legacy/afsic/organic-productionorganic-food-information-access-tools.

U.S. Department of Agriculture. 2022. *U.S. Department of Agriculture: Economic Research and Service*. Governmental Website. Irrigation & Water Use. 2022. www.ers.usda.gov/topics/farm-practices-management/irrigation-water-use/.

USDA Agricultural Marketing Service. 2024. *USDA Certified Organic: Understanding the Basics*. United States Department of Agriculture. www.ams.usda.gov/services/organic-certification/organic-basics#:~:text=Organic%20is%20a%20label%20that,biodiversity%2C%20and%20preserve%20ecological%20balance.

USDA Animal and Plant Health Inspection Services. 2022. *USDA Wildlife Services Posts Fiscal Year 2022 Data on Management Actions and Funding Sources*. United States Department of Agriculture. www.aphis.usda.gov/news/program-update/usda-wildlife-services-posts-fiscal-year-2022-data-management-actions-funding.

USDA, Economic Research Service. 2023. *Organic Agriculture: Overview*. United States Department of Agriculture. www.ers.usda.gov/topics/natural-resources-environment/organic-agriculture.aspx.

Wender, Melanie. 2011. "Goodbye Family Farms and Hello Agribusiness: The Story of How Agricultural Policy Is Destroying the Family Farm and the Environment." *Villanova Environmental Law Journal* 22 (1): 141–67.

Wolfe, Linnie Marsh. 1979. *John of the Mountains: The Unpublished Journals of John Muir*. Madison, WI: University of Wisconsin Press.

Young, Samuel Hall. 1915. *Alaska Days by John Muir*. New York, NY: Fleming H. Revell Company.

# 5

# THE IMPORTANCE OF LOCAL FOOD FOR THE ETHICAL OMNIVORE DIET

Every year, the Moscow Farmers Market begins their season on May 4, when some local products are finally ready to be harvested and sold. It is a popular Saturday morning event in a small town in Idaho, near where I live. Like clockwork, farmers will travel from around the region to town and residents of the Palouse fill the streets. The market began in 1976 with a few farmers, but the venture is now going strong, as hundreds of vendors offer fresh fruits and vegetables, meats, homemade baked goods, nursery plants, cheeses, flowers, handmade crafts, and local delicacies. I particularly enjoy the locally made hot sauces and tamales. My spouse and I often arrive early to talk with farmers, as they unload their beautiful offerings. It is a whirlwind of local fruits and vegetables, honey, huckleberries, and music. The vendors are passionate about their products, delighted in discussing their farms and how their foodstuffs were produced. The Scandinavian baker, for example, will often talk about the time and care she puts into sourcing high quality and culturally appropriate ingredients for her insanely good treats. Down the row from her, the beekeeper offers samples of his various honeys, each uniquely flavored, as the bees fed-off different types of flowers. Buckwheat honey is as dark as blackstrap molasses and rich, while wildflower honey is as golden as the sun over the Palouse prairies. This is a historically important pastime, he will tell you, as beekeeping flourished around world. The Etruscans maintained beehives on boats and the Aztecs mastered the production of monofloral and multifloral varietals. When in season, the pepper farmers will bring in over 50 different types and explain how each is unique and flavorful. Perhaps my favorite farmers are the fruit vendors, with their sweet offerings. They'll often cut a slice off different peaches or offer you several types of cherries, so that you can compare the tastes. I always learn something new when I visit the

DOI: 10.4324/9781003215189-5

Moscow Farmers Market and feel connected to my community and place. Then, end sneaks up on us and the market it over. The vendors wrestle canvas roof tents back into their traveling cases and pack up boxes of their unsold bounties. The community disperses, traveling back to their homes, and we eaters wait patiently until the next market day.

## The Importance of Local Food for the Ethical Omnivore Diet

This chapter explores the many ways that ethical omnivores embrace buying "local" or the local food movement. As readers know, the ethical omnivore diet is built on eating food that is produced in ethically and environmentally friendly ways. This includes supporting organic and regenerative production methods, as well as pasture raised and free-range animal agriculture. Popular websites and books often recommend that omnivores buy locally produced foods, as well. But why is this? Local farmers could embrace many agricultural practices, including industrial production methods. If it's just about distance, then it doesn't seem to fit with the rest of the recommendations. It seems that an organically produced tomato would be preferable to a conventionally grown one, even if the conventional one was from the farm next door. One reason why ethical omnivores embrace local food could be that eating products produced within a 100-mile radius could reduce farming's environmental footprint, or the product's food miles (Noll and Werkheiser 2017). Food miles are the distance, food is transported from the farm to the consumer. This argument is relatively straightforward. The food that we buy in grocery stores is often grown in other states and even other countries. Let's look at some of my favorite fruits, as an example. Many of the bananas and pineapples sold in the store are grown in Costa Rica. California grows around 90% of U.S.-produced strawberries, yet many grocery stores carry strawberries grown in Mexico, as this country is one of the largest importers to the United States (Wu et al. 2021). Another of my favorite products, coffee, is produced all around the world and, yet, that morning cup of joe is available across the country. So, it is understandable that buying local features prominently next to buying organic in the ethical omnivore diet.

However, reducing food miles is only one of the reasons why local food is important. For example, detractors argue that environmental benefits of buying local are overblown (Singer and Mason 2007; de Bres 2016), as transportation makes up only a small amount of agriculture's greenhouse gas emissions (Weber and Matthews 2008). Peter Singer and Jim Mason (2007) have gone so far as to argue that local food is unethical. We should be supporting impoverished farmers in other countries with food dollars, rather than the well-off farmers in the United States. This argument fits with his utilitarian mindset, but it is problematic. Not only is this argument built on a gross misunderstanding of the financial plight of American farmers (many are a few harvests away from losing their farms), but it is also blind to the various reasons why people buy local products. It's not just about reducing food miles.

When we focus on how food is produced, then the recommendation to buy locally produced food takes on a different meaning. It is true that, from a general perspective, buying local means purchasing products grown close to home. However, it also means so much more. Buying that local tomato or pint of strawberries is a way for eaters to support community agriculture projects, farmers who care about the environment, and producers who prioritize animal welfare. This is especially the case when you can talk to the farmer or visit the farm itself. These and other interactions provide eaters with opportunities to learn about how their food is produced and agriculture, more generally. This deepens our understanding food systems and how our food choices impact the environment, animals, and other communities. Buying that locally grown tomato helps to support alternative food systems, and thus challenges the industrialized, global food system one meal at a time. Supporters argue that this alternative food system is revolutionary, as it embraces environmental sustainability, animal welfare, resilience, and the importance of protecting local communities from economic hardships.

This chapter explores why ethical omnivores embrace local food. To do this, we will define what local food is and explore the reasons why eaters are embracing locavorism. (Here, a locavore is simply someone who prioritizes eating local food and locavorism is the social moment surrounding this practice.) It should be no surprise to the readers that these projects can take on many forms. In fact, the local food movement is not static, but should be understood as a diverse initiative that includes several distinct types of food projects. It then discusses the many connections between ethical omnivorism and local food movements. In a way, the ethical omnivore diet and locavorism share the same roots in the organic agriculture movement. As such, both are simultaneously a food ethic and a social initiative aimed at bringing about structural changes to agriculture, or how we produce food. They are also deeply intertwined, as we will see, helping to bolster each other. We will end with the exploration of local food as a heuristic (Thompson 2023) and how increasing personal knowledge and developing habits are important for eaters.

## What Are Local Food Projects and Why Do They Matter?

Books and articles urging us to eat locally are now commonplace, as popular authors such as Wendell Berry, Barbara Kingsolver, and Michael Pollan urge readers to buy locally produced foodstuffs. In fact, local food initiatives are steadily popping up in communities and neighbourhoods around the country. They have diverse goals and can take many forms, such as farmers markets, urban farms, community-supported agriculture projects (or CSAs), and even small gardens in schools (Holt-Gimenez et al. 2011; DeLind 2011; Martinez et al. 2010). I'm sure many readers have gone to a farmers' market, buying fresh produce, eggs, and other delicious goods. I personally go to the Moscow Farmers Market near my home and take for granted that it will be open every Saturday after May. According to the USDA (2022), there are approximately 8770 farmers markets in the United States, up from 1755 in 1994. That is substantial growth, for sure. However, even the 1994 numbers are impressive, as the history of direct-to-consumer food sales is a bleak tale. The geographer Allison Brown (2001) provides a riveting summery of this history in a little-known paper blandly titled "Counting Farmers Markets." Brown begins her overview with the story of pear growers in Marin County, California. In 1943, they openly flaunted authorities, loading trucks with their produce and selling their goods in central San Francisco, where thousands of residents lined up to buy fresh fruit at a steep discount, often 65% below market value. John Burcato, San Francisco Water Authority Officer and farmer described these markets as "a way to handle produce gluts resulting from World War II labor and transport shortages while smashing the monopoly of regional produce brokers" (p. 655). Readers might be familiar the politics of fruit production in California, as the industry was painted in a poor light in John Steinbeck's novel *The Grapes of Wrath*. There were other black-market operations around country, such as Spokane, Washington's dairy smuggling operation.

An important takeaway from this history is that farmers markets were already struggling during this time. Post-World War II construction of irrigation infrastructure in the West and the interstate highway system sounded the death knell for these ventures. By 1970, only 340 were left and those few were populated by resellers, rather than farmers. Their numbers continued to dwindle until the passage of the Direct Marketing Act of 1976 by Congress, which legitimized direct-to-consumer marketing and sales, freeing up the USDA to work with farmers to rebuild local markets. This policy and regulatory change, coupled with the work of popular agrarian authors, such as Wendell Berry, helped to popularize buying local. Today, farmers markets are commonplace in the United States and around the world.

## From Buying Local to the Organic Movement

The push to rebuild local markets is interconnected with the growing popularity of organic farming practices. As discussed earlier in the book, the Organic Movement began to take root in the 1940s, when concerned farmers were worried that new farming techniques (what we today call industrial farming) could negatively impact sustainability, soil health, animal populations, and human communities (Rodale Institute 2021; Conford 2001). This movement continued to gain in popularity, as giants in sustainable agriculture (such as Wes Jackson and Robert Rodale) provided additional critiques of industrial production and championed the benefits of growing and eating organic products. Before the 1980s, most farmers entered into organic production because of their deeply held environmental, philosophical, or spiritual values (Guthman 2014). Following in the footsteps of organic pioneers, early adopters attempted to put their written ideas into practice and continue refining regenerative farming methods. An excellent example of this is the Rodale Institute, founded in 1947 to perform the longest running scientific experiments on organic production. They sought to use the power of science to demonstrate that organic methods perform as well, if not better, than conventional methods. Like local farmers markets, organic production also saw explosive growth in the 1980s. Changes in agricultural policy, the creation of tariff barriers, and shifting commodity supports impacted how growers make their planting decisions. Simultaneously, citizens started to become aware of how food is produced and became increasingly concerned with what I call the Trifecta of Food Concerns. These are: (a) environmental impacts, (b) animal welfare failures, and (c) human health effects. We discussed each of these in previous chapters. Eaters in the 1980s began to demand that food be produced in ways that align with their values.

Local farmers market numbers rose, and these venues gave consumers an opportunity to impact agricultural production, far more than they could before. Individual citizens could write to the USDA but they have very little power when it comes to agricultural policy and regulations. Also, without direct contact with farmers, as purchases are mediated through the market, they also have limited control over how their food is produced. For example, once a farmer sells their corn to the granary, it loses its connection to the farm, as it comingles with corn produced by other farmers, who used a variety of practices. By the time consumers buy corn, they usually have no idea how it was produced, unless they buy it from a farmer. Local farmers markets changed all this. With the blessing of Congress, direct-to-consumer marketing and sales are now legitimized. Farmers had an opportunity to create boutique products that meet the needs and desires of local eaters. Producers could charge a premium for these products, creating additional streams of income to support their operations. By the 1990s, farmers market numbers grew to 1755 and continued to increase annually (USDA 2022). In addition, numbers of other direct-to-consumer venues also rose, including CSAs, teaching farms, school gardens, etc.

From a historical perspective, it is not surprising that ethical omnivores embrace local food. Being able to talk with farmers and get to know how your food is produced is an essential part of being an ethical omnivore. When we look at the Trifecta of Food Concerns (environmental impacts, animal welfare, and human health effects), each are important for those embracing this diet and lifestyle. Local food venues have risen to the challenge, providing opportunities for eaters to find food that aligns with what they care about. Today, these once boutique products are becoming mainstream, especially after the USDA (2021) implemented the National Organic Standard in 2002 and local produce began to be featured prominently in food venues. In addition, other labels were created (Certified Humane, Wild Caught, etc.) to help eaters get a better understanding of how their food is produced. Now, a wide range of organically produced foodstuffs are available for purchase at your local grocery store, removing the need to buy directly from your farmer. However, as we can see from the USDA numbers, the growth of local food venues continues.

## Eating Local as an Ethical Omnivore

Part of the reason for this growth is that local food initiates satisfy several needs of individual consumers and communities. Local food movements can be broken down into three sub-movements, each with their own ethical commitments (Werkheiser and Noll 2014). As we'll see, there are: (a) individual-focused initiatives, guided by dietary concerns, (b) systems-focused initiatives, or those intended to bring about change at the policy and regulatory level, and (c) community-focused initiatives, or those with the goal of empowering local communities and bolstering food sovereignty. In this chapter, we'll be spending a lot of time discussing individual focused projects, as ethical omnivores are quite concerned with how foodstuffs impact personal health. A common justification for switching to this diet is that it's healthier. Though, does this mean that ethical omnivores are simply consumers demanding boutique products that fit with their values, or is there something more here? Before we tackle this topic, I want to briefly mention that systems-focused initiatives are also important for ethical omnivores, which should come as no surprise to readers.

These projects often focus on bringing about change at the policy or regulatory level. The United States has a long history of using policy to support both small- and large-scale agricultural systems. Policy tools, such the US Farm Bill, have been used to fund an array of agricultural and food programs that provide various social benefits, such as ensuring that the nation has an adequate food supply, that food prices are fair, and that consumers have access to locally and regionally produced goods (USDA 2024a). As the ethical omnivore diet comes out of the Organic Movement, we have already discussed several examples of how leaders in organic agriculture have transformed the agricultural landscape of the United States, Great Britian, and beyond. The Rodale Institute's role helping to develop the USDA National Organic Standard, being but one of many examples. Another is the National Organic Certification Cost-Share Program, which was included in the 2014 Farm Bill (USDA 2024b). This assists producers with the cost of gaining organic certification. The increasing popularity of organic foodstuffs has helped to bolster policy initiatives, but there is still much to do. Organic agriculture is not nearly as supported as conventional production. In addition, current organic standards may fall short when it comes to soil health and animal welfare. As such, change at the policy level is an effective tool to influence food systems. These changes could greatly impact ethical omnivore's ability to source appropriate foodstuffs that align with their diet.

## Local Food: Catering to Eater's Values

This brings us to the individual-focused sub-movement. Recommendations for eaters to buy environmentally sustainable produce and humanely raised meats, dairy, and eggs align well with these types of local food projects. The individual-focused sub-movement (or IF) can be understood as the "face" of local food (Werkheiser and Noll 2014). I'm sure many readers have come across magazine articles or op-eds touting the benefits of buying local. I've even seen quite a few bumper stickers and cloth bags with pithy sayings along these lines. The sociologist Laura B. Delind (2011) captures this point nicely when she discusses the "locavore" phenomenon:

> Locavores and would-be locavores (theoretically the public-at-large) are told repeatedly through popular films (e.g., Supersize Me, Fast Food Nation, King Corn, Fresh, Food, Inc.), and books (e.g., Omnivore's Dilemma, In Defense of Food, Animal, Vegetable, Miracle) and media features (e.g., PBS, NYT, Yes!, Mother Jones, Business Week) that they—as individuals— can effect change one vegetable, one meal, and one family at a time. It suggests that what is wrong with the world (from monocultural practices, to obesity, to global warming) can be addressed through altered personal behavior.
>
> *(276)*

What Delind is getting at here is that locavorism is very popular, but it also embraces certain commitments, such as that: "1) food is a product which is purchased, 2) people are individual consumers of food, and 3) change happens when… individual choices have cumulative impacts on health, lifestyle, environment, animal welfare, farm workers, the local community, and so on" (Noll and Werkheiser 2017). Value-driven diets, from vegetarianism to ethical omnivorism, tend to accept this basic understanding of how we "vote with our dollars," or bring about change one meal at time. This is the idea that the best way to bring about positive change is through economic processes driven by individual consumer choices. For locavores, buying regional products has several benefits. As mentioned above, supporters claim that this diet could mitigate environmental harms associated with agriculture, as local food is shipped shorter distances and often grown using fewer petrochemicals (if the crops are organic). It also helps support farmers using environmentally friendly methods and who are committed to animal welfare. Additionally, they argue that local food supports regional businesses and growers rather than large corporations, and thus builds more resilient local economies (Noll and Werkheiser 2017). From the perspective of personal health, farmers markets provide ample access to wholefoods and those produced without the use of potentially harmful pesticides, herbicides, and other inputs. As you can see from this list, there is quite a bit of overlap between the values of locavores and ethical omnivores, especially concerning agricultural production methods. As we will see, ethical omnivores, and indeed all ethically minded eaters, need local food systems to help ensure that their products align with their values.

### Eating Organic Is Not Enough

In short, ethical omnivores need local food systems to properly source foodstuffs. Most articles on ethical omnivorism stress how dietary decisions can make a large environmental impact. However, in today's corporate controlled food system, it's more complicated than ever to find food that aligns with these values (Kelloway and Miller 2019). For example, in *The Vegetarian's Guide to Eating Meat*, Marissa Landrigan (2011) explores what it means to be a mindful omnivore. For her, this diet requires knowing where your food comes from, as eating a vegetarian diet or even buying organic is not enough. When we analyze our food choices using a wider lens, many vegetarian and vegan options become problematic, especially foods of convenience. "Big Food" is very good at using labels and claims (such as Organic, All Natural, Fat Free, Cage Free, etc.) to virtue signal, making eaters think that their products are more ethical than they actually are. When watching a person buy vegetarian products at a grocery store, Landrigan (2011) wonders if:

> he knew that Hain Celestial was a subsidiary brand of Heinz Corporation, one of the top twenty food producers in the world, or if he could name any other Heinz brands. Smart Ones frozen meals maybe, or Boston Market frozen entrees—both of which the Heinz company makes with chicken bought from Tyson. Tyson, the largest meat producer in the world. Tyson, who in the last decade has paid more than $7.5 million in fines for felony violations of the Clean Water Act.
>
> *(138)*

She goes on to ask herself what good she was personally doing buying many of these products, as their parent companies are tied to big-tobacco, Smithfield Foods, and Tyson, to name a few? Over the last 40 years, economies of scale have substantially reduced prices of food, but at the same time, a handful of giant multinational corporations have taken control of the American food supply chain. As these own several different brands, we're presented with an illusion of choice, as the seeds that farmers plant to the nut butter that you buy in grocery stores are produced by a small number of companies, making profits catering to your preferences. In reality, our purchases often support many agricultural practices that do not align with our values, as the brand's parent companies are engaged in these activities. What does it matter if your veggie burger is vegan, if you're supporting a company that slaughters billions of chickens annually? For Landrigan (2011), then, we need to look beyond the brand to determine if our foodstuffs are produced in ethically acceptable ways.

Some ethical omnivores may argue here that this is why we have agricultural regulation and standards. Unlike the messy food landscape for vegetarian eaters, ethical omnivores simply need to look for the certified organic label and all will be well. However, this is not necessarily the case. For instance, Landrigan (2011) agrees with supporters of Regenerative Organic that our current Organic Standard doesn't go far enough to protect the environment and animals from harms. The crux of the critique is that the Organic Standard is, itself, problematic. Early supporters of organic agriculture were pure in their intentions to create an alternative production method. However,

> when the organic food industry became popular with consumers, food processing corporations decided to get in on the growing market, and began buying up smaller, struggling organic farms wherever they could. Gerber, Heinz, Dole and ConAgra all created or purchased organic brands. So, the USDA got involved and started regulating what it meant to stamp the word —organic on a food product.
>
> *(Landrigan 2011, 128)*

This caused an ideological rift within the organic food scene, as tensions arose between organic as an ideology vs a marketing strategy. With a governmental standard in place, corporations could now find ways to adhere to those regulations, while increasing the size and scope of organic production, well beyond what the original Organic Movement intended.

Today, the USDA allows organic factory farms, which seems like a contraction in terms. As Landrigan (2011) notes, "I felt as if buying organic from ConAgra ran counter in some ways to the intention, I had in buying organic… Can an organic industry still represent what it means to be organic?" (128). From an ethical omnivore perspective, the answer is yes and no. It is true that the USDA Organic Standard allows for organic "factory" farms, meaning that large-scale production is allowed, as is monocropping. Also, organic dairy farms are not required to provide a minimum amount of pasture for their cows, though any land used must be certified organic. They also have a large amount of leeway concerning feed, if it is certified organic. Many industrial dairies, such as Horizon Cows, are in areas where pasture is not possible, requiring the use of dry feedlots and that organic feed be shipped into the area. For Landrigan (2011) and like-minded eaters, industrial dairies are anathema to the ideal of organic food, leading to common misconceptions. The point they are trying to make isn't that all organic farms are big agriculture in disguise, taking advantage of customers and mistreating animals. Rather, the bucolic notion of organic farming that many eaters have is not accurate.

For purists, regenerative organic agriculture requires the use of practices that are hard to scale up. For big-organic, only large-scale production is competitive and cost-effective. Supporters of industrial organic will argue that it is cost-effective enough for the average person to afford eating these products. Any person who has ever gone to a farmers' market knows this well, as they find staggering price tags next to those beautiful fruits and vegetables, grown on a small farm. Purists will reply that the founders of organic agriculture desired to revamp the way we farm, rather than simply offering healthier and cost-effective food products to the masses. Modifying organic production methods to fit into existing industrial agricultural systems could be seen as an ideological betrayal, sacrificing too much at the altar of marketing and convenience. Though, for many busy professionals today, convenience is exactly what we need. The USDA Organic Standard was created to help eaters identify organic products quickly and better incorporate these foodstuffs into our wider food system. Thus, for some eaters, "the purists lost. As anyone who has ever eaten an Amy's frozen pizza or a Rising Moon burrito can tell you, there is such a thing as organic processed food, in which additives and synthetic chemicals are permitted" (Landrigan, 131). The nutritionist Jane Dye Gussow (1997) went to far as to show that even an organic twinkie is possible within current regulations.

This doesn't mean that buying industrially produced organic foodstuffs is meaningless or that our food choices don't matter. From a systems perspective, increasing the demand for organic products helps to bolster policy initiatives, as it shows that there is a need for a new standard, addendum to the U.S. Farm Bill, updated policy, etc. For example, eaters wanted security that the products they are buying were produced using organic methods, and a certification program was developed. If nobody wanted organic yogurt or pizzas, then there wouldn't be a need for this standard. However, buying organic products isn't doing the heavy lifting that many people think that it is. The purists make a good point about the founders of organic agriculture's desire to revamp the way we farm. For ethical omnivores, individual food choices should be driven by production concerns, such as environmental impacts, overall sustainability, and animal welfare. This is where the local food movement comes into play, connecting eaters to farmers and agriculture, more generally.

## Local Food as an Alternative to Big Organic

Local food systems help to address some of the failings of big-organic in a few ways. First, as Barbara Kingsolver et al. (2009) argue in their book *Animal, Vegetable, Miracle: A Year of Food Life*, farmers markets are important because they connect us to the place where we live, in terms of food and people. Kingsolver et al. calls this "stalking the vegetannual," or the act of rediscovering seasonality. There is much we can learn from even a single plant. The entire growing season is encapsulated in its development, from the formation of roots to the leaf and flower, fruit to shell. It's not natural for plants to flower out of season. When we buy our food locally, we get to experience the natural cycle writ large in the produce offered at farmers' markets. This connection is very important for eaters, as it helps us to learn what crops the land can grow, who are neighbors are, and what foodstuffs are culturally significant. In these ways, we connect ourselves to our shared place. For Landrigan (2011), "learning all that about the people and the land around us is the first step to placing ourselves within that giant quilt, the beginning of finding our own identity within the fabric of a place." (227). For the agrarian philosopher Paul Thompson, this is part of the transformative power of local food.

In a market saturated by industrial agricultural products and confusing food labels, local food can help ground eaters in the larger food system and provide learning opportunities to better know how foodstuffs are produced. In "The Reshaping of Conventional Farming: A North American Perspective," Thompson (2001) poignantly states the following:

> The dilemma of sustainable agriculture in North America is how to marry consumers' self-interested concern about healthy diets to a philosophical vision of agriculture in which this form of self-interest is symptomatic of a hopelessly corrupted social framework—one that has little chance of righting itself so long as people continue to order their lives according to norms of preference satisfaction.
>
> *(227)*

When we simply purchase products at the grocery store based upon our preferences, we lose sight of larger entanglements, such as those Landrigan (2011) discussed. Those cage free eggs or veggie burgers might, at face value, align with your ideals, but this may not be the case, when you look behind the veil. Corporate decision-making and agricultural production methods often fail to meet eater's ethical standards, especially those of vegetarians and ethical omnivores, alike.

In his newest work, *From Silo to Spoon: Local and Global Food Ethics*, Thompson (2023) provides a potential answer to the above dilemma of how to connect self-interest to a transformative vision of food systems —highlighting how locavorism, as heuristic, could act as a "gateway philosophy" for the local food movement and thus help create a new public, where personal identity as consumer is supplanted or replaced by that of citizen. Many agrarians, from Thomas Jefferson to Wendell Berry and later Joel Saltin, critique the social conditions of their day, arguing that citizens often fail to realize that we are embodied and environmentally situated beings. Thus, it is common in this literature for scholars to advocate for "a therapy that reconnects body and earth through farming and through a deeper understanding of food" (Thompson 2023, 92). These authors expose an infection in modern societies, but satisfying food preferences is not an adequate cure. For Thompson (2023), "the adoption of agrarian practices will bring about the transformation that allows us to leave the choice-making shopper behind, once and for all" (94). As we discussed in the food ethics chapter, locavorism could act as a powerful heuristic or a framework to help us consider the wider normative implications of our food choices. Learning more about local food could ease consumers into a more rewarding relationship with what's on their plate.

A mature and full-bodied food ethic reflects myriad considerations. While participating in community food systems still fulfills dietary preferences, it also sharpens the eaters' ethical evaluation of those choices. This type of critical evaluation and agricultural knowledge sensitizes readers to big-organic's problematic products. In this way, locavorism as a heuristic transforms the simple act of shopping from a naïve formulation of a consumption ethic, where a consumer simply tries to spend their money in ways that harness market forces in support of better outcomes, to an ethical orientation (Thompson 2023). This highlights the tension between eater as consumer and eater as citizen. Consumers base their choices on the satisfaction of preferences. In contrast, "when we act as citizens we take a more idealistic standpoint. We evaluate political choices not so much in what they have for ourselves as in whether they lead to a better world" (Thompson 2023, 98). Thus, we are back at the dilemma discussed in Thompson's (2001) essay. How do we marry consumers' self-interested concern about healthy diets to a better vision of agriculture and eating?

## Ethical Omnivore Diet: From Heuristic to Habit

One way to answer to this question is to tout the benefits of the locavore movement. Local food, as a heuristic, helps those who embrace the consumer relationship with food gradually broaden their understanding of agriculture and place. It helps them transform from consumer to citizen. Another answer, however, is provided by the ethical omnivore diet. As it is grounded in the Organic Movement, environmental citizenship and consumer preferences are wed to a more idealistic standpoint, one that embraces a vision for better agriculture and a better world. Local markets help ethical omnivores source food that aligns with their values, but it also reiterates the interconnectedness at the heart of a healthy food system. In this way, it helps eaters form habits important for living life as an ecological citizen. Henry David Thoreau believed that everyday experiences, such as building a fence, planting beans, and sourcing our foodstuffs, are important for the development of human character. Agrarian pragmatists embrace the view that the natural world, including farms, are a reliable guide for the development of character and a self-reliant personality (Anderson 2000; Corrington 1990; Thompson 2008). In fact, Thoreau's teacher and friend Ralph Waldo Emerson firmly believed in the superiority of self-discovered knowledge. When eaters embrace the view that we are embodied and environmentally situated beings, we begin to grasp that norms can be selected by ecological processes.

The idea behind this is straightforward. Even in a society where self-interest is prioritized, environmental carrying capacity will ultimately curtail some land practices (Thompson 2008). The Dust Bowl of the 1930s is great example of this. American and Canadian prairies experienced a period of intense dust storms that caused widespread ecological and agricultural damage. These storms were caused by environmental changes, including a period of severe drought, and the failure of producers to use dryland farming and topsoil preservation methods to prevent erosion. Farmers who embraced agricultural methods in line with their environment (i.e., ecologically stable habits) continued to thrive, while those in areas impacted by dust storms lost their farms. Lessons gleaned from this event shaped agricultural policy until the 1970s. For pragmatist philosophers, the term "habit" captures these types of norms, which are non-reflective responses to situations or unconscious behavioral patterns (Thompson 2008). We fall into habitual behavior patterns all the time. How many readers have driven to work in the morning without consciously thinking that you should put the car into gear, merge into traffic, etc.? Much of what we do falls outside of conscious thought. Habits are different from conscious choices, as they are often unreflective behaviors.

This work is important for ethical omnivores in two ways. First, local food as a heuristic helps eaters to better understand the ecological limits of the area where they live. By engaging with producers, the hope is that eaters gradually glean agricultural information about the crops that thrive in their area and those that do not, when it's the best time to harvest foodstuffs, and other important matters. For example, Barbara Kingsolver et al. (2009) spent most of *Animal, Vegetable, Miracle: A Year of Food Life* discussing the myriad types of crops their home state of Kentucky can support, when they're perfectly ripe to eat, and the ecological realities of their production. They also discussed the foods their family craves but that cannot be produced locally. Through the local food heuristic, we learn the habits of the land, by engaging with producers who are shaped by that land. We develop new habits, as we "stalk the vegetannual," and rediscover seasonality one meal and one farmers market trip at a time. We also learn how choices are "framed" within the governmental and social landscape, as food policy shapes what products are available and who can sell these products. We saw the power of regulation when we talked about the far-reaching consequences of the Direct Marketing Act of 1976, which legitimized direct-to-consumer sales and harkened in our age of abundant farmers markets.

Social mores and norms also frame our decisions in important ways. These can be understood as unwritten cultural expectations and requirements that are deeply ingrained in citizens. For example, people can get very angry when a person skips ahead in line. There's no law against line skipping but it is a social norm, and we know that we shouldn't do this. As Thompson (2008) states, "even in individual behavior, decision makers never give consideration to the full range of possible options available. There are always a limited set of 'ends-in-view,' and a similarly limited set of plausible means that are given consideration" (123). Here, he's getting at the idea that freedom of choice is an illusion, especially for eaters, as ecological, governmental, and social landscapes limit the choices that we even consider. For instance, a resident of Moscow Idaho probably wouldn't think of eating insects for dinner, while I have several friends who live in other countries where insects are on the menu.

Habits and framing are interesting but what do they have to do with the ethical omnivore diet and the power of local food? For agrarian pragmatists, understanding how individual choices are limited and shaped by framing contributes to better decision-making (Thompson 2008). For instance, the philosophers Mark Johnson and George Lakoff (1999) argue that thinking within frames helps citizens make ecologically appropriate choices, especially when we have limited time. Frames and habits are either successful in helping citizens negotiate their environments or they are not, and people who adopt less-successful frames and habits tend to struggle. For example, eaters who develop healthy habits, like eating fruits and vegetables, tend to have better health outcomes then those adopting a diet of processed meat products. Framings and habits also greatly impact eaters' ability to conceptualize whether a specific situation is ethically important. For instance, frames orient eaters towards distinct possibilities and, as philosophers note, particular conceptions of what issues are normative. When we move away from framing food as consumer choice to an ecological act, for example, different ethical issues rise to the surface. Consumers are often worried about factors that impact themselves and their family, such as food safety, nutritional content, and availability. While ecological eaters are worried about environmental impacts, sustainability, mitigating climate change harms, wildlife habitat, and other issues. Framing matters not only for our choices but also for shaping our lifeworld.

Framing and habits are elements of human behavior that emerge from our routine activities with people, places, and things (Thompson 2008). When we engage with the products of our home soil and the people who have devoted their lives to nurturing these products, we develop important habits and shift how food issues are framed in our minds. This shift weds consumer concerns with the ecological, broadening the eater's understanding of food and agriculture. To answer Paul Thompson's (2001) question, how do we marry consumers' self-interested concern about healthy diets to a better vision of agriculture and eating? The ethical omnivore diet and local food both hold important insights for eaters grappling with the realities of food systems. Big-organic seeks to simplify food choices, reducing them down to a label. Their answer to this question is to trust in their promises that marketing slogans and descriptions align with our values. But, as Landrigan (2011) pointed out, our purchases often support practices that go against package labeling and promises, and we need to look beyond the brand to determine if our foodstuffs are produced in ethically acceptable ways. The illusion of choice in grocery stores hides the larger social framings of processed foods, while cultivating potentially problematic habits, as these overly processed "organic" foodstuffs contain unhealthy amounts of sugar, salt, and additives. It also hides the tensions between organic purists and industrial production advocates, giving the impression that all organic production is the same. As we've learned, it is not. There are many different methods that we can use to produce food, some better than others. The organic standard and big organic are not without their critics.

## Local Food Needs Ethical Omnivorism

Thus far, we've discussed how ethical omnivores' are enriched by engaging with local food projects. However, it is also important to at least mention here that locavorism also benefits from ethical omnivorism. This is because omnivore diets allow for more flexibility when sourcing food from our immediate area and allow for the most land-use efficient agricultural practices. Many eaters are lucky to live in areas that can produce a cornucopia of foods, but others are not so lucky. For example, the state of New York can feed a large percentage of its population from the vast agricultural areas that make up most of the state (Landrigan 2011). Many people think of New York City when the state is mentioned, but cities are often surrounded by a "charmed circle" of farmland, originally intended to feed city populations before the invention of refrigeration (Atkins 2012, 53). Indeed, pre-modern cities themselves were often areas of intense agricultural production, growing delicate vegetables in hot houses and even housing livestock (Noll 2017). What is surprising about the state of New York is not that it has agricultural lands, however, but that it can feed so many people on lower quality land, not fit for growing crops

(Landrigan 2011). Much of the state is devoted to producing meat and dairy products from grazing animals, like cattle. Pasture is of lower quality than cropland, but is more widely available. This is a relatively common situation globally, as many societies rely on grazing animals for food in areas not fit for crop production.

As an aside here, this problematizes a common justification for vegetarian diets, in that they require less land per person and so should be prioritized. This is true at face value, but the devil is in the details. Vegetable and fruit production require more high-quality land, which there isn't a lot of in many areas. These lands are also stressed, as industrial agriculture ignores topsoil health at our peril. In contrast, omnivorism gives eaters greater flexibility to eat foods that align with place and the natural rhythms of the seasons. While a person can certainly eat a vegetarian diet in many states, eating in alignment with the environment may demand a more diverse diet. As Landrigan (2011) poetically noted, "humans can't eat everything in front of us. By using animals as a sort of middleman in our digestive system, we can make more efficient use of what we have. Eating some cattle lets us eat grass" (151). Omnivorism provides this flexibility and, this flexibility in turn, helps eaters to eat local more days out of the year.

## Ethical Omnivorism and Environmental Health

Local food advocates also need ethical omnivores to adequately combat environmental critiques of locavorism. Buying local is often touted as an effective strategy to reduce the number of miles that food travels from farm to the table and thus its environmental impact. The agricultural sector radically changed over the last 75 years, with international trade in food increasing fourfold since the 1960s and domestically produced food traveling farther distances (Singer and Mason 2007, 135). In this larger context, local food products are often framed as more environmentally friendly alternatives to big agriculture. However, food scholars are increasingly critical of this claim. Helena de Bres (2016), for example, questions whether food miles really matter that much for the environment. Her reasoning goes like this:

> To accurately assess the respective carbon footprints of… a local and a 'distant' tomato, we need to consider the amount of fuel used across the entire life cycle of each. Especially if you live in the Northern hemisphere, a 'life cycle assessment' of this kind will often reveal that the distant tomato has burnt up less fuel by the time it gets to your kitchen than the local one has.
>
> (6)

That seems like a bold claim, yet it is echoed in the work of Peter Singer and Jim Mason (2007). They argue that most of the fuel used to get food to local markets is spent on the production side, well before products are transported to markets (de Bres 2016). In this vein, Weber and Matthews (2008) argue that transportation is a relatively small drop in the energy bucket, accounting for only 4% of the total energy used to produce and transport food to U.S. consumers.

As agricultural production relies on petrochemicals, it is energy-intensive and even more so in some countries. For instance, "countries with warmer climates or higher rainfall (generally located nearer the equator or in the Southern hemisphere) don't need heated greenhouses or extensive irrigation to produce crops, thus burning much less fuel" (de Bres 2016, 6). For this reason, and due to economies of scale, distant farms might be more energy efficient than local farms, because they have an environmental advantage that translates into more fossil fuel efficiency, even when we account for the transportation phase. Hammering this point home, detractors also argue that the mode of transportation makes a big difference when calculating food miles (Desrochers and Shimizu 2012, 99). Boats use less fuel than trucks and can carry more cargo and, thus, have a lower environmental impact than using multiple trucks to transport goods. Locavores often fail to include the miles that consumers travel to local farms and markets in their calculations, in contrast to the one-stop shopping that supermarkets allow for (de Bres 2016). Additionally, detractors argue that the benefits of "non-food miles" are often overstated, as these are bundled with other environmental advantages, such as promoting biodiversity, improving land conservation, and reducing packaging. Finally, there are other environmental costs that accrue when we grow food in places not suited for such production, such as the use of massive amounts of water and fertilizers, soil degradation, etc. The takeaway here is that if we want to limit the environmental impact of food production, then local food isn't the way to do so. Rather, we should be strengthening international regulations to ensure that food trade is done in environmentally friendly ways.

However, there are glaring issues with the above analysis, that de Bres (2016) does not try to hide. First, when framing the arguments against eating local, she is careful to note that the analysis doesn't take different production methods into account. As we discussed above, local food could be produced using a wide array of farming methods, some of which are environmentally friendly. As such, this type of nuance was not included in the analysis. I find this position highly problematic, as criticisms of locavorism take for granted that products are being produced using industrial methods. They seem to be saying that the dominant way of growing food is industrial, so we should simply assume that all production is so. However, ethical omnivores are very sensitive to the production side of sourcing food. Even the organic standard, let alone regenerative organic, is highly critical of the use of petrochemicals during production. Second, many producers are sensitive to the carrying capacity of the land, tailoring agricultural methods and diets to place. This commitment is what is driving the push for regenerative organic. I agree that food miles account for a small percentage of energy use when analyzing conventional agriculture. However, the argument that it is more energy efficient to grow crops in other regions is only applicable if you're eating foodstuffs out of season. But, as we've seen, locavorism is devoted to eating foods in line with local ecological rhythms. When you do this, hot houses, extra fertilizers, and massive amounts of water may not be used during production. It all depends on the crop, environmental conditions, season, and other shifting factors. Thus, the above argument is built on the assumption that consumers will continue to buy products out of season, which isn't necessarily the case. Agriculture is tied to ecological services, which are in flux. Weather patterns can shift from day to day, so these general claims are of limited use. Eaters grounded in their environments, sensitive to the habits and wisdom formed by local producers, are in a much better position to determine what foods align with ecological values.

Finally, criticisms lump all eaters into a single category, that of consumer. However, as we've seen, not all eaters embrace this role. Others strive to live their lives as an ecological citizen, rather than passive consumer of agricultural products. The power of participating in local food projects for ethical omnivores lies in being able to identify foodstuffs that align with eater's values. Not all local foods are environmentally friendly, but many local products are. Embracing Thompson's heuristic, habits, and being sensitive to framing help eaters glean important knowledge concerning their food. Different products will have different ecological impacts. It is the responsibility of eaters to determine which fit better with their values. As we "stalk the vegetannual," and rediscover seasonality, we develop the knowledge needed to be an active ethical eater, not simply one who assumes all local foodstuffs are the same. Ethical omnivorism provides the tools necessary for local food enthusiasts to truly embrace what it means to be an ecological eater and citizen. Agricultural knowledge is power.

## Ethical Omnivorism and Local Food

In these ways, the ethical omnivore diet seeks to improve human and ecological thriving, in that it pushes eaters to embrace the role of ecological citizen. It also pushes eaters to take responsibility for their food choices, as we actively increase our understanding of local agriculture and food systems. In many ways, ethical omnivorism and local food movements are intertwined. The values and goals guiding each overlap significantly. For example, both attempt to provide an alternative to corporate-led, industrialized agricultural systems by reconnecting food with environmental health and sustainability and the importance of place (Levkoe 2011). Supporters often argue that people dependent on industrial agriculture often lose control over their diet, as governmental agencies and large corporations frame choices in sometimes problematic ways. In modern grocery stores, the wide range of food choices that eaters could make are often reduced to shallow choices concerning brand name recognition and marketing ploys. This illusion of choice is only effective when eaters lack knowledge of the realities of food production, such as how foodstuffs are produced and processed.

Embracing local food, as a heuristic, helps ethical omnivores to steel themselves against the siren call of big agriculture and big organic. Cultivating contextually appropriate habits and understanding how food choices are framed could help individual eaters and communities regain their power over the food they eat and the systems that produce it. In these ways, supporting local food projects moves us one step closer to cultivating regenerative food systems, which prioritize self-actualization, eater autonomy, and the cultivation of better relationships between producers and the environment. From this perspective, it's not difficult to see why ethical omnivores place eating locally produced foodstuffs alongside eating organic. Both recommendations align with their values in important ways and are a central part of what it means to be an ethical omnivore.

## References

Anderson, Douglas. 2000. "Wild Farming: Thoreau and Agrarian Life." In *The Agrarian Roots of Pragmatism*, edited by Paul Thompson and Thomas Hilde, 153–63. Nashville, TN: Vanderbilt Press.

Atkins, P. 2012. "Introduction." In *Animal Cities: Beastly Urban Histories*, edited by P. Atkins, 1–19. Burlington: Ashgate Publishing Inc.

Bres, Helena de. 2016. "Local Food: The Moral Case." In *Food, Ethics, and Society*, edited by Anne Barnhill, Mark Budolfson, and Tyler Doggett. Oxford: Oxford University Press.

Brown, Allison. 2001. "Counting Farmers Markets." *Geographical Review* 91 (4): 655–74.

Conford, Philip. 2001. *The Origins of the Organic Movement*. Glasgow: Floris Books.

Corrington, R.S. 1990. "Emerson and the Agricultural Midworld." *Agriculture and Human Values* 7:20–26.

DeLind, Laura B. 2011. "Are Local Food and the Local Food Movement Taking Us Where We Want to Go? Or Are We Hitching Our Wagons to the Wrong Stars?" *Agriculture and Human Values* 28 (2): 273–83.

Desrochers, Pierre, and Shimizu Hiroko. 2012. *The Locavore's Dilemma*. New York, NY: Public Affairs.

Guthman, Julie. 2014. *Agrarian Dreams: The Paradox of Organic Farming in California*. University of California Press.

Guzzow, Joan Dye. 1997. "Can an Organic Twinkie Be Certified?" In *For All Generations: Making World Agriculture More Sustainable*, edited by P Madden. Ames, IA: WSAA.

Holt-Gimenez, Eric, and Y Wang. 2011. "Reform or Transformation?: The Pivotal Role of Food Justice in the U.S. Food Movement." *Race/Ethnicity: Multidisciplinary Global Contexts* 5 (1): 83–102.

Kelloway, Claire, and Sarah Miller. 2019. *Food and Power: Addressing Monopolization in America's Food System*. Open Markets Institute. https://static1.squarespace.com/static/5e449c8c3ef68d752f3e70dc/t/5ecdafcece92da449232f534/1590538191983/190322_MonopolyFoodReport-v7.pdf.

Kingsolver, Barbara, Camille Kingsolver, and Steven L. Hopp. 2009. *Animal, Vegetable, Miracle: A Year of Food Life*. Harper Collins.

Lakoff, G, and M Johnson. 1999. *Philosophy in the Flesh: The Embodied Mind and Its Challenge to Western Thought*. New York, NY: Basic Books.

Landrigan, Marissa. 2011. "The Vegetarian's Guide to Eating Meat." *Iowa State University Digital Repository*, Graduate Theses and Dissertations,, 251.

Levkoe, Charles. 2011. "Towards a Transformative Food Politics." *Local Environment* 16 (7): 687–705.

Martinez, Steve, Michael Hand, Michelle Da Pra, and Susan Pollack. 2010. *Local Food Systems Concepts, Impacts, Issues*. Vol. 97. Washington, DC: US Department of Agriculture.

Noll, Samantha. 2017. "Food Sovereignty in the City: Challenging Historical Barriers to Food Justice." In *Food Justice in US and Global Contexts: Bringing Theory and Practice Together*, edited by Ian Werkheiser and Zach Piso, 95–111. New York, NY: Springer Publishing.

Noll, Samantha, and Ian Werkheiser. 2017. "Local Food Movements: Differing Conceptions of Food, People, and Change." In *Oxford Handbook of Food Ethics*. Oxford: Oxford University Press.

Rodale Institute. 2021. *The Leaders Who Founded the Organic Movement*. Rodale Institute. https://rodaleinstitute.org/blog/leaders-organic-movement/.

Singer, Peter, and Jim Mason. 2007. *The Ethics of What We Eat: Why Our Food Choices Matter*. Potter/Ten Speed/Harmony/Rodale.

Thompson, Paul. 2001. "The Reshaping of Conventional Farming: A North American Perspective." *Journal of Agricultural & Environmental Ethics* 14:217–29.

Thompson, Paul. 2008. "Agrarian Philosophy and Ecological Ethics." *Science and Engineering Ethics* 14:527–44.

Thompson, Paul. 2010. *The Agrarian Vision: Sustainability and Environmental Ethics*. University Press of Kentucky.

Thompson, Paul. 2023. *From Silo to Spoon: Local and Global Food Ethics*. Oxford: University of Oxford.

U.S. Department of Agriculture. 2021. *U.S. Department of Agriculture: National Agricultural Library*. Governmental Website. Organic Production/Organic Food: Information Access Tools. 2021. www.nal.usda.gov/legacy/afsic/organic-productionorganic-food-information-access-tools.

U.S. Department of Agriculture. 2024a. *214 Farm Act: Local and Regional Foods*. U.S. Department of Agriculture. www.ers.usda.gov/topics/farm-bill/2014-farm-bill/local-and-regional-foods/.

U.S. Department of Agriculture. 2024b. *Organic Agriculture*. U.S. Department of Agriculture. www.ers.usda.gov/topics/farm-bill/2014-farm-bill/local-and-regional-foods/.

U.S. Department of Agriculture: Economic Research Service. 2022. *Growth in the Number of U.S. Farmers Markets Slows in Recent Years*. US Department of Agriculture. www.ers.usda.gov/data-products/chart-gallery/gallery/chart-detail/?chartId=104402.

Weber, Christopher, and H. Scott Matthews. 2008. "Food Miles and Relative Climate Impacts of Food Choices in the United States." *Environmental Science and Technology* 42 (10): 3508–13.

Werkheiser, Ian, and Samantha Noll. 2014. "From Food Justice to a Tool of the Status Quo: Three Sub-Movements Within Local Food." *Journal of Agricultural and Environmental Ethics* 27 (2): 201–10.

Wu, Feng, Zhengfei Guan, and Alicia Whidden. 2021. *An Overview of the US and Mexico Strawberry Industries*. University of Florida Extension. https://edis.ifas.ufl.edu/publication/FE971

# 6

# FOOD JUSTICE ON THE PLATE

## Respecting Food Sovereignty

I spent a summer helping to run the Eastside Community Garden in Lansing, Michigan. I was a recent transplant to the state, from my home in Pennsylvania. Where my family is from, corn grows higher than children playing in the yard, sprouting from some of the richest soil in the country. Generations of farmers, using sustainable methods, wrapped the Appalachian Mountain foothills and valleys in ribbons of color, bursting with earth's bounty. My own family farmed on one of the highest spots in Berks County. In contrast, Lansing was built in swampland. It's close to sea level and is home to some of the biggest car manufacturers in the world. Ford and General Motor plants grew into behemoths, with neighborhoods in between, each with their own communities and struggles. The Eastside Neighborhood is highly diverse and densely populated, with single family homes in neat rows down streets and local businesses along a main corridor. Hunger is a problem here, as well as access to fresh foods. This is where the Eastside Community Center and their garden comes into play. The garden and greenhouse are in Hunter Park, a popular part of the neighborhood, with a public pool and a paved path for walking. It is a community supported agriculture project, where neighbors can purchase a share of the produce produced or donate their time to offset the costs of this produce. Everyday residents and children would join us to weed the beds, water, plant crops, and harvest. We'd cut baby lettuce and laugh at each other's stories and share recipes.

The garden is built into the park, so that it's easily accessible to the neighborhood. I often watched children run around munching on carrots that they helped grow and harvest. (Of course, we washed them first.) Crops were intentionally interspersed in the park itself, so that anyone who was hungry could pick fresh fruits and vegetables. The old non-food producing trees were

DOI: 10.4324/9781003215189-6

replaced with fruit trees, blueberry bushes were planted, and even the flowers were edible varieties. It is a beautiful place, with butterflies and bees buzzing around. Rabbits were often spotted in the morning dew and finches sang on fruit trees. Rain ran down chains to fill a barrel and the water was used to nurture plants that will in turn nurture us. Peas, cucumbers, and even tomatoes were trellised, with their little shoots reaching out like fingers searching for the twine, so that they can climb ever higher. Farmers and volunteers' hands guided them to the best spots. The compost pile was turned and added to, last year's plants and cast-offs becoming the nutrients for next year's harvest. And, the whole cycle started again and will start again. While the Hunter Park Garden is small, it produces a lot of food and directly serves some of the needs of the surrounding neighborhood. It's not meant to replace a grocery store, per say, but it provides easily accessible fresh fruits and vegetables to the community. It's about as "farm to table" as you can get. For me, this little garden in the middle of a neighborhood in Michigan is a wonderful example of environmentally friendly and community focused food production.

## A Movement Grounded in Respecting Food Justice

So far, we discussed the ethical omnivore diet, as a diet, but one that has deep normative roots. Eating and drinking are ethical acts and practicing an ethic of seeing is important for thoughtful omnivores (King 2007). Every day we think about what to eat and what not to eat. When making food decisions, we impact our personal health, the well-being of food and agricultural workers, domesticated animals, and the environment, more generally (Fanzo and McLaren 2020). The food ethics guiding the ethical omnivore diet is sensitive to normative concerns that arise from farm to table, as the way foods are produced, processed, distributed, marketed, and prepared all have impacts beyond the plate. Last chapter, our discussion of the interconnections between local food projects and the ethical omnivore diet widened our analysis to include social concerns, beyond personal eating habits. Unlike local food initiatives that cater to eaters' preferences and desires, systems focused projects embrace the idea that food choices are always embedded or "framed" by social institutions. It's not enough to vote with our dollars. Rather we should be advocating for regulatory and policy changes, by engaging with political structures (Werkheiser and Noll 2014). For example, by creating food standards enforced by governmental agencies, such as the USDA, we can hold producers accountable, mandating that they follow those standards.

This chapter deepens our analysis even further by placing justice considerations on the plate. Having access to safe and nutritious foods is important, but it's also important to recognize that the pursuit of "public goods" informs both diets and agricultural policy. For instance, eaters who buy local often do so for environmental and community reasons. They want their food to be produced in ecologically friendly ways, their food dollars to go towards supporting local farmers who embrace these methods, etc. On the policy side, The U.S. Farm Bill, a package of legislation passed every 5 years, has a tremendous impact on how food is grown, what kinds are grown, and farming livelihood (Elliot and Raziano 2012). It funds programs aimed at increasing access to nutritious foodstuffs, but there are also programs devoted to conservation, rural development, farm worker safety, crop insurance, etc. These "public goods" programs address concerns well beyond consumer access to agricultural products. Many of these duties can be distilled down to the idea that we should treat others fairly, and are thus built on social justice commitments, as well as ethical commitments. Ethical omnivores' engagement with community focused local food projects highlights the important role that food and environmental justice play for these eaters.

In addition to the pursuit of "public goods," maintaining the food sovereignty of communities is another justice issue that guides eaters and food movements, alike. At the most basic level, food sovereignty simply means that communities exercise greater control over where and how they obtain food. Lots of food projects embrace food sovereignty, as an ideal, guiding action on the ground. These could include neighborhood gardens, community-supported agricultural projects, farmers markets, and other initiatives where communities exercise greater control over their food system. Local food projects like these are typically called "community-focused" initiatives (Noll and Werkheiser 2017). A commitment to food sovereignty is one way they are distinct from both individual- and policy-focused projects. Where individual-focused projects are an overlap of local food with lifestyle politics, community-focused initiatives are an overlap of local food with community-based food justice movements. Given this commitment to fairness and equity, local food projects are important because they help communities exercise meaningful control over their food practices in ways that strengthen and preserve their community and individual identities. Food acts as a powerful touchstone, translating abstract ideals and principles into practice in real life.

This chapter uses community-centered food projects to explore how ethical omnivorism is built on social justice commitments. It begins by defining food justice and food sovereignty. Then, it draws connections between important components of ethical omnivorism and justice-oriented food movements. When we recognize that ethical omnivorism is deeply connected to the local food movement, several normative commitments discussed earlier in the book make more sense. In particular, this connection at least partially explains why ethical omnivores are committed to ensuring that food products support small-scale sustainable farming methods. Additionally, the flexibility concerning what products can be eaten is compatible with food sovereignty. Respecting food traditions is an important part of food justice initiatives, as foodways are deeply connected to cultural identity. Thus, respecting diverse foodways is a part of enabling the autonomy of individuals and groups. Both food justice and food sovereignty overlap with ethical omnivorism in interesting ways, as we will see.

## What Is Food Justice?

Food justice is commonly defined as the commitment that everyone should have access to healthy, safe, and culturally appropriate foodstuffs, no matter your economic status, social identities, national origin, cultural origin, or disability (Schanbacher 2010; Whyte 2016). In this way, the umbrella of food justice includes distributive concerns, as advocates grapple with how benefits and harms of food systems are distributed to various individuals based on social group membership (Noll and Murdock 2020). As Glennie and Alkon (2018) argue, food justice advocates seek "to understand how inequalities of race, class and gender are reproduced and contested within food systems" (2). Here, food systems are not separate from the societies we live in but are connected to the realities of our lives. Our access to food is mediated through social structures, which could both cause and reinforce unequitable treatment. For example, in the United States alone, approximately 50 million people are food insecure, 90% of whom are people of color (Atkinson 2016; Holt-Giménez and Harper 2016). According to Atkinson (2016):

low-income communities of color, concentrated at the fringes of our most thriving urban centers, have been targeted by fast food chains and ignored by corporate grocery store chains due to the perceived lack of economic opportunity, also known as 'grocery store redlining,' instituted through historical zoning laws that established racial segregation.

*(1)*

Due to this history, supermarkets are often absent or much farther away than fast food restaurants (Gallagher 2006; Howerton and Trauger 2017). A slew of health and nutritional harms are the result. Rural areas have also been hit hard, as they constitute less than two-thirds of counties in the United States, yet 9 out of 10 counties with the highest food insecurity rates in the country are rural (Feeding America 2024). Lack of access to fresh fruits and vegetables in these areas are distributive justice issues but are also deeply connected to a wide range of inequalities, exacerbating and reinforcing them.

In addition, food justice also includes how benefits and harms are distributed within agricultural systems themselves. Discussing this dimension, Kyle Whyte (2016) and other justice scholars (Alkon and Agyeman 2011; Jayaraman 2013) define it as: "the norm that everyone who works within a food system, from restaurant servers to farm workers, should be paid livable and fair wages and work in safe conditions no matter one's national origin, economic statuses, social identities, cultural membership, or disability" (Whyte 2016, 1). There is a long history of agricultural workers being treated unfairly. For food justice scholars, these inequities need to be addressed. For example, the Regenerative Organic standard demands that farm workers be paid a living wage and work in safe environments. For supporters of this certification program, the U.S. Organic Standard may be great for eaters, but it fails to shield producers from injustices within food systems. By adding these two requirements, the hope is that current practices will shift to better align with minimum standards of equitable treatment. Along this line, The United Farm Workers union spent years fighting for the "dignity and respect for America's farm workers through better working conditions and a living wage" (United Farm Workers 2014). Similarly, the Restaurant Opportunities Center organization is committed to improving "wages and working conditions for the nation's restaurant workforce" (Restaurant Opportunities Center 2024). By including these in an organic certification program, the ethical omnivore's commitment to buying organic includes a social justice component.

Another dimension of food justice, particularly important for ethical omnivores, is the demand that we value food in relation to the self-determination of individuals and communities (Whyte 2016; Werkheiser and Noll 2014). This type of food justice is often discussed in terms of specific communities obtaining "food sovereignty" (Adamson 2011; Alkon 2009; Alkon and Agyeman 2011; Holt-Giménez and Shattuck 2011). The first global forum on Food Sovereignty penned "The Declaration of Nyéléni," which includes an excellent definition of the term:

> Food sovereignty is the right of peoples to healthy and culturally appropriate food produced through ecologically sound and sustainable methods, and their right to define their own food and agriculture systems. It puts the aspirations and needs of those who produce, distribute and consume food at the heart of food systems and policies rather than the demands of markets and corporations.
>
> *(La Via Campesina 2006, n.p.)*

As you can see from this definition, advocates for sovereignty also discuss many of the aforementioned justice issues, such as improving the fairness of food production, processing, and distribution, and working to mitigate racial, gender, and class injustices. However, their solutions to problems demand that communities exercise greater control over food systems. The reason why food sovereignty advocates frame food in this way is because they embrace definitions of "food" and "people" that differ greatly from other local food projects (Werkheiser and Noll 2014). For most eaters, food is typically seen as some kind of interchangeable commodity, and people are autonomous individuals acting in their own self-interest, typically as consumers. We want to make dinner and so, go to a grocery store to exchange our money for desired products. In contrast, food sovereignty advocates see food is an essential part of culture that is deeply connected to community and personal identity. Food ways act as a touchstone, reinforcing social ties that bind us together, and change happens when communities come together to protect these traditions, through acts of solidarity and collective action (Desmarais et al. 2010; Whyte 2016; Noll 2020). An important part of collective action is having a chair at the table when food-related decisions are made. In these ways, food sovereignty supporters call for greater control and for "justice as recognition" in agricultural systems, as both are important for fully exercised community sovereignty. Thus, decision-making processes should be fair and, when possible, include impacted parties, (Coolsaet and Neron 2020; Rosol and Blue 2022).

The ideal of justice as recognition is complex and has a long philosophical history, but it is important for understanding the power of food sovereignty. Two justice scholars Axel Honneth and Nancy Fraser provide key insights into why recognition and participation are important for food justice. Honneth (2000) describes recognition as the "moral grammar of social conflicts," as it confronts the ways we respect diverse peoples, cultural practices, personal identities, and systems of knowledge (Coolsaet and Neron 2020; Noll and Bhar 2023). This definition is sensitive to issues of self-respect and self-worth and sees recognition and participation as intertwined. Here, being respected in institutional spheres is important for people's dignity and places participants in "networks of solidarity," or community groups with shared values. Similarly, Nancy Fraser argues that the "most general meaning of justice is parity of participation" (Fraser 2005, 5). Parity happens when members of a society feel free to interact with each other as peers. This may seem simplistic, but parity of participation is sometimes impeded in social spheres. Material exploitation (economic injustice), social subordination (cultural injustice), and political disenfranchisement could each render citizens unable to participate (Coolsaet and Neron 2020; Fraser 1995; Fraser and Honneth 2003).

The above discussion of food justice and sovereignty is interesting, but readers are probably wondering how this connects to ethical omnivorism. By placing such a strong normative emphasis on production and environmental health, these eaters become more sensitive to food justice considerations. In addition, ethical omnivorism may be useful for food sovereignty projects, especially if their goal is to preserve and protect traditional foodways. Food ethics activists have a history of attacking community foodways, especially if hunting is involved. The online bullying of an Alaska Native teenager for participating in his village's whale hunt is but one of many examples (O'Malley 2017). Food ethics and diets insensitive to justice considerations can be problematic when applied to complex social contexts. As we will see, food sovereignty, justice of recognition, and distributive justice are important for ethical omnivores. In particular, we will begin this discussion by looking at how the ethical omnivore diet opens eaters' eyes to food justice and why distributive justice issues should matter for all eaters, irrespective of place.

## From Personal Health to Distributive Justice

Distributive justice concerns often prompt ethical omnivores to think more critically about their food choices. This is because their diet is sensitive to connections between personal and environmental health, which is fertile ground for thinking about distributive justice issues in agriculture and beyond. Omnivores are unusually cognizant of their biological nature, due to the ecological framing of their diet. According to the ethicist Kathryn Paxton George (1990), when we embrace our omnivorous nature, we appeal "to our biological nature and to the interests we have in the nutrition and health of our bodies" (174). She goes on to argue that sourcing sufficiently nutritious and safe foodstuffs should be prioritized over other ethical considerations, as asking individuals to violate their personal safety in pursuit of other ethical goals is, itself, unethical. Her position makes sense, especially when we recognize that eaters are socially situated and often navigate conflicting moral precepts. For instance, my grandmother once ate food that was offered to her at a friend's house, even though she knew she was mildly allergic, because she didn't want to break the ethical mandate between host and guest. Not slighting the host was more important to her than her safely. While this is laudable, I can think of very few ethicists who would support putting your health at risk for such a cause. Similarly, for George, by appealing to our biological and ecological nature, it is important to listen to our bodies when determining what to eat. This idea is echoed on the Ethical Omnivore Movement website, where it reiterates the point that we should be sourcing nutritious foodstuffs that improve personal health, as well being sensitive to how food production methods impact the environment. For this diet, ecological and personal health are equally important and are often intertwined.

Health and the environment might seem like two separate issues, but this is not the case for founders of The Organic Movement and thus some ethical omnivores. In this vein, Wendel Berry (1994) argues that health is about wholeness. For Berry, "the word 'health,' in fact, comes from the same Indo-European root as 'heal,' 'whole,' and 'holy.' To be healthy is literally to be whole; to heal is to make whole" (n.p.). Agriculture, as a heuristic, helps to connect personal and environmental health, by stressing the interconnections between the two. When we see ourselves as an ecological citizen, to use both Aldo Leopold and Paul B. Thompson's words, we see ourselves embedded in a greater environmental whole. As the English agriculturist Sir Albert Howard said, in *The Soil and Health*, "the whole problem of health in soil, plant, animal, and man [is] one great subject" (quoted in Berry 1994, n.p.). This perspective nudges us to think wholistically about food and health, breaking down boundaries between agricultural production, food consumption, and the environmental realities of both activities. Thus, the ethical omnivore diet recognizes that personal health holds ethical significance, but also that how we farm impacts general thriving. For these thinkers, and ethical omnivores who embrace organic ideals, when presented with a choice between technological innovation in agriculture and the health of the human and ecological community, they choose the health of the community.

Analyzing food systems from the perspective of an ecological citizen brings into focus how agriculture can both benefit and harm eaters, producers, and the environment. Let's look at impacts to personal health, as an example. Many eaters, especially those living in urban areas, begin by thinking about how food impacts their health, the health of their family, and that of their community. To use Thompson's (2023) words, these concerns often prompt the beginning of our food journey, and thus the heuristic process. For example, Michael Pollan argues that eaters typically begin learning about agricultural systems by trying to figure out what to eat. It seems simple but it's quite complicated. Pollan (2009) ponders "but for all the scientific and pseudoscientific food baggage we've taken on in recent years we still don't know what we should be eating" (x). Should we eat more sugar or less sugar, more fats or less fats? What about carbohydrates? What carbohydrates are good? How can we tell if they're good? Should we be eating certain foods together to get maximum good effects? What about artificial foodstuffs, like sweeteners? Going down this rabbit hole soon leads us to how our food is produced, as the age of produce when processed, when they're picked, and even soil quality can impact nutritional content. On the flip side, understanding agriculture sharpens our understanding of potential harms associated with food production. Conventional agriculture uses a wide range of inputs, such as herbicides, pesticides, and fertilizers. Some of these inputs could be harmful to farmers and eaters' health. Thus, even for eaters only worried about personal health, agriculture production factors should play a role in determining what they eat.

## Distributive Justice Concerns on the Plate

The concerns that eaters have about food production are usually connected to wider food justice issues. For example, let's look at two commonly used agricultural chemicals and their potential harms: DDT and glyphosate. You probably recall from earlier chapters that Rachel Carson's book *Silent Spring* alerted the world to the ecological and human health dangers of DDT. This insecticide was once called the "savior of mankind" because of its effectiveness controlling insect-borne diseases during World War II (Anonymous 2024). In fact, it was so useful at stopping the transmission of typhus, that DDT has been credited with saving millions of lives during the war. After World War II, the "miracle" chemical was used in extremely large quantities, in homes and for insect control in crop and livestock production. DDT was popular because it was cheap, readily available, and potent. Farmers could occasionally apply the pesticide and still enjoy its benefits over a long period, as it remains toxic for years. While it breaks down easily in sunlight, half of DDT in soils will take 2–15 years to break down, depending on the type of soil (Washington State Department of Health 2024). Yet, even with its long life, the government and chemical industry both heavily supported its use. We now know the environmental risks of using this pesticide, and that human exposure is associated with breast cancer, diabetes, reduced fertility, miscarriages, and impaired neurodevelopment in children (NIH). This farmer's fairy dust was banned from agricultural use in 1989 but is still used in some countries to control malaria (NPIC 1999).

In addition, another popular herbicide making public health headlines is glyphosate, commonly known as Roundup. It's used to control broadleaf weeds and grasses and is frequently applied in agriculture and on lawns. Glyphosate is truly marvelous from a production standpoint. If you plant Roundup Ready crops, for example, and spray glyphosate, everything will die except the desired crop. It's an excellent tool for increasing yields. The U.S. Environmental Protection Agency has also said that it is not likely to produce cancer in humans, if you follow the instructions on the label (EPA 2017). However, scientific research is inconclusive and not everyone follows instructions. In 2023, for example, a paper published in the *Journal of the National Cancer Institute* found that people exposed to glyphosate have biomarkers linked to the development of cancer (Chang et al. 2023). This isn't conclusive, but it is concerning. When exposed, we also know that glyphosate can impact the kidneys, liver, and nervous system. In addition, the EPA (2017) stated that there are substantial risks for birds, mammals, and terrestrial and aquatic plants.

In addition, both DDT and glyphosate are associated with epigenetic damage, meaning that future generations could be harmed. The geneticist Michael K. Skinner has done extensive research on both agricultural inputs. According to a recently published paper on the subject, "while some toxicants do not impact the directly exposed generation, the later generations that are transgenerational or ancestrally exposed suffer health impacts" (Korolenko et al. 2023, 241). The experiments focus on fish and mammals. When applied to humans, who are also mammals, what this could mean is that individuals exposed may not experience any adverse effects, but their grandchildren and great children could be harmed. Potential harms could include increased rates of certain cancers, infertility, obesity, etc. The bioethicist William Kabasenche and Michael Skinner (2014) connect these harms to food and environmental justice. In particular, they argue that, due to emerging work on epigenetic effects, we now have good reason to believe that DDT will "negatively impact future generations" (2). Alexandra Korelenko, Samantha Noll, and Michael Skinner (2023) make a similar claim concerning glyphosate in a paper published in the *Yale Journal of Biology and Medicine*. Epigenetic research raises intergenerational environmental justice concerns. The point here is not that we should do away with agricultural inputs, but rather eaters should be aware of the risks imposed during production and that these risks are justice issues. This is especially the case, as the intensive use of chemical fertilizers and pesticides are on the rise globally, increasing the chances that eaters and workers will be exposed to residues (Lam et al. 2017).

As eaters gain a better understanding of the harsh realities of food production, the distribution of benefits and harms comes into greater focus. The two cases above highlight key food justice concerns. A distributive justice lens helps to highlight how our individual food choices impact: (a) ecosystems, (b) farmers and workers, (c) rural communities, and (d) our future children. As we saw above, historical criticisms of DDT focused on environmental justice concerns. Wildlife and ecosystems were overly harmed, while humans enjoyed the benefits of using this pesticide. Today, intensive use of chemical pesticides and fertilizers places pressure on ecosystems, as excess residues and toxins find their way into surface water and groundwater (Matson et al. 1997). These impacts beyond the farm harm ecosystem functioning and neighboring communities, alike. Second, health concerns of agricultural inputs, like DDT and glyphosate, could greatly impact farmers and farm workers if they are exposed, as well as communities living near agricultural zones (Donley et al. 2022). Rural communities are often put at risk by industrial plant and animal operations (Twiss 2019). The health of farm workers and local communities are important food injustices. Finally, potential health impacts lead us to consider intergenerational justice. Making sure that pesticide and herbicides are not harmful to workers and eaters is not enough to ensure that their use is just. Environmental impacts matter, but intergenerational harms are also on the table, as we saw. Each of these concerns are food justice issues. Matters of equity and fairness are important aspects of agriculture, as we see from looking at just two of the thousands of potential agricultural inputs.

## The Food Sovereignty Diet

We are men and women of the earth, we are those who produce food for the world. We have the right to continue being peasants and family farmers, and to shoulder the responsibility of continuing to feed our peoples. We care for seeds, which are life, and for us the act of producing food is an act of love. Humanity depends on us, and we refuse to disappear.

*(La Via Campesina, Maputo Declaration 2008)*

Another important aspect of food justice is food sovereignty, or the demand that we value food in relation to the self-determination of individuals and communities (Whyte 2016; Desmarais and Wittman 2013; Werkheiser and Noll 2014). In fact, the environmental ethics scholar, Robert Figueroa (2017) argues that social justice cannot be obtained without considering both distributive justice and justice as recognition. This "bivalent" approach is typically applied to environmental inequities but is also useful for understanding food justice concerns. So, what does the food sovereignty of communities have to do with the ethical omnivore diet and its recommendations, such as eating local foodstuffs? To better understand the connections between the two, we need to discuss the birth of the global food sovereignty movement.

The international farmers organization La Via Campesina is a great example, as it was founded in 1993 by 182 organizations from 81 countries (Desmarais and Nicholson 2013). This landmark event was prompted by the finalization of the Uruguay Round of the General Agreement on Tariffs and Trade (GATT). For the first time, the GATT included agriculture and food in its negotiations. This Act along with the World Trade Organization marked a shift away from controlled national economies to ones dominated by the global economic market. Organizational representatives of small farmers, indigenous peoples, and farm workers from the Americas, Europe, Asia, and Africa pushed back, worried that these regulatory changes would nudge nations to dismantle agrarian programs and structures that help ensure the viability of small-scale farming and protect national food security.

Today, La Via Campesina is a massive global force, but its roots stretch back into the 1980s, as farmers began to face hardships caused by accelerating industrialization of agriculture (Desmarais and Nicholson 2013). It was during this time when farmer leaders found that they shared common concerns with other communities. For supporters of food sovereignty and farmer rights:

> Everywhere, the industrialization and liberalization of agriculture – imposed through structural adjustment programs and regional free trade agreements – were leading to an acute agricultural crisis caused by the restructuring of agriculture, the destruction of biodiversity, further degradation of the environment, increased disparity, greater impoverishment in the countryside accompanied by the consolidation and concentration of agri-business corporations. Increasingly, peasants and small-scale farmers everywhere were being driven off the land.
>
> *(Desmarais and Nicholson 2013, 4)*

For small agrarian communities, cash-crop and monoculture intensive industrial agricultural was transforming the way that they farm and, subsequently, the very structure of their communities. As we learned from the agrarian pragmatists, agriculture sets the tone for societies, as we glean important information by engaging with the earth (Thompson 2008). The rhythms of seasons and other environmental realities frame our daily lives and provide hard limits for our behavior. Some actions help us thrive, while other actions spell our doom, especially when it comes to food production. For agrarian societies, industrial agriculture broke with centuries of tradition, throwing away time-tested strategies for thriving. The relationships between producer and land, forged over centuries were broken. Additionally, it increased the risks to farmers, as they transitioned to new ways of doing agriculture. This was problematic for many groups, as producers began to fail, losing their land. With expensive seeds and inputs, a few bad crops spelled disaster. Farmers were going out of business, sometimes drinking the herbicides and pesticides meant for crops in an act of despair (Bonovoisin 2020). These harsh realities galvanized the 182 organizations from 81 countries that make up La Via Campesina. By 1993, they mobilized and today advocate for greater recognition of food sovereignty, as a counterpoint to rising industrialization and consolidation.

For La Via Campesina, this isn't a conflict between farmers in the global north and global south, as some ethicists like to frame it. Rather, it's a struggle between two divergent paradigms of economic and social development (Desmarais and Nicholson 2013). One the hand, agriculture is conceived as a profit-making activity that is increasingly concentrated into the hands of a few large agro-industry corporations. On the other hand, "La Via Campesina envisions a very different, more humane, rural world: one in which 'food is first and foremost a basic human right,' agriculture is based on… small-scale production, uses local resources and is geared to domestic markets" (Desmarais and Nicholson 2013, 4). Advocates embrace the idea that a food sovereignty framework mandates that communities have a right to produce culturally significant foodstuffs in their territories and that agriculture plays important social and ecological functions, as well as an economic one. From this perspective, greater consolidation in the name of increased efficiency is ethically suspect, as it works against both community control and local benefits of food systems.

## Food Sovereignty and Eating Local

As readers can see, there is an agrarian undercurrent in food sovereignty movements important for our analysis concerning ethical omnivorism. Indeed, these eater's concerns overlap quite well with several issues discussed above, including ecological and social inequities. They are also worried about greater industrialization and consolidation of agriculture, as this could undermine environmental thriving. In the Global North, for example, the numbers of farms have been steadily dropping for years. According to Melanie J. Wender (2011), most of the food that we eat today isn't produced on family farms. The

United States has seen a shift in farm production to larger operations, typically referred to as agribusinesses. Today, "approximately ninety-eight percent of America's food supply is produced by agribusinesses" (1). Agribusinesses are larger farming operations that outproduce smaller family farms, so this shift isn't surprising. It should be noted that many large farms are still "family farms," in that a family owns them. However, as technological agricultural innovations transformed the industry, many small producers couldn't keep up and went bankrupt. These farms were then bought by other producers, creating larger farms. Today, it's common for farms to be over 1000 acres. The literature typically describes this as falling off the "technological treadmill," so to speak. The growth of these large-scale farms led to fewer producers and harmed rural communities around the globe. Consolidation means fewer farmers and their families in rural communities. This means that fewer people need the services available in small towns and these towns then struggle.

For agrarians, farming is the lifeblood of society. When agricultural methods change, this shift has a wider impact, beyond the farm itself. Increased demand for organically produced products and the local food movement are helping to reverse this trend. For La Via Campesina and other food sovereignty advocates, the consolidation of farms into the hands of a few families or corporations is problematic, because it reduces the control that citizens have over their food systems (Desmarais and Nicholson 2013, 4). There are wider social costs that are not considered when we adopt industrial production methods. Yes, yields typically do increase. However, biodiversity is reduced, the environment is degraded, and the countryside is impoverished, as agricultural resources are consolidated. Small-scale farmers are driven from the land, and more of us purchase food in plastic containers in supermarkets divorced from the realities of food production.

Ethical omnivore's dietary recommendations push back against this trend and embrace many of the same values as food sovereignty initiatives. Their commitment to eating organic and regeneratively produced foodstuffs, for example, is driven by environmental concerns. Biodiversity levels matter and farms are important environments that can be managed in sustainable and ecologically friendlier ways. Organic also has the added benefit of empowering producers to demand more for their products, helping to support these types of operations. Organic production methods are also often embraced by small-scale producers (Glazebrook et al. 2020), helping them to survive in a cut-throat agricultural environment. This then helps to increase the numbers of these farms—operations that act as a counterpoint to decades of consolidation. Locavorism also has several benefits. For example, farmers markets and other direct to consumer selling ventures provide eaters with a way to support small-scale production. These projects also use local resources in the community and help to bolster local food security. In fact, resilient local food systems have been linked to greater food security, especially during times of crisis (Bene 2020).

In a contextual way, La Via Campesina's vision of a "more humane, rural world" is built on an ethical commitment to locavorism, where communities can benefit from and inform local food systems. Here, local food networks can be understood as "sites of resistance" (Portman 2014, 1), becoming "both the symbol and substance for structural change" (Delind 2005, 123). Buying local products can help to empower eaters to work towards bettering their communities. It supports local producers, for sure. More generally, food security is important for maintaining a thriving society. Thus, building a more resilient local food system could greatly contribute to revitalization efforts. However, the ethicist Helena de Bres (2016) is quite dismissive of these claims, arguing that "public regulation is often necessary for large-scale, sustainable change... To the extent that locavorism distracts individuals from higher-impact political reform, the concerns underlying the political argument could point away from rather than toward buying local food" (25). Her argument has merit but fails to adequately recognize benefits associated with increasing food sovereignty of local communities. When placed in the context where industrial agriculture is displacing agrarian communities, helping to maintain a thriving local food system is, itself, an act of resistance. In addition, creating smaller food systems, where producers farm within ecological limits for the benefit of their immediate community, is a type of ideological resistance, where food sovereignty frameworks are bolstered, and industrial paradigms are weakened. In a world with two divergent paradigms of economic and social development, locavores embrace opportunities to vote with their dollars. While policy and regulation are important for bringing about change, policy-centered local food initiatives are already doing this work. There's no need for community-centered programs to shift focus away from their goals to lobby for changes to the Farm Bill, for example. Local food initiatives are diverse and embrace different strategies for bringing about change.

The ethical omnivore, by embracing organic and buying local, helps to bolster the food sovereignty of their communities. This, in turn, creates opportunities for eaters to play a role in their food system, and thus bolsters justice as recognition. Both food sovereignty and local food advocates are worried about the consolidation of agricultural resources into the hands of a few producers and corporations. Local food, as heuristic, provides eaters with opportunities to learn about agricultural production, and has the added benefit of bolstering their engagement with food systems. As such, their transition into that of ecological citizen is necessitated on adding more chairs to the table and increasing the numbers of individuals empowered to make agricultural decisions. Drawing from Axel Honneth (2000), opportunities for engagement also helps eaters become a part of "networks of solidarity," or community groups with shared values. If Nancy Fraser is correct, that the "most general meaning of justice is parity of participation," then local food projects play an important role bolstering the just treatment of communities and eaters (Fraser 2005, 5), regardless of whether policies are reformed. It's fascinating how this diet intersects with wider social movements, as agrarian ideals are built into its recommendations.

## Ethical Omnivorism and Culturally Appropriate Foodstuffs

Finally, the ethical omnivore diet is important for food sovereignty because it is sensitive to community's call to make their own food choices. Food justice, generally, embraces the idea that people should have access to culturally acceptable foodstuffs. For example, Kyle Whyte (2016) rightly states the following:

> Another dimension of food justice, which is found in the words and writing of advocates but is perhaps less commonly appreciated, is that food justice should account for the value of food in relation to the *self-determination* of human groups such as urban communities of color, Indigenous peoples and migrant farmworkers, among many other groups.
>
> *(1)*

Advocates often claim that we should recognize the value of foodways in relation to personal and social self-determination. Societies, communities, and ethnic groups around the world have unique traditions centered on foods. Food sovereignty advocates see food is an essential part of culture that is deeply connected to community and personal identity. Foodways, then, are a strategy for reinforcing social ties and our personal identities. For Whyte, this is an essential norm of food justice. The ethical omnivore diet is sensitive to the demand that eaters should determine what's on their plates. It provides the flexibility necessary to exercise self-determination, going forward. Many ethically based diets, and the food ethicists who support them, do not accept this mandate to respect cultural aspects of diets. Nor do they recognize a need to bolster justice as recognition, as they provide their view of what everyone should be eating. For example, the ethicists Peter Singer (2015) and Tom Regan (2004) are not shy when advocating for a vegetarian or vegan diet, even going so far as to argue that it's the only ethically acceptable diet. When placed in conversation with sovereignty and food justice frameworks, however, these recommendations smack of authoritarianism. If food systems differ based on place, then universal analyses will fall short. While such recommendations make sense when applied to large industrial agricultural systems, ethical omnivores and food justice advocates alike embrace the contextual and local food system. Thus, eaters and producers will have a better understanding of the benefits and harms associated with production in their homes. In addition, regardless of the production method, communities should be respected, as they make sometimes difficult food-related decisions, especially when it comes to traditional foodstuffs and foodways. Food ethics, and their recommended diets, insensitive to justice considerations can be problematic, especially when applied to complex social contexts. While not everyone is an ethical omnivore, my point here is that the diet is sensitive to justice demands in aways that other diets are not.

Unlike food ethics that focus on one normative issue (such as improving animal welfare, increasing ecological sustainability, etc.), ethical omnivorism is committed to a flexible ethical framework and to mitigating distributive injustices. This mandates that individual and community sovereignty be respected. It also requires that communities be involved in the process of determining what foods are available (and how these foods are produced) in their local food systems. In other words, justice requires equal representation when making important food-related decisions that impact communities three times a day. Ethical omnivorism, as a social movement, places special emphasis on achieving these wider social justice goals.

## References

Adamson, Joni. 2011. "Critical Environmental Justice Studies, Native North American Literature, and the Movement of Food Sovereignty." *Environmental Justice* 4 (4): 213–19.

Alkon, Alison Hope. 2009. "Breaking the Food Chains: An Investigation of Food Justice Activism." *Sociological Inquiry* 79:289–305.

Alkon, Alison Hope, and Julian Agyeman. 2011. *Cultivating Food Justice: Race, Class, and Sustainability*. Cambridge, MA.: MIT Press.

Anonymous. 2024. *Section II: Uses of DDT*. Online Ethic Center for Engineering and Science. https://onlineethics.org/cases/section-ii-uses-ddt.

Atkinson, Sarah. 2016. *What's Missing from the Discussion of 'Food Deserts'?* Berkley Nature. https://nature.berkeley.edu/classes/es196/projects/2016final/AtkinsonS_2016.pdf.

Bene, Christophe. 2020. "Resilience of Local Food Systems and Links to Food Security- A Review of Some Important Concepts in the Context of COVID-19 and Other Shocks." *Food Security* 12:805–22.

Berry, Wendell. 1994. *Health Is Membership*. Center for Faith and Learning Scholar Program. www1.villanova.edu/dam/villanova/mission/faith/Readings/fall-2020/Health%20is%20Membership%20by%20Wendell%20Berry.pdf.

Bonovoisin, Toby, Leah Utyasheva, Duleeka Knipe, David Gunnell, and Michael Eddleston. 2020. "Suicide by Pesticide Poisoning in India: A Review of Pesticide Regulations and Their Impact on Suicide Trends." *BMC Public Health* 20:251.

Bres, Helena de. 2016. "Local Food: The Moral Case." In *Food, Ethics, and Society*, edited by Anne Barnhill, Mark Budolfson, and Tyler Doggett, 495–510. Oxford: Oxford University Press.

Bruin, Annemarieke de, Imke de Boer, Niels Faber, Gjalt de Jong, Katrien Termeer, and Evelien de Olde. 2024. "Easier Said than Defined? Conceptualising Justice in Food System Transitions." *Agriculture and Human Values* 41 :345–62.

Chang, Vicky, Gabriella Andreotti, Maria Ospina, Christine Parks, Dangping Liu, Jospeph Shearer, Nathaniel Rothman, et al. 2023. "Glyphsate Exposure and Urinary Oxidative Stress Biomarkers in the Agricultural Health Study." *Journal of the National Cancer Institute* 115 (4): 394–404.

Coolsaet, Brendan, and Pierre-Yves Neron. 2020. "Recognition and Environmental Justice." In *Environmental Justice: Key Issues*, edited by Brendan Coolsaet, 52–62. New York: Routledge.

Delind, Laura. 2005. "Of Bodies, Place, and Culture: Re-Situating Local Food." *Journal of Agricultural & Environmental Ethics* 19 (2): 121–46.

Desmarais, Annette Aurelie, and Paul Nicholson. 2013. *La Via Campesina: An Historical and Political Analysis*. La Via Campesina. https://viacampesina.org/en/wp-content/uploads/sites/2/2013/05/EN-10.pdf.

Desmarais, Annette Aurelie, Nettie Wiebe, and Hannah Wittman. 2010. *Food Sovereignty: Reconnecting Food, Nature & Community*. Fernwood.

Donley, Nathan, Robert Bullard, Jeannie Economos, Iris Figueroa, Jovita Lee, Amy Liebman, Dominica Martinez, and Fatemeh Shafiei. 2022. "Pesticides and Environmental Injustice in the USA: Root Causes, Current Regulatory Reinforcement and a Path Forward." *BMC Public Health* 22 (708): 1–23.

Elliot, Patricia, and Amanda Raziano. 2012. *The Farm Bill and Public Health: A Primer for Public Health Professionals*. American Public Health Association. www.apha.org/-/media/files/pdf/factsheets/farm_bill_and_public_health.pdf.

EPA. 2017. *EPA Releases Draft Risk Assessments for Glyphosate*. United States Environmental Protection Agency. www.epa.gov/pesticides/epa-releases-draft-risk-assessments-glyphosate.

ethicalomnivore.org. n.d. *Why Ethical Omnivorism?* Accessed July 24, 2024. www.ethicalomnivore.org/why-ethical-omnivorism/.

Fanzo, Jessica, and Rebecca McLaren. 2020. "An Overview of the Ethics of Eating and Drinking." In *Handbook of Eating and Drinking: Interdisciplinary Perspectives*, edited by Herbert Meiselman, 1095–1115. New York: Springer.

Feeding America. 2024. "Why Hunger Is More Common in Rural Areas." Feeding America. www.feedingamerica.org/hunger-in-america/rural-hunger-facts.

Figueroa, Robert. 2017. "Bivalent Environmental Justice and the Culture of Poverty." *Rutgers University Journal of Law and Urban Policy* 1 (1): 27–42.

Fraser, Nancy. 1995. "From Redistribution to Recognition? Dilemmas of Justice in a 'Post-Socialist' Age." *New Left Review* 1 (212).

Fraser, Nancy. 2005. "Reframing Justice in a Globalizing World." *New Left Review* 36.

Fraser, Nancy, and Axel Honneth. 2003. *Redistribution or Recognition? A Political-Philosophical Exchange*. London/New York: Verso.

Gallagher, M. 2016. *Examining the Impact of Food Deserts on Public Health in Chicago*. Chicago: Gallagher Research and Consulting Group.

George, Kathyrn Paxton. 172AD. "So Animal a Human..., Or the Moral Relevance of Being an Omnivore." *Journal of Agricultural and Environmental Ethics* 3 (2): 1990.

Glazebrook, Trish, Samantha Noll, and E Opoku. 2020. "Gender Matters: Climate Change, Gender Bias, and Women's Farming in the Global South and North." *Agriculture* 10 (267): 1–25.

Glennie, Charlotte, and Alison Alkon. 2018. "Food Justice: Cultivating the Field." *Environmental Research Letters* 13:1–14.

Holt-Gimenez, Eric, and Breeze Harper. 2016. "Dismantling Racism in the Food System." *Food First* 1:1–7.

Holt-Giménez, Eric, Annie Shattuck, Miguel Altieri, Hans Herren, and Steve Gliessman. 2012. "We Already Grow Enough Food for 10 Billion People ... and Still Can't End Hunger." *Journal of Sustainable Agriculture* 36 (6): 595–98. https://doi.org/10.1080/10440046.2012.695331.

Honneth, Axel. 2000. *Disrespect: The Normative Foundations of Critical Theory*. Cambridge: Polity Press.

Howerton, Gloria, and Amy Trauger. 2017. "'Oh Honey, Don't You Know?' The Social Construction of Food Access in a Food Desert." In *ACME: An International Journal for Critical Geographies* 16 (4): 740–60.

Jayaraman, S. 2013. *Behind the Kitchen Door*. Ithica, NY: Cornell University Press.

Kabasenche, William, and Michael Skinner. 2014. "DDT, Epigenetic Harm, and Transgenerational Environmental Justice." *Environmental Health* 13 (1): 62.

King, Roger. 2007. "Eating Well: Thinking Ethically about Food." In *Food and Philosophy*, by Fritz Allhoff and David Monroe, 177–91. New York: Blackwell Publishing.

Korolenko, Alexandra, Samantha Noll, and Michael Skinner. 2023. "Epigenetic Inheritance and Transgenerational Environmental Justice." *Yale Journal of Biology and Medicine* 96:241–50.

Lam, Steven, Giang Pham, and Hung Nguyen-Viet. 2017. "Emerging Health Risks from Agricultural Intensification in Southeast Asia: A Systematic Review." *Journal of Occupational Environmental Health* 23 (3): 250–60.

Matson, P.A., W.I.J Parton, Alison Power, and M.J. Swift. 1997. "Agricultural Intensification and Ecosystem Properties." *Science* 277 (5325): 504–9.

Noll, Samantha. 2020. "Local Food as Social Change: Food Sovereignty as a Radical New Ontology." *Argumenta* 5 (2): 215–30.

Noll, Samantha, and Tuhina Bhar. 2023. "The Five Pillars of Urban Environmental Justice: A Framework for Building Equitable Cities." *Philosophy of the City Journal* 1 (1): 84–99.

Noll, Samantha, and Esme Murdock. 2020. "Whose Justice Is It Anyway? Mitigating the Tensions Between Food Security and Food Sovereignty." *Journal of Agricultural and Environmental Ethics* 33:1–14. https://doi.org/10.1007/s10806-019-09809-9.

Noll, Samantha, and Ian Werkheiser. 2017. "Local Food Movements: Differing Conceptions of Food, People, and Change." In *Oxford Handbook of Food Ethics*. Oxford: Oxford University Press.

NPIC. 1999. *DDT: General Fact Sheet*. National Pesticide Information Center. http://npic.orst.edu/factsheets/ddtgen.pdf.

O'Malley, Julia. 2017. *A Teen Whaler in the Age of Cyberbullies*. Hakai Magazine. https://hakaimagazine.com/features/teen-whaler-age-cyberbullies/.

Pollan, Michael. 2009. *Food Rules: An Eater's Manual*. New York: Penguin Books.

Portman, Anne. 2014. "Mother Nature Has It Right: Local Food Advocacy and the Appeal to the 'Natural'". *Ethics and the Environment* 19 (1): 1–30.

Regan, Tom. 2004. *The Case for Animal Rights*. Berkeley, CA: University of California Press.

Restaurant Opportunities Center. 2024. *About Us.* https://rocunited.org/mission/#sth ash.0iRkmMqO.dpuf.

Rosol, M, and G Blue. 2022. "From the Smart City to Urban Justice in the Digital Age." *City* 26 (4): 685–705.

Schanbacher, William D. 2010. *The Politics of Food: The Global Conflict Between Food Security and Food Sovereignty.* Santa Barbara, CA: ABC-CLIO.

Singer, Peter. 2015. *Animal Liberation: The Definitive Classic of the Animal Movement.* Open Road Media.

Thompson, Paul B. 2008. "Agrarian Philosophy and Ecological Ethics." *Science and Engineering Ethics* 14:527–44.

Thompson, Paul B. 2023. *From Silo to Spoon: Local and Global Food Ethics.* Oxford: University of Oxford.

Twiss, Pamela. 2019. "Rural Social Work and Environmental Justice." *Contemporary Rural Social Work Journal* 11 (1): 1–21.

United Farm Workers. 2014. *The Movement at a Glance.* https://ufw.org/_page. php?menu=about&inc=fwmglance.html

Via Campesina. 2006. *[Nyeleni] DECLARATION OF NYÉLÉNI.* 2006. https://nyeleni. org/spip.php?article290

Washington State Department of Health. 2024. *DDT.* Washington State Department of Health. https://doh.wa.gov/community-and-environment/contaminants/ddt#:~: text=DDT%2C%20DDE%2C%20and%20DDD%20in,on%20the%20type%20 of%20soil

Wender, Melanie. 2011. "Goodbye Family Farms and Hello Agribusiness: The Story of How Agricultural Policy Is Destroying the Family Farm and the Environment." *Villanova Environmental Law Journal* 22. https://digitalcommons.law.villanova.edu/ cgi/viewcontent.cgi?article=1016&context=elj

Werkheiser, Ian, and Samantha Noll. 2014. "From Food Justice to a Tool of the Status Quo: Three Sub-Movements within Local Food." *Journal of Agricultural and Environmental Ethics* 27 (2): 201–10.

Whyte, Kyle. 2016. "Food Justice and Collective Food Relations." In *Food, Ethics, and Society: An Introductory Text with Readings*, edited by Anne Barnhill, Mark Budolfson, and Tyler Doggett, 122–135. Oxford: Oxford University Press.

# 7

# THE ETHICAL OMNIVORE ANIMAL ETHIC

Thanksgiving is a traditional time when many American families come together to share a festive meal. In rural Pennsylvania, my family members will travel far distances to celebrate good news and catch up with friends and relatives. It's a joyous occasion filled with laughter and good-hearted banter. I admit that I sometimes dream about my grandmother's Dutch apple pie, made with love and plenty of black walnuts from the big tree in her backyard. It's divine. I also love hearing my cousin's stories, as we share a slice a la mode. But, if our Thanksgiving is any indication, conversations can also get quite heated. Besides my uncle Bob's loudly shouted political views, what's on the table is a surprising area of contention.

The Nolls are a large family and we're a diverse bunch, especially when it comes to diets. For example, this last Thanksgiving, I shared a lovely meal with meat lovers, various omnivores (including a local food advocate), pescatarians, and a smattering of vegetarians. Everyone has strong views on food and ethical commitments run deep concerning what's on our plate. A couple of my aunts like to stay true to traditional dishes, so they don't like to make substitutions. They argue that culture matters and dishes are a historical touchstone that need to be respected and preserved. Other family members are avid hunters, as filling the deep freezer with provisions for the year is important. Pennsylvania has more deer than people and they have few natural predators. Controlling the population is important for maintaining ecological balance, as well as conserving forests and native plants. But, other family members are committed to diets that push back on these practices. For example, a cousin returning from college is a vegan, committed to not eating animal products of any kind, including dairy products and eggs. Animal agriculture goes against her ethical views, and she chooses not to support

DOI: 10.4324/9781003215189-7

these practices, one meal at a time. Other cousins are also committed to not eating meat, but they follow a vegetarian diet. They have different definitions about what that means, though, so only one can still enjoy a piece of apple pie with ice cream, as these are made with cream and butter. No brawls have occurred *yet*, but there have been heated conversations on everything from "who is the true vegetarian," to "why won't Aunt Alice substitute butter with a vegan alternative?" Give it time. As you can guess, arguments abound at the table, as we break bread together. This is because what's in the bread matters.

This chapter deals with the cow in the room, so to speak, when we talk about eating ethically. But, before we dig into the meat-eating debate, let's go over the ethical omnivore recommendations concerning meat eating. As we discussed previously, ethical omnivores embrace organic and regenerative organic agricultural standards. When many people think of organic, they tend to think of vegetables and fruits. As you walk down the produce isle in your local grocery, you will inevitably be confronted with large brightly colored signs proudly proclaiming the organic origin of various vegetables, along with sometimes questionably high-price tags. Additionally, the USDA National Organic Standard, created in 2000, includes strict requirements for meat, dairy, and egg production (USDA 2013). For example, animals must be fed and managed organically, allowed year-round access to pasture or the outdoors, as appropriate for the species, raised on certified organic land and pasture, and cared for following animal welfare standards. They also need to be raised in a manner that is sensitive to environmental conservation and biodiversity. The USDA is quite strict and performs yearly farm inspections to ensure that the farmer's organic plan and their management plans align. Believe me, this is certainly the case. Even the marshmallows we gave the pigs as treats at the MSU Student Farm needed to be certified organic.

However, several critics argue that the Organic Standard doesn't go far enough to ensure high animal welfare standards (ASPCA 2023; Rodale Institute 2024). For example, while animals are required to have outdoor access, there are no clear requirements mandating the type of outdoors or the length of time animals should spend outside. Similarly, it doesn't require a minimum amount of space per animal, and even allows for physical alterations, such as tail docking, debeaking, and castration. Some of these may be needed but others, such a debeaking, are only needed in industrial facilities. Due to these concerns, Robert Rodale, of the Rodale Institute, coined the term "regenerative organic" to distinguish a kind of food production that goes beyond organic production requirements. It mandates that farmers follow the "the "Five Freedoms," a more robust animal welfare standard. This requires that animals should be grass-fed and pasture raised, when appropriate. It does not endorse the use of concentrated animal feeding operations, as well. Regenerative organic can be seen as step closer to meeting the ethical omnivore's ethical requirements. But just what are these requirements?

Ethical omnivores (also known as compassionate carnivores in the literature) typically embrace two positions (Sandler 2014). The first is that people should be allowed to eat meat, if certain conditions are met. In fact, in some situations, eating meat may be the best course of action, otherwise food would go to waste. For example, there are cases where animals need to be culled for health or ecological reasons. This is the case with invasive species, such as lionfish in Florida, which cause widespread ecological harm if not removed. Another example are elk in the Pacific Northwest. We are currently experiencing an outbreak of elk hoof disease, which harms the membrane attaching the hoof to the rest of the foot. Infected elk often lose their hoofs and walk on bone. As readers can guess, it's very painful and also highly contagious. As researchers at Washington State University try to find a cure, sick animals are being culled from herds to limit the spread and reduce animal suffering. These animals are edible, as humans are in no danger of contracting the disease. With numbers of food insecure families on the rise, it would be wasteful to throw away perfectly good food. Here, the argument is relatively straightforward. Ecological health and/or animal welfare demands that we cull certain animals. And, the byproducts of these conservation actions should not be wasted. However, this is a drop in the bucket, so to speak, concerning meat eating. What about farm raised animals that eaters typically consume daily?

A more philosophical argument supporting meat eating is known as the "new omnivorism" position in the literature. Here, theorists such as Andy Lamey (2007) and especially Josh Milburn and Christopher Bobier (2022) argue that omnivorism should be taken seriously as a food ethic. They argue that eaters who embrace this diet typically observe that: (a) animals suffer in industrialized plant-based agriculture and (b) that there are relatively harm-free methods of raising animals for food. Lori Gruen and Robert Jones (2016) grapple with the dark realities of food production, when they observe that "all aspects of consumption in late capitalism involve harming others, human and nonhuman" alike (Gruen and Jones 2016, 157). Land clearing, field traps, pesticides, and mechanical harvesting all harm a wide range of animals. Some of the harms are intentional (e.g. removing pests), while other harms are unintentional (e.g. accidently destroying a field mouse nest while tilling). As Milburn and Bobier (2022) note, examples are quite easy to find if concerned eaters look for them. Mammals, birds, and reptiles are killed during land clearing for agricultural use (Finn & Stephens 2017; Fraser and MacRae 2011); field animals are routinely killed by mechanical harvesting (Archer 2011; Davis 2003); and fertilizers and pesticides kill birds and fish (Fischer and Lamey 2018). These are just a few examples of the myriad ways other species are harmed in plant-based agriculture. When you think about how ecologies function, this isn't surprising. We are in competition with other animals for resources. Rabbits, birds, deer, and other animals live in natural areas before they're turned into farms and they desire the crops, after farms are created. New omnivores argue that, paradoxically, allowing for some meat eating could reduce the suffering of sentient animals, when producing food. This argument goes as follows: (1) Both plant-based and animal industrial agriculture cause harms to sentient animals. (2) As ethical eaters, we have a duty to minimize harm to sentient animals when we produce food. (3) Supporting farms that embrace ecologically healthy practices and high animal welfare standards will reduce these harms. Ecologically sustainable agriculture relies on animals to provide needed nitrogen to grow food, as they don't use petroleum-based inputs. This is called the nitrogen cycle. Thus, a diet of mostly plants and some animal protein, from sustainable farms, will minimize harm to animals in food production, while also maintaining high yields.

I want to quickly mention Michael Pollan's additional argument that if we didn't raise many of our domesticated animals for food, then they would go extinct. (The interdisciplinary scholar Donna Haraway also supported this view in a talk she gave in 2015.) People typically don't raise cows, pigs, water buffalo, and other farm animals as pets. They raise them as part of productive farms. When they're no longer needed for agriculture, they tend to die out, as we've seen with heritage breeds not suitable in industrial systems. From this view, some species would face extinction if they weren't raised for food. But he goes on to argue that this doesn't mean that food animals should be treated badly. Pollan observes that "[p]eople who care about animals should be working to ensure that the ones they eat don't suffer, and that their deaths are swift and painless" (Pollan 2006, 328). Other animal ethicists, such as Temple Grandin and those who support animal welfare standards, agree. Whether or not you agree, an important takeaway from these arguments is that how we grow and raise our food matters. If you truly care about limiting animal suffering, then it's not enough to eat a vegetarian diet. For ethical omnivores, you need to eat some animals to save them. However, what are animal welfare standards? Will these frameworks reduce animal harm like supporters of new omnivorism think they will? The next section explores what we mean by animal welfare and places the ethical omnivore animal ethic in historical context. The demand to treat animals well and eat them too did not start with Michael Pollan, as has been suggested in the literature, though he is an eloquent defender of omnivorism. Humans have been debating diets and animal use for thousands of years. I ask readers to take a walk through history, as debates concerning meat eating inform today's diets.

## Placing the Debate in Context to Understand the Beef

People have been grappling with the ethics of meat eating for a very long time. Before looking at current debates, we need to place the conversation in context. In the 6th century BC, Egyptian priests did not use any animal-based products, including food and clothing items (Crowley 2016). They believed that the human soul is immortal and, upon death, can be passed into the body of other living species. This idea is important for many religions, such as Hinduism, Buddhism, and Jainism. One of my favorite stories is of a Tibetan monk who would stop to pick up earthworms while helping a farmer, placing them back into the soil, so as not to cause harm. While meat eating is not strictly forbidden, many practicing Buddhists do not eat meat, drawing from religious texts as justification. Similarly, the Greek philosopher and mathematician Pythagoras believed that eating meat sullied the soul and was like eating one's kin (Corse 2010). In both examples, killing an animal is unethical and thus eating one is too. While not against killing, Medieval monks in Europe also ate a largely vegetarian diet, indulging in fish or small portions of meat only during special occasions (Zwart 2000). This practice was thought to reduce temptation and help bolster the ideals of frugality and temperance. The desire to live a virtuous life, in line with Christian ideals, influenced every aspect of a Monk's life, including their dietary habits.

Other types of diets were popular, as well, and had ethical justifications. Many cultures embraced an omnivore diet, which could include meats, vegetables, grains, berries, and other edibles. Indeed, humans can eat a surprising number of things! For example, *The Apicius*, also known as *De re culinaria* (On the Subject of Cooking) is one of the oldest known collections of recipes, compiled in the 5th century CE (Apicius and Vehling 1977). It provides a unique glimpse into Roman tastes and diets and preparations for an astonishingly vast number of fruits, vegetables, and animals. There are entire passages on keeping truffles, olives, citron, and other ingredients fresh. Another section provides recipes to prepare quadrupeds, which includes everything from wild boar and venison to dormouse. In a review at the beginning of the first translation, the translator Joseph Dommers Vehling stresses that we are the cooking animal and that cookery deals with natures work. They provide key insights into how the environment works and our place in the larger ecosystem, to use a modern term to describe an old idea. He recognizes that some readers may shy away from the sections detailing animal death, but those committed to eating in line with nature will prevail. This quote is particularly evocative, "If they were told that they must kill before they may cook—that might spoil the appetite and dinner joy of many a tender-hearted devourer of fellow-creatures" (Vehling 1977, 39). In reply, the author goes on to declare "Heaven forbid! Being real children of nature, and behaving naturally, nature likes them…" This focus on embracing a diet aligned with nature is not surprising, as the Romans revered Ancient Greek thought. The philosopher Aristotle argued that acting in accordance with nature is a key part of living an ethical life. As we explored in the introduction, eating is an important part of cultivating personal virtues. There are many other examples of omnivore diets in history and their popularity continues today, across the globe.

When looking at the history of food ethics, remarkable shifts occurred on this topic. As we just discussed, historically, food ethics was a matter of dietetics or the consumption of food. As the food scholar Hub Zwart so aptly notes, "ancient dietetics was basically a private morality [and] in the course of history, several basic models for reflection on food emerged" (2000, 114). Food began to take on personal and cultural significance, often acting as a signal that the eater embraces a certain faith or philosophical conviction. For instance, certain religious groups will abstain from eating certain types of meat, such as pork. While Greek dietetics focused on temperance, religious food ethics often starts with distinctions between what is allowed and what is not. Modern food ethics grew from this foundation but was broadened to include issues of production. In the streets of Seattle, it's not uncommon to come upon a vegan proudly proclaiming that they've washed their hands of the ethical abuses associated with eating meat. In the former example, abstaining from eating a specific food signifies a religious conviction, while the latter eater is expressing a moral commitment. What's fascinating is that today issues relating to consumption and food production have merged. For example, ethical vegetarians and vegans often justify their dietary choices by discussing poor animal welfare on industrial farms. In this way, how animals are treated and what happens on the farm influence what we choose to put on our plates. As we will see, animal welfare now plays a major role in meat eating debates.

### Animal Welfare and Why It Matters

Views on animal welfare shifted and influence many eaters' diets. Since the early 18th century, society's attitude toward animals have transformed significantly. Particularly in Northern Europe, the anti-vivisectionist movement gained popularity, as public opinion turned against experimentation on live animals (Franco 2013). In the United States, the rise of the animal welfare movement is an absorbing tale with heroes and villains and even a stolen dalmatian named Pepper. It's an important story, as it shows how changes in community attitudes influence personal actions, policies, and regulations, alike. This story begins on the streets of New York. Early modern cities were often places of suffering for domesticated animals, such as horses, dogs, and pigs. When reading descriptions, I'm often surprised by the numbers and types of animals on the streets. For instance, a lithograph of Five Points (a New York neighborhood) published in 1827 clearly shows roaming pigs and dogs, with horses pulling carriages (Unknown 1855). Other accounts describe turtles on their backs kept outside restaurants (turtle soup was quite popular) and livestock being herded through neighborhoods to slaughter facilities. It was on streets like these where The ASPCA (American Society for the Prevention of Cruelty to Animals) was born (Freeberg 2020; Ingram 2020). Its founder Henry Bergh was a wealthy New Yorker who was an American diplomat assigned to Russia under President Lincoln's administration. He traveled extensively and was applauded by the horrific animal abuse he witnessed, from bullfighting to the whipping of horses unable to continue pulling carts. After consulting with a friend in the United Kingdom on their animal cruelty laws, Bergh returned to the United States and made it his mission to help the "mute servants of mankind" (Freeberg 2020). He helped to draft the Declaration of the Rights of Animals, created the ASPCA in 1866, and the following week, the first anti-cruelty laws were passed in the United States, granting ASPCA agents the right to enforce these laws on the streets.

Fast forward to the 1900s and several states followed suit, also passing anti-cruelty laws to protect animals from abuse (Davis 2024; Freeberg 2020). Animal advocate groups then took the fight to Washington, pushing for sweeping federal welfare legislation. However, the numbers of animals used for biomedical research greatly increased during this time, as well (Hajar 2011). Research advocacy groups were highly critical of any push that could reduce their supply of readily available research subjects. The result was a stalemate in congress, as both groups advocated for wildly different directions concerning animal use and care. Surprisingly, though, this stalemate was resolved after the Lakavage family's Dalmatian Pepper was stolen from their farm in Pennsylvania in 1965 (National Agricultural Library 2019). The family let the dog out to play in their yard and he disappeared. After searching for several weeks, they found out that Pepper had been sold to a research facility in New York City and was already euthanized. The Lakavage's family story was not unique, as the demand for new animal research subjects led to kidnappings and black-market auctions of beloved pets across the country. Even the labs at the National Institutes of Health had stolen dogs in their labs. Pepper's theft and eventual death (as well as popular dog-napping movies, such as 101 Dalmatians) caused a public outcry. The scales were tipped to favor animal advocate groups, as Rep. Joseph Resnick (D-NY) introduced a Laboratory Animal Welfare bill in Congress. He jokingly called himself "dogs best friend" in Washington (Nolen 2016). The Animal Welfare Act (AWA) was passed in 1966 and strengthened throughout the years to ensure that labs embrace high animal welfare standards. This legislation mirrored similar changes to animal use around the globe.

Our definitions of animal welfare have changed throughout the years, as we gain a greater understanding of species needs. Marisa Erasmus, a professor at Purdue in the Department of Animal Sciences does a wonderful job discussing how our views have evolved over the years (Erasmus 2020). Animal welfare extends beyond how animals are treated, which was the focus of early state laws. Since Dr. Donald Broom's definition published in 1986, organizations such as The American Veterinary Medical Association and the World Organization for Animal Health expanded their definitions to include animal responses to environmental and living conditions. Additional frameworks include the Five Freedoms developed by the Farm Animal Welfare Council in the United Kingdom, after they published The Brambell Report on farm animal conditions in 1965 (Elischer 2019). This report was highly critical of current standards, arguing that animals should be able to "stand up, lie down, turn around, groom themselves and stretch their limbs" (quoted in Elischer 2019, n.p.). The result was one of the most well-known animal welfare frameworks used today. The Five Freedoms include the following: (1) Freedom from hunger and thirst; (2) freedom from discomfort; (3) freedom from pain, injury or disease; (4) freedom to express normal behavior; and (5) freedom from fear and distress (Webster 2016). These are widely used by organizations and professionals who evaluate animal welfare for a living. Another important framework developed in 1997 is called the Three Pillars of Animal Welfare (Erasmus 2020). This definition includes three key concepts: First, we need to respect an animal's emotions or affective states. They should not be stressed, in pain, or frustrated. Second, an animal should be able to perform natural behaviors. If it's in a being's nature to create nests or roost, then they should be able to do so. If they are nocturnal, then it's not acceptable to keep them in a lighted room 24/7, for example. Finally, an animal should be healthy and have good biological functioning.

Today, each of these components inform animal welfare definitions and standards. As Marisa Erasmus so eloquently stated, "animal welfare is about how the animal is doing, and how the animal is perceiving its environment… To effectively evaluate or measure animal welfare, all three concepts (behavior, affective state and health and biological functioning) need to be considered" (2). With these frameworks as a guide, animal welfare scientists use species-specific measures (body condition and behavior), resource-based measures (do they have access to food and water), and other tools to assess their health and overall wellbeing. While these measures have gotten more sophisticated over the years, their ethical foundation remains the same. Like Henry Bergh, animal welfare frameworks don't critique animal use, unless this use is overly cruel. For example, many organizations, such as the ASPCA, are staunchly against blood sports, such as dog and cock fighting, while still supporting pet ownership. These frameworks tacitly accept the position that humans should use animals for their own purposes, be that for research, food, fiber, or companionship. The ethical rub here concerns how we treat and house them, not that we use them.

Animal welfare standards play an increasingly important role in eater's decisions. How animals are raised, treated, and slaughtered are important issues that eaters have agonized over for the last 20 years. So much so that consumers are changing their food and purchasing habits (Verbeke et al. 2009). Recent studies have shown that animal welfare may play a significant role determining what affluent consumers purchase and the money they're willing to pay for premium products. In fact, a recent paper even went so far as to call welfare a critical theme for the future success of commercial livestock production (Verbeke and Viaene 2000).

Interestingly, though, this growing concern is not solely due to the ways animals are treated. Research indicates that consumers are concerned with animal welfare, though for two different types of reasons (Nocella et al. 2009). First, they're concerned with zoocentric concerns, or those that relate to how animals are treated. But, they are also worried about anthropocentric concerns, or how animal welfare impacts the quality and safety of foodstuffs. Several other studies, including those by Bailey Norwood and Jayson Lusk (2007) support this view that consumers are willing to pay more to support production systems that improve animal welfare. This is important because it shows that consumers truly care about welfare, rather than simply saying that they do. People tend to pay more for things that they care about. For instance, this weekend I saw a line of people paying $15 for 2 pounds of cherries at the local farmers' market. Cherries were less half the cost at the grocery store, but these eaters care about the quality of the fruit and where they're grown. Some also genuinely want to support local producers. In the next stall, another farmer was selling pork products made from Berkshire heritage pigs raised on his farm.

Ethical omnivores embrace welfare standards on the farm. As Michael Pollan (2024) states, "a truly sustainable agriculture will involve animals, in order to complete the nutrient cycle, and those animals are going to be killed and eaten" (n.p.). He goes on to say that he respects vegetarians and vegans because they've done the hard work of thinking through the consequences of what's on their plate. But, his own examination has led him to the conclusion that eating small amounts of meat from farms with high welfare standards is something that he feels good about. I had a conversation with Temple Grandin, a professor of animal science and autism spokesperson, and she largely comes to the same conclusion. Though both respect individuals who grapple with the ethics of their food choices, as the process is important. For supporters of small-scale sustainable agriculture, animals play a key role on the farm. They provide much needed nitrogen, replacing environmentally harmful or unsustainable petroleum-based fertilizers. They provide important labor, so to speak, as farm animals such as pigs are excellent at rooting around in soils, aerating and tilling it. Chickens are amazing at pest control and can be great partners on a farm. As we discussed, the ethical omnivore diet has grown out of The Organic Movement, meaning that sustainability and environmentally friendly practices are paramount. The other side of this coin is animal welfare. If farm animals are seen as indispensable partners on a farm, then animal welfare becomes important. Ethical omnivore cookbooks and websites tend to prioritize animal welfare. Not all meat is the same. Eating animals raised in a sustainable manner, with high animal welfare standards fits the bill. For many eaters, this means eating less meat and far more vegetables than is typical in industrial countries. Raising animals in farms with high standards means that farms will raise fewer animals and thus meat products will cost more.

## From Animal Welfare to Animal Rights

But eater's perceptions are guided by many ethical commitments, some of which challenge animal use, especially when we use them for food. Historically, we largely used animals for agriculture and transportation, as they're great at providing fiber, food, and locomotion. And, agricultural success largely depended on having healthy animals. Thus, good husbandry and good care was enforced by an ethic based on self-interest and anti-cruelty (Rollin 2012). But with the emergence of new types of "normal" animal use, most notably animal research and intensive agriculture, suffering occurs that falls outside this anticruelty ethic. For the veterinary health ethicist Bernard Rollin, animal welfare frameworks are an attempt to replace this historical ethic—an ethic that was short-circuited. Changes in animal use forced society to create new animal ethics to help guide us. But there are three questions that we need to grapple with, as a society, when doing this. I remember Rollin discussing these at a conference several years ago, when I was a graduate student. He was quite the character, rolling in on a Harley Davidson motorcycle and talking about animal welfare, while wearing a biker jacket and chaps. As one of the first ethicists to teach in a School of Veterinary Medicine, he had many stories and even more insights. The three concerns that Rollin wants to grapple with are as follows: First, what entitles humans to use animals for our benefit, especially in ways that hurt, harm, kill, or distress them? Second, how can we justify animal use? For him, the only justifiable argument for using human beings in these ways is utilitarian, meaning that their sacrifice generates more benefits than costs. For example, humans are often a part of medical research, with the hope that the information we glean will help develop new treatments, vaccines, and standards of care. With protections in place, we, as a society, accept that the potential harm of trying a new medication for the first time is outweighed by societal benefits. Rollin argues that we can use this same logical argument to support some animal research, but many of the ways that we use animals would not be justified.

He goes on to argue that many people disregard the previous two ethical concerns. Billions of animals are being used for research and food and this use is not producing the greatest good for the greatest number. As such, we are left with a third concern. Specifically, Rollin argues that:

> if researchers fail to attend to the question of our right to use animals in invasive ways and ignore the clear-cut moral demand that the benefits from the research outweigh the costs to the animals, at the very least common sense and common decency dictate that animals...be treated as well as possible.
>
> (s5)

From this perspective, animal welfare arguments do not grapple with these two other ethical concerns. The current debate about meat eating really comes down to an ethical conflict between these three concerns. For some eaters, we are not justified in using animals for food, be that meat, eggs, or dairy. For others, we can use animals to benefit us, but only if these benefits outweigh the costs. Peter Singer argued that a utilitarian ethic would not support the majority of industrial animal agriculture. However, this doesn't mean that all animal use is off the table. He contentiously stated that primates used to develop lifesaving treatments could be justified depending on the situation. We will discuss Singer's ethic more below, but the tension is palpable here. Finally, there are those who defend animal use, such as through stewardship or environmental ethics. However, there appears to be little common ground between those who embrace the first concern and the third. This begs the question: Are there acceptable ethical justifications for using animals? This is a contentious issue that's sparked many a debate at the family table and online.

Interestingly, the publication that led to the development of the Five Freedoms also helped to launch the Animal Rights Movement. Let's turn back time to 1964, a year before the Brambell Report was published. Ruth Harrison's book called "Animal Machines" was just released, which presented a scathing review of industrial agriculture, describing intensive livestock practices of the time. Harrison's work prompted the British government to appoint a committee, led by Professor Roger Brambell (Elischer 2019). The result was the "Report of the Technical Committee to Inquire into the Welfare of Animals Kept under Intensive Livestock Husbandry Systems," which is commonly known at The Brambell Report. The Animal Rights movement also began to gain traction during this time, as well. In an interview, the well-known ethicist Peter Singer claims that Harrison's work inspired his own. Singer and other animal rights advocates push back against the very idea that we are entitled to use animals for our own purposes. As we will discuss, their work harkened in an age where raising animals for food is questioned.

Similar to Harrison, Singer grapples with the plight of both research and food animals in the book *Animal Liberation: A New Ethics for Our Treatment of Animals*, first published in 1975. It is an excellent example of how public criticisms expanded beyond animal research to include agriculture and meat eating. The book helped to spark the Animal Rights Movement in the United States, with its poignant and logical arguments. In this foundational text, he tries to persuade readers that we're acting in "speciest" or discriminatory ways towards other species, in that we are treating them differently simply because they are not human. Thus, it is a type of discrimination. He likens the animal rights movement to civil rights and feminist movements, as it also combats a type of discrimination or prejudice. It's wrong to treat people differently simply because of their gender, ethnicity, or race. Likewise, it's wrong to treat animals differently, just because they are a member of another species. Once we do away with these biased arguments, we are left with the reality that all beings capable of suffering (including animals) are worthy of ethical consideration. This doesn't mean that they're ethical agents, in that we should hold them to human standards. Singer isn't saying that wolves should be brought up on murder charges when they kill a deer, for example. That's what it means to be an ethical agent. This is when you have ethical responsibilities and are held the ethical standards concerning actions. Rather, non-human animals are moral patients, meaning that we should consider their welfare and interests when making decisions. A child, for instance, is often treated as a moral patient, rather than a fully formed moral agent. We don't hold them completely accountable for their actions, as they're not fully developed rational agents. This is why we appoint guardians and proxy decision-makers, especially when stakes are high, such as when making medical or legal choices. We're not going to ask a 6-year-old to choose which cancer treatment is better for them. They're not mature enough to make these decisions on their own, yet. The other side of the coin is human exceptionalism, or the idea that humans have a capacity (such as abstract thought, empathy, a community, or even the ability to lie, etc.) that gives them moral status, while other species are exempt. This is the other side of the speciesism coin, so to speak. Singer and other animal rights theorists challenge both views, maintaining an egalitarian ethic, where humans and other animals are all morally considerable.

For the last 40 years, there is growing consensus that we should treat animals as vulnerable beings, worthy of ethical consideration. They are not simply property that we can do what we want with. Each experiences the world from a unique point of view. They direct their own lives and attempt to thrive. Members of several species experience anxiety and pain and joy, like humans. For Singer (2015), at the most basic level, all mammals don't want to suffer. You could say that they have "an interest" in not suffering from injury, lack of necessities, or poor environmental conditions. And for

Singer, this is all you need to be considered a moral patient. If you can suffer, you have an interest in not suffering. If you have interests, then these should be considered when a decision is made that affects you. This holds for humans and non-human animals alike. Singer is a utilitarian, so for him this means that the best action is the one that produces the greatest good for the greatest number. Roughly, when deciding, we should identify all individuals whose interests will be impacted. Then, determine what action produces the best outcomes for the most beings, overall. This is a gross simplification of utilitarianism and Singer's work, but it highlights how he thinks about animal ethics. We need to grapple with the consequences of our choices and impacts to animals matter. Other thinkers provide similar justifications for treating animals ethically, but recommend that we apply different ethical frameworks, or rules of thumb.

Other thinkers make similar arguments, placing animals in the ethical sphere. For example, Tom Regan published *The Case for Animal Rights* in 1983. This is also considered a foundational text for the Animal Rights Movement. In it, Regan (1995) argues that all experiencing "subjects-of-a-life" have inherent value and thus should be treated ethically. For this thinker, all mammals are subjects-of-a-life and thus fall within our ethical purview. As Dale Jamieson (1990) explains, inherent value means that beings have "value that is logically independent of the value of their experiences and of their value to others" (350). Inherent value often makes me think of the philosophy of Immanuel Kant and his ethical recommendation that we should treat others as an end in themselves, and not merely as a means. To have inherent value means that you have value in-and-of yourself, regardless of whether your useful to others or society. For example, when you get a cup of coffee from your local coffee house, if you treat the barista like they're only valuable as coffee dispensers and their lives and feelings don't matter, then you're not respecting their inherent value. For Regan, all entities who have inherent value possess it in equal measure, meaning that you either do or you don't have it. It's not a matter of degrees (Regan 2004). It doesn't matter what color hair you have, or sex, or species membership. If you are a subject-of-a-life, you are valued as much as all others who have inherent value (Abbate 2015).

Here, both Singer and Regan are largely in agreement that animals should be treated ethically, though they made unique arguments to get there. However, Regan (1995) applies a different ethic to help us determine how to best treat animals. He's very critical of Singer's approach, as he argues that you can't clean up unjust institutions by tidying them up. They either are or are not just. Utilitarian ethics allows some animal testing and some animal agriculture, but that's a wrongheaded approach. Additionally, as this framework focuses on consequences, it has a rather glaring blind-spot. Regan uses the example of the fictional Aunt Bea to explain his concern. Imagine, you have an Aunt Bea and she has a lot of money. She has several children and grandchildren who would benefit from having that money. It would make their lives substantially better if she were gone. So, should we kill her? If we're only worried about consequences, then there could be a world where it is ethical to take Aunt Bea out. But most people will answer that it's wrong to kill her. Aunt Bea's life matters, regardless of her (or her money's) usefulness to others. If this is the case, then all individuals who have inherent value matter in the same way. Regan concludes that subjects-of-a-life have a right to be treated respectfully, which includes the right to not be harmed merely because others would benefit.

Thus far, we've been focusing on Peter Singer and Tom Regan's theories as they each played an important role developing the literature. In fact, the animal ethicist David DeGrazia (1991) argues that their work, along with Raymond Frye's, make up the "first generation" of animal ethics (49). However, this characterization might do a disservice to their work, as they have both continued to produce new work for decades. Both Singer and Regan have been polishing and refining their work throughout the years. As I write this, both have contributed a staggering number of publications. Additionally, *Animal Liberation* is in its fifth edition, along with an expanded and edited anniversary edition, and Regan's *The Case for Animal Rights* has been in print since it was first published in 1983. With this being said, today the literature is quite large, as several theorists provide their unique arguments and contributions. Accounts of animal rights have been developed using a diverse array of theoretical frameworks, such as utilitarianism, social contract theory, Kantianism, the capabilities approach, feminist frameworks, and even Aristotelian and Ancient Greek philosophy (Regan 2004; Rowlands 2009; Nussbaum 2007; Palmer 2010; Rollin 2016). There is also the political turn in animal ethics, as scholars grapple questions surrounding citizenship, social membership, and political representation of animals (Donaldson and Kymlicka 2013). Finally, there is a growing area of legal scholarship that explores the possibility of legal personhood and redefining animal rights law, using long-term litigation campaigns and legal arguments (Francione 1995; Wise 2000).

As you can see, the research has blossomed and pulls from several traditions. For example, Clare Palmer, in her book *Animal Ethics in Context* (2010), is highly critical of "capacity"-based ethics, or those that argue that a specific trait (such as the ability to suffer or reason) is acceptable justification for treating animals ethically. For Palmer, context, history, and our relationships with certain animals are important ethical factors. Animals that live independently in the wild aren't our moral business. We're not going walk into Yellowstone and ethically sanction buffalo, for example. But what about our domesticated animals? For Palmer, if an animal is dependent on humans, through selective breeding or the destruction of habitats, then we have a responsibility to help them. Relationships matter. We recognize this in daily life. Parents often accept the fact that they have special obligations to their children. Children recognize that they have a responsibility to their parents, especially when they need end of life care. These relationships are important and entail ethical duties and rights, in that we often feel like we have a duty to our children, family, friends, and other important figures in our lives. The relationships we have with dependent animals are similar, in that they also entail duties. For instance, I have a duty to my dog called Turtle. She relies on me for food and water, shelter, exercise, and affection. Different contexts create different moral relationships. Bernard Rollin agrees with Clare Palmer that, at the very least, we have a duty to animal's dependent on humans. However, he uses the Aristotelian conception of telos to guide actions. He proposed that we should follow the "Maxim to Respect Telos" when deciding how to treat animals (Rollin 2016, 1995). This maxim is, roughly, that if we have dealings with animals, we need to respect their needs and desires.

## The Case for Vegetarianism

If we agree that animals should be treated with respect, then can we use them for food? The answer depends on who you read, but most animal rights theorists argue that we should reduce or eliminate all industries and practices that treat animals as resources. For example, strong animal rights theories like Regan's are abolitionist in nature, meaning that they require the end of animal testing, industrial agriculture, and other practices that exploit animals. The animal ethicist Cheryl Abbate (2015) expresses this sentiment well, when she states that many rights theories demand "that we, as moral agents, employ a 'hands off' policy of noninterference in our dealing with nonhuman animals... This entails that we not 'trespass' into their lives and that we just let nonhuman animals be" (Regan 2004, 357). With Regan's criticisms of utilitarianism, you would think that Singer would advocate for more balanced approach, even concerning animal agriculture. However, this is not the case. Singer has been highly critical of meat eating for his entire career (Singer 2007; 2015). Looking back at *Animal Liberation*, it's not hard to see why.

Well-written logical arguments are only one of the reasons why this book influenced so many people. Another reason is because of the way that the text tugged at reader's heartstrings concerning animal research and agriculture. The book was an emotional read, especially with the inclusion of gruesome pictures of laboratory subjects and scathing critiques of animal agriculture. For example, Singer discusses starvation, electric shocks, and the physical and psychological torture of animals used for research. Concerning farming, Singer and other animal ethicists are united in their criticism of current practices. Most farm animals in the world are raised in factory farms, or facilities that prioritize efficiency and cost-efficacy rather than animal welfare.

He is highly critical of these types of farms, juxtaposing them against smaller more idyllic farms, where animals are raised on pasture and given plenty of space to roam. Singer then goes on to describe unhealthy conditions, including starvation, overcrowding, callus handling, and slaughter in detail. With close to 100 billion animals raised annually for food, the ethical toll is dire. This critique of industrial agriculture forms the emotional foundation for animal ethics, modern vegetarianism, and ethical omnivorism as well. So, what is the solution?

For Singer and Regan, it's vegetarianism or veganism, of course. Let's do away with factory farming and the ethical wrongs of animal agriculture will be righted (Singer 2007, 2015; Regan 2004). Rights-based approaches rightly point out that we're using livestock to obtain food, not as an end in themselves. While some animal use could be defended by utilitarian ethics, the current amount of suffering caused by factory farming renders this argument mute. The bioethicist James Rachels (2016) simplifies this position, arguing that we only need to accept one principle to see that vegetarianism is the ethical diet. Specifically, if we accept that it's wrong to cause harm unless there is good enough reason, then meat is no longer what's for dinner. This argument hinges on how we justify raising and slaughtering animals for food. If billions of animals are living in crowded and stressful conditions, then the enjoyment of eating a steak is not enough to justify the harm caused. It also takes us back to Bernard Rollin's three concerns. The first grapples with how we justify using animals, especially when we cause harm. Animal rights ethicists have provided an answer to this question. For many thinkers in this tradition, there is rarely a good enough reason to do so. Better to have the salad, than the chicken or fish. For other animal ethicists, however, the answer isn't so simple. For example, Rollin argues that we should turn back many industrial practices and embrace farming methods that prioritize animal welfare, rather than efficiency. And, Claire Palmer (2010) urges us to think about our relationships with animals, including food animals, and recognize the ethical duties bound up with this relationship. Even Peter Singer has argued in the past that it might be acceptable to eat animals that have enjoyed a good life, though this is highly problematic due to environmental concerns (Schiffman 2023). This aligns well with his utilitarian ethic. My point here is that this is a contentious topic in the literature, with different ethicists providing novel recommendations. There is a good amount of consensus, as well. Most agree that animals should be treated ethically and that we're failing them.

What I find fascinating here is that there is agreement in the ethical literature concerning industrial agricultural practices. Whether you're talking to an animal rights advocate, an animal welfarist, a vegetarian, or ethical omnivore, they're all likely to be concerned about the way farm animals are being treated. The animal rights movement launched 50 years ago, so you would expect there to be change. But, in a recent interview, Singer stated the following:

> Europe and the U.K. have banned some of the worst forms of confinement for chickens where they can't even spread their wings, as well as California and several other U.S. states. The confinement of calves in veal stalls so that they can't turn around — that's also prohibited in some places. Confining breeding sows in tiny stalls has also been banned in Europe and elsewhere. But in much of the U.S., conditions haven't changed very much, and in some respects they have gotten worse. Chickens are being bred to grow so fast that the birds no longer support their body weight. For the last couple of weeks, they are in pain just standing up, and they can't sit down because they are raised on a kind of litter — wood shavings that are full of their droppings and has such a high level of ammonia in it that if they sit down, it gives them skin burns on their legs and chest. There is no legal control, and market forces demand the cheaper chickens that can be raised that way. Overall, the breeding of chickens, which is the largest number of farm animals, has intensified. It's actually gotten worse.
>
> (Schiffman 2023)

He goes on to state that, like Europeans, Americans also reject many of these practices. For example, referendums to improve the lives of farm animals are quite popular, often passing by substantial majorities. But, the agricultural industry is powerful and plays a large role in U.S. politics, defeating attempts to change federal policy. The AWA doesn't apply to farm animals. Indeed, there are no federal laws regulating the treatment of billions of food animals while they're on the farm. Agricultural gag laws also erode trust, as they block people from recording or documenting animal cruelty abuses. Paradoxically, this blockade strategy is ultimately a losing one, if the numbers are correct below. It allows harmful conditions to continue and it's also angering citizens, as consumers reject industrial animal agriculture with their dollars and votes, when possible. Eaters increasingly turn to local food systems, and other standards that include animal welfare requirements, such as USDA Organic, Animal Welfare Approved, and Certified Humane, among others.

As discussed above, animal welfare is an important consideration for eaters today. According to a recent Gallup Poll (2020), one in four U.S. adults have cut back on eating meat, and this seems to be a trend. Though, they go on to argue that this doesn't mean vegetarianism is on the rise, as these numbers have been holding steady for the last 20 years at 4–5%. There could be many reasons for this change, such as rising prices, recommendations to eat less meat, inflation, etc. For instance, The New York Times best-selling book *How Not to Die* by Michael Greger (2015) recommends that we eat a mostly vegetable-based diet for our health. In addition, a study by Nocella et al. (2009) specifically linked this trend to animal welfare, as well as human thriving. Their research has shown that "the most frequently reported motivations for a meat-reduced or meat-free diet are ethical concerns about animal welfare" (1). Frey and Pirscher (2018) go so far as to argue that deontology, utilitarianism, and a mixture of the two approaches play an important role in motivating the willingness to pay more to support higher welfare standards in production systems. The animal rights movement did a great job educating the public about animal abuses and urging them to think more deeply about how we treat livestock. Today, the public is increasingly doing this, and they are changing their eating habits, accordingly, be that by reducing meat consumption or embracing an ethics-based diet. This change might not be the abolitionist response that Regan advocated for, but it is an important change, nonetheless.

And, this returns us to animal welfare. For some eaters, no animal use is acceptable. For others, we are justified in our use of animals for food, but we need to ensure that livestock are well taken care of. Henry Bergh, the founder of the ASPCA, never questioned whether humans should be using animals, nor is this topic typically brought up in current welfare legislation debates. Like animal rights advocates, ethical omnivores have given a good amount of thought to the animal use question. They don't take it for granted that we have dominion over the fish of the sea, fowl of the air, cattle, and every creeping thing on the earth, to paraphrase Genesis. Nor do they accept the abolitionist position that we should do away with animal agriculture. Rather, ethical omnivores recognize that they share many views that vegetarians also share, but they disagree on one very important point. Terence Cuneo (2015) does a wonderful job describing this overlap, as well as the beef between these two ethics. In *Conscientious Omnivore*, Cuneo argues that supporters of both views agree that killing farm animals for food is problematic. By killing animals, we are doing a harm to them. They also agree that there are good reasons not to kill animals for food and that its better if we don't raise animals simply for food. Finally, both would at least consider the argument that the badness of killing animals could be offset if they lived good lives, though they might disagree on how much its offset (33).

So, where do they disagree? Here's where his argument gets tricky. He argues that "conscientious omnivores believe that, while we may have moral reasons not to kill these animals for food, we would not wrong these animals were we to kill them for food" (33). In this way, family farming is distinct from industrial agriculture. The latter violates the rights of animals, while family farming does not. By giving animals good (though short) lives, they're not humiliated and degraded. They're also not treated disrespectfully, as if their lives and welfare don't matter, as they only have instrumental worth. Critics might point out that animals are killed in both instances, so there is little difference ethically between the two farming systems. However, in family farms, animals are not killed simply for the pleasure that we get from eating meat. Cumeo goes on to say that family farms also provide "food that sustains and nourishes us, which is (for many) very pleasurable to eat… This food, in turn, sustains a variety of rich social practices that many value a great deal" (34). So, many important traditions revolve around the table, such as cookery, holiday celebrations, animal husbandry, and shared meals. Love is derived from the middle English word for "breaking bread," after all. We share our food with those who are important to us and this sharing, in turn, reinforces relationships.

## Living Well with Animals and the Planet

So, there is a core ethic that both animal rights advocates and ethical omnivores can agree on. This ethic is built on respecting the rights of animals not to be treated cruelly and not to be killed just for the pleasure we get from killing or eating them. Violating these rights means that we're treating animals instrumentally, or like their lives and well-being don't matter. Thus, they are both critical of industrial practices. Also, they both advocate for eating less meat, as sustainable animal production is time-consuming and produce a much smaller yield than industrial farming. Where they differ is their proposed solution to right the wrongs of current animal husbandry methods. Unlike animal rights advocates, ethical omnivores embrace a complex vision of farming, where animal husbandry is important for more than putting bacon on your plate. The moral life is not only about how to act well but also how to live well, for both humans and non-human animals, alike (Cuneo 2015, 25). Though, here I do want to mention that Cuneo's use of "family farm" is problematic for many ethical omnivores. Most farms in the United States are technically "family farms," in that they're owned by specific families. However, they tend to be large and practice industrial methods, as discussed early in the book. These are not the operations Cuneo is describing, as he's clear that family farms are distinct from industrial operations. For him, then, the family farm is one that aligns with The Organic Movement, meaning that it's small scale, sustainable farming, like the farms discussed earlier in this book. If this is so, then other animal omnivores would agree with his assessment.

For example, EOM founder, Lana Joe Salant (2023) has written extensively on the ethical omnivore movement and commercial agriculture. On the EMO website, Salant argues that she needs to state, first and foremost, that they do not endorse animal confinement operations. That the basic needs of farm animals should be met. They should be given appropriate food, for example, as chickens and pigs are omnivores, not vegetarians. They deserve to have access to their dietary requirements. She continues, stating that "our food animals deserve the best possible lives and the best, most reverent deaths we can afford them or quite frankly we don't deserve to eat them" (n.p.). This also includes hunting and fishing (for food). In short, for this organization, the essence of ethical omnivorism is raising, "growing, hunting and gathering our own food sustainably… Using the animal from nose to tail and the plant from root to shoot as far as possible. That's the essence of ethical omnivorism" (n.p.). They encourage eaters to grow their own food, support local farmers, eat organic produce and ethically sourced meats, dairy, and eggs. Above all, their core values push eaters to embrace a diet that aligns with mother nature, as everyone and everything is connected.

So, an ethical omnivore embraces an animal welfare ethic and rather stringent one, as they do not endorse factory farming. Farmers in the United States are committed to animal welfare, though standards are lower than in Europe. However, it also includes an environmental ethic, as well. The EOM list of core values clearly states this. They implore eaters to support organic and sustainable agriculture and think about how their food choices impact Mother Nature. This is like Michael Pollan's (2024) food ethic discussed earlier, where he argues that animals play a key role in farms not reliant on petroleum-based inputs. Their manure is needed to complete the nutrient cycle, and I would add that they also provide important services, such as pest control and tilling, as they live their lives on the farm. Finally, the ethical omnivore diet grew out of The Organic Movement, so embracing sustainability and environmentally friendly practices is part of its DNA, so to speak. It is an ethic of interconnections, recognizing that what we eat has far reaching consequences for our health, our animals, and the environment. Pulling from the four pillars of food ethics, this approach is sensitive to impacts to: (1) society, (2) individuals, (3) the environment, and (4) animal welfare. As Terrence Cuneo (2015) so aptly noted, the moral life is not only about how to act well but also how to live well, for both humans and non-human animals, alike (25).

So, is there such a thing as ethical meat eating? For ethical omnivores, it is ethical to eat meat, but not all meat is the same. Eating animals raised in a sustainable manner, with high animal welfare standards fits the bill. For many eaters, this means eating less meat and far more vegetables than is typical in industrial countries. Raising animals in farms with high standards means that farms will raise fewer animals and thus meat products will cost more. For ethical omnivores, eating in balance with nature is worth it. But, the food fight will continue, as families gather on holidays and in social media. The moral overlap between vegetarians and ethical omnivores may be substantial, but they disagree when it matters. The next chapter will explore ethics of meat eating even further, as we move away from the farm and into the forest.

# References

Abbate, C.E. 2015. "Comparing Lives and Epistemic Limitations: A Critique of Regan's Lifeboat from an Unprivileged Position." *Ethics and the Environment* 20 (1): 1–21.

Abbate, C.E. 2020. "Animal Rights and the Duty to Harm: When to Be a Harm Causing Deontologist." *Journal for Ethics and Moral Philosophy* 3:5–26.

Apicius, Marcus Gavius. 1977. *Apicius: Cookery and Dining in Imperial Rome.* Translated by Joesph Vehling. Dover Publishing.

Archer, Michael. 2011. "Slaughter of the Singing Sentients: Measuring the Morality of Eating Red Meat." *Australian Zoologist* 35 (4): 979–82.

ASPCA. 2023. *The 'USDA Organic' Label and Farm Animal Welfare.* ASPCA. www. aspca.org/shopwithyourheart/advocate-resources/usda-organic-label-and-farm-animal-welfare#:~:text=In%20reality%2C%20the%20current%20standards,virtually%20indistinguishable%20from%20factory%20farming

Corse, Taylor. 2010. "Dryden's 'Vegetarian' Philosopher: Pythagoras." *Eighteenth-Century Life* 34 (1): 1–28.

Crowley, Maureen. 2016. "History of Vegetarianism." *The Pretty Nostalgic Compendium* 1:1–7.

Cuneo, Terence. 2015. "Conscientious Omnivorism." In *Philosophy Comes to Dinner*, edited by Andrew Chignell, Terence Cuneo, and Matthew Halteman. New York: Routledge.

Davis, Janet. 2024. *The History of Animal Protection in the United States.* Organization of American Historians. www.oah.org/tah/november-2/the-history-of-animal-protection-in-the-united-states/.

Davis, Steven. 2003. "The Least Harm Principle May Require That Humans Consumer a Diet Containing Large Herbivores, Not a Vegan Diet." *Journal of Agricultural and Environmental Ethics* 16 (4): 387–94.

DeGrazia, David. 1991. "The Moral Status of Animals and Their Use in Research: A Philosophical Review." *Kennedy Institute of Ethics Journal* 1 (1): 48–70.

Donaldson, Sue, and Will Kymlicka. 2013. *Zoopolis: A Political Theory of Animal Rights.* Oxford: Oxford University Press.

Elischer, Melissa. 2019. *The Five Freedoms: A History Lesson in Animal Care and Welfare.* Michigan State University Extension. www.canr.msu.edu/news/an_animal_welfare_history_lesson_on_the_five_freedoms

Erasmus, Marisa. 2020. *Animal Welfare and Animal Rights: Ethics, Science and Explanations.* Purdue University Extensions. www.extension.purdue.edu/extmedia/AS/AS-662-W.pdf

Finn, Hugh, and Nahiid Stephens. 2017. "The Invisible Harm: Land Clearing Is an Issue of Animal Welfare." *Wildlife Research* 44 (5): 377–91.

Fischer, Bob, and Andy Lamey. 2018. "Field Deaths in Plant Agriculture." *Journal of Agricultural and Environmental Ethics* 31:409–28.

Francione, Gary. 1995. *Animals Property & The Law (Ethics and Action).* Philadelphia, PA: Temple University Press.

Franco, Nuno Henrique. 2013. "Animal Experiments in Biomedical Research: A Historical Perspective." *Animals* 3 (1): 238–73.

Fraser, D, and MacRae. 2011. "Four Types of Activities That Affect Animals: Implications for Animal Welfare Science and Animal Ethics Philosophy." *Animal Welfare* 20 (4): 581–90.

Freeberg, Ernest. 2020. *A Traitor to His Species: Henry Bergh and the Birth of the Animal Rights Movement*. New York: Basic Books.

Frey, Ulrich J., and Frauke Pirscher. 2018. "Willingness to Pay and Moral Stance: The Case of Farm Animal Welfare in Germany." *PLOS ONE* 13 (8): 1–20.

Greger, Michael. 2015. *How Not to Die: Discover the Foods Scientifically Proven to Prevent and Reverse Disease*. New York: Flatiron Books.

Gruen, Lori, Robert Jones, Ben Bramble, and Bob Fischer. 2016. "Veganism and Aspiration." In *The Moral Complexities of Eating Meat*. Oxford: Oxford University Press.

Hajar, Rachel. 2011. "Animal Testing and Medicine." *Heart Views* 12 (1): 42.

Hargreaves, Shila, Antonio Raposo, Ariana Saraiva, and Renata Zandonadi. 2021. "Vegetarian Diet: An Overview through the Perspective of Quality of Life Domains." *International Journal of Environmental Research and Public Health* 18 (8): 4067–92.

Harrison, Ruth. 2013. *Animal Machines: The New Factory Farming Industry*. Wallingford, Oxfordshire: CABI.

Ingram, Darcy. 2020. "The Strange Case of Henry Bergh's 'Declaration of the Rights of Animals.'" *Society and Animals* 30 (4): 1–13.

Jamieson, Dale. 1990. "Rights, Justice, and Duties to Provide Assistance: A Critique of Regan's Theory of Rights." *Ethics* 100 (1): 349–62.

Lamey, Andy. 2007. "Duty and the Beast." *Journal of Social Philosophy* 38 (2): 331–48.

Mccarthy, Justin, and Scott Dekoster. 2020. *Nearly One in Four in U.S. Have Cut Back on Eating Meat*. Gallup. https://news.gallup.com/poll/282779/nearly-one-four-cut-back-eating-meat.aspx#:~:text=16%2D30%20Gallup%20telephone%20poll,report%20%22never%22%20eating%20meat

Milburn, Josh, and Christopher Bobier. 2022. "New Omnivorism: A Novel Approach to Food and Animal Ethics." *Food Ethics* 7 (5): 1–17.

National Agricultural Library. 2019. *Animal Welfare Act Timeline*. U.S. Department of Agriculture. www.nal.usda.gov/collections/exhibits/awahistory/list

Nocella, Giuseppe, Lionel Hubbard, and Riccardo Scarpa. 2009. "Farm Animal Welfare, Consumer Willingness to Pay, and Trust: Results of a Cross-National Survey" *Applied Economic Perspectives and Policy* 32 (2): 275–97.

Nolen, Scott. 2016. "50 Years Later, Animal Welfare Act Is a Work in Progress." *American Veterinary Medical Association*. www.avma.org/javma-news/2016-10-01/50-years-later-animal-welfare-act-work-progress

Noll, Samantha, and Brittany Davis. 2020. "The Invasive Species Diet: The Ethics of Eating Lionfish as a Wildlife Management Strategy." *Ethics, Policy, and Environment* 23 (3): 320–35.

Norwood, Bailey, and Jayson Lusk. 2007. "The Dual Nature of Choice: When Consumers Prefer Less to More." Southern Association of Agricultural Economics. https://ageconsearch.umn.edu/record/34850/?ln=en&v=pdf.

Nussbaum, Martha. 2007. *Frontiers of Justice: Disability, Nationality, Species Membership (The Tanner Lectures on Human Values)*. Cambridge: Belknap Press: An Imprint of Harvard University Press.

Palmer, Clare. 2010. *Animal Ethics in Context*. New York: Columbia University Press.

Pollan, Michael. 2006. *The Omnivore's Dilemma: A Natural History of Four Meals*. New York: Penguin.

Pollan, Michael. 2024. *Animal Welfare: Frequently Asked Questions*. Michaelpollan. Com. 2024. https://michaelpollan.com/resources/animal-welfare/.

Rachels, James. 2016. "The Basic Argument for Vegetarianism." In *The Animal Ethics Reader*. New York: Routledge.

Regan, Tom. 1995. "Obligations to Animals Are Based on Rights." *Journal of Agricultural & Environmental Ethics* 8:171–80.

Regan, Tom. 2004. *The Case for Animal Rights*. Berkeley, CA: University of California Press.

Rodale Institute. 2024. *Regenerative Organic Certified*. Rodale Institute. https://roda leinstitute.org/regenerative-organic-certification/.

Rollin, Bernard. 1995. *Farm Animal Welfare: Social, Bioethical, and Research Issues*. Ames, IA: Iowa State Press.

Rollin, Bernard. 2012. "The Moral Status of Invasive Animal Research." In *Animal Research Ethics: Evolving Views and Practices*, edited by Susan Gilbert, Gregory E. Kaebnick, and Thomas Murray. Garrison, NY: The Hasings Center.

Rollin, Bernard. 2016. *A New Basis for Animal Ethics: Telos and Common Sense*. Columbia, MO: University of Missouri.

Rowlands, Mark. 2009. *Animal Rights: Moral Theory and Practice*. New York: Springer.

Salant, Lana Joe. 2023. "About the Ethical Omnivore Movement." *Ethical Omnivore Movement*. www.ethicalomnivore.org/about-eom/.

Sandler, Ronald. 2014. *Food Ethics: The Basics*. New York: Routledge.

Schiffman, Richard. 2023. *Beyond Factory Farms: A New Look at the Rights of Animals*. YaleEnvironment360. https://e360.yale.edu/features/peter-singer-interview.

Singer, Peter. 2015. *Animal Liberation: The Definitive Classic of the Animal Movement*. Open Road Media.

Singer, Peter, and Jim Mason. 2007. *The Ethics of What We Eat: Why Our Food Choices Matter*. Potter/Ten Speed/Harmony/Rodale.

Unknown. n.d. *Five Points from Valentine's Manual (1855)*. cuny.edu. Accessed June 17, 2024. https://shec.ashp.cuny.edu/items/show/1713.

USDA Agricultural Marketing Service. 2013. *Organic Livestock Requirements*. U.S. Department of Agriculture. www.ams.usda.gov/sites/default/files/media/Orga nic%20Livestock%20Requirements.pdf.

Vehling, Joesph. 1977. "Introduction." In *Apicius: Cookery and Dining in Imperial Rome*, by Marcus Gavius Apicius, translated by Joesph Vehling, xi–xvii. Dover Publishing.

Verbeke, Wim, Federico Perez-Cueto, Marcia de Barcellos, Athanasios Krystallis, and Klaus Grunert. 2009. "European Citizen and Consumer Attitudes and Preferences Regarding Beef and Pork." *Meat Science* 84 (2): 284–92.

Verbeke, Wim, and Jacques Viaene. 2000. "Ethical Challenges for Livestock Production:Meeting Consumer Concerns about Meat Safety and Animal Welfare." *Journal of Agricultural and Environmental Ethics* 12 (2): 141–51.

Webster, John. 2016. "Animal Welfare: Freedoms, Dominions and 'A Life Worth Living.'" *Animals (Basel)* 6 (6): 35.

Wise, Steven. 2000. *Rattling The Cage: Toward Legal Rights For Animals*. New York: Perseus Publishing.

Zwart, Hub. 2000. "A Short History of Food Ethics." *Journal of Agricultural and Environmental Ethics* 12 (2): 113–26.

# 8

# FROM WILD LANDS TO TABLE

## Hunting, Heritage, and the Environment

Hunting and angling are two popular activities, especially in my home state. I have wonderful memories fishing with my grandfather (affectionately called Pop-pop) during the first day of rainbow trout. This was the best day when I was a girl, even more so than a holiday. We'd look over our tackle the day before and head out early in the morning to the river, down by the covered bridge one of my ancestors designed. It was so very picturesque, as grand old willow trees stretched over the water, creating long strips of shadow. He taught me to watch the flow of the current to better identify pockets where fish would congregate, like the elderly denizens of our family church on Sundays. By the end of the day, we'd have a small basket of fish that we caught together. Pop-pop had a strict rule that if you caught a fish, then it was your responsibility to clean it. We would go home with our catch, and he'd set up the smoker, using apple or cherrywood from his orchard to process them. We'd then spend the next day filling the yard with the most wonderful scents, a promise of what was to come. One of my favorite memories was running around the yard with a whole smoked trout in my hands, happy that I helped catch, clean, and prepare it.

Hunting, fishing, and foraging are important activities that bolster food security for my family and for many others. The winters are long, and grocery stores are expensive. There's not much to forage, as the watercress, berries, and dandelions wither (all of which we ate, as a family). It's easy to find yourself with an empty belly and only a bucket of snow to show for your troubles. My mother knew these harsh realities well, as she spent her childhood in a drafty shack, with only a single stove for warmth and no running water or plumbing. When I was a child, she was determined to make sure we were well-fed and made it her mission to go out every season and take a deer to help feed her

DOI: 10.4324/9781003215189-8

children. She once came home in tears, as hunting your own food can be difficult emotionally.

My mother's pain underscored the difference between hunting for sport and for necessity. She'd sometimes process the deer in the garage, and we'd help with butchering. Everything was used. I particularly loved the bologna sandwiches after school. We'd also go out as a family picking raspberries, blackberries, mulberries, and, well, all the berries when they were ripe. Hunting, angling, and foraging are common subsistence practices for families in Pennsylvania. Woe to the family who doesn't fill their stores before the winter sets in. While today we have grocery stores, this lesson was passed down from generation to generation. As Pennsylvanians weather the economic storms of modernity, the old wisdom serves us well.

These activities are also important for environmental conservation and for reconnecting people to the land. In our modern world, wilderness is being lost, as land is developed and changed for human use. I felt this loss viscerally as a child, when entire wooded areas (and productive fields) where my brothers and I would play were turned into shopping malls and parking lots. I remember seeing the bulldozers trucked in and trees fell one by one. Entire environments were removed in the name of progress. There would be no more berries to pick, or honeysuckle flowers to lick the sweetness from. We are becoming a people overly reliant on technology and motorized vehicles and equipment. We go from air-conditioned house to air-conditioned office and back again. As we lose touch with the environment around us, natural areas are increasingly in jeopardy. Hunting, angling, and foraging help us to connect to the world around us. As we learn its rhythms and glean secrets about other species, we also learn about ourselves. Building-off the previous chapters, this chapter goes on to provide an overview of the ethical dimensions of hunting and fishing, trying to capture the reasons why ethical omnivores embrace these practices.

Ethical omnivores largely support hunting and fishing within certain parameters, as we will see. For example, the Boone and Crockett Club (2024a) endorses a strict hunter ethic, stressing fair chase, and sustainable use. The analysis below utilizes the environmental ethicist Gary Varner's (2002) distinction between three types of hunting: Therapeutic, subsistence, and sport hunting. Each are important for understanding ethical omnivores' position on hunting and fishing, as they involve distinct focal practices and are justified by different ethical arguments. We will find that, unsurprisingly, ethical omnivores support therapeutic and subsistence hunting for both animal welfare and environmental reasons. As they are critical of industrial agriculture, both subsistence and therapeutic hunting provides an alternative way to obtain meat products. The latter can be justified on both environmental and animal welfare grounds, if we target mandatory management species. We end with a discussion of care ethics, as ethical omnivores gain important knowledge about food systems by interacting with nature and their insights bolster personal ethical growth. For these reasons, and due to the North American hunting model, they also support sport hunting, as well.

## From Wild Lands to Table

As we talked about in previous chapters, the ethical omnivore diet is largely made up of ethically sourced high-quality meats, fruits, vegetables, seeds, and nuts. Being mindful of how your food is produced is vital for these eaters. It's important to buy local products sourced from organic producers and farms and ranches that embrace high animal welfare standards. Industrial food production involves harming others, including ecosystems and humans and nonhumans, alike (Gruen and Jones, 2016, 157). Hunting, fishing, and foraging are strategies that ethical omnivores use to reduce some of these harms.

According to some estimates, 7.3 billion animals are incidentally killed annually on harvested cropland, which is more than the number of pigs or cattle slaughtered (120 million and 40 million, respectively) in the United States every year, though closer to the number of broiler chickens killed (roughly 9 billion) (Archer 2011; Davis 2003; Fisher and Lamey 2018). Other scholars put forth lower, yet still startling statistics. The animal scientist Steven Davis (2003) estimated that in the United States, 1.8 billion wild animals are killed yearly during the production of plant-based foods. Demetriou and Fischer (2018) go even farther, arguing that vegans could save animal lives, if they converted part of their diet to meat harvested from animals, they themselves hunted and killed. They are also worried about harms to animal dignity, as field animals lose house and home to the agriculture process, living in abject terror of the combine harvester.

While the number of animals killed is contested, as it's difficult to get an accurate count, the range of figures helps us to better conceptualize the sheer scale of animal suffering caused by industrial vegetable production. Land clearing, field traps, pesticides, and mechanical harvesting all harm a wide range of animals, in myriad ways. As Anthony and Varner (2020) argue, "hunters recognize that by eating commercially available, plant-based foods they kill animals *indirectly*, however, and that by substituting some hunted animals, they can lower the total number of animal deaths for which they are responsible, either directly or indirectly" (215). This argument holds for ethical omnivores, as well. Hunted and foraged foodstuffs sidestep many of the harms associated with agriculture, empowering eaters to take responsibility and control over their impacts. Not only will cropland deaths be reduced, but animal welfare could be increased, as wild animals live outside human control. In addition, these activities could reduce the ecological impacts of food procurement, especially if we focus on harvesting animals that outstrip ecological carrying capacity or harm environmental health and stability, such as invasive species.

While these positions are interesting, there is a lot philosophically to unpack here. Supporters of hunting make distinct arguments that stress specific aspects of these practices. First, there is the argument concerning animal welfare and death, which includes the assumption that fewer animals are harmed when we obtain wild foodstuffs, and/or that culling via hunting is less harmful than culling in industrial agriculture (Anthony and Varner 2020). These arguments often connect with a wider "care ethic" that hunters use to defend their practices. Then, there is the ecological argument, or the idea that hunting better aligns with an environmental ethic. If we target species that outstrip ecological carrying capacity, then these practices become important wildlife management strategies. Finally, there are justifications for specific types of hunting and fishing. Not all types are the same, as we do these activities for different reasons. Are we talking about therapeutic, subsistence, or sport hunting, for example? Is one ethically better than another? Contemporary hunters typically embrace a strong hunting ethic, which includes commitments to fair chase and reducing suffering (BHA 2024). Distinctions between moral and immoral hunting practices stress the need to demarcate different types of hunting. The next section discusses these different types of hunting, before going on to explore ethical omnivore's justifications for the position that many are ethically acceptable.

## Different Types of Hunting

Due to the different purposes hunting is supposed to serve, we can separate this activity into three distinct categories (Varner 2002). The first type is called "therapeutic hunting," which is motivated by the desire to secure overall welfare of the target species or the integrity of its ecosystem. An excellent example of this type of hunting is the removal of lionfish from Florida's waters, as they have no natural predators and are decimating local reef fish populations (Noll and Davis 2020). The second type is called "subsistence hunting," which primarily centers on securing food for human beings. Later, we will talk about the contested definitions of this term and what this conflict means for ethical omnivores, as procuring food is important for the diet. Finally, we have "sport hunting," which is aimed at maintaining cultural or religious traditions, reenacting historical practices, or securing trophies. Gary Varner (2002) intentionally collapses hunting for ritual and hunting for sport, as both types are driven by human needs that are less fundamentally important than securing food and maintaining ecosystem services. These are abstract archetypes, but each capture key motivations for the removal of animals from an ecosystem. However, it should be noted that they do overlap, sometimes necessarily so. For instance, many states have laws against wanton waste, making it illegal to hunt without taking meat and/or hides from the animal. Also, all regulated hunting is therapeutic to some extent even when the target species is below its objective population, as hunters are typically allowed to take surplus animals. The money from selling tags and licenses goes into the system responsible for bringing the population of that species up to the objective number. Additionally, one can simultaneously hunt for food and for sport, for example, as maintaining cultural traditions is not in conflict with obtaining foodstuffs. This overview helps us to better understand ethical omnivore's defense of hunting as an activity, as well as criticisms. For example, a common justification for hunting is that it's necessary to prevent overpopulation and environmental degradation. This is clearly a defense of therapeutic hunting, rather than sport or subsistence activities.

### Is All Hunting Acceptable?

As we saw from ethical omnivores' position on hunting, these eaters largely embrace therapeutic and subsistence justifications. If industrial agriculture causes environmental harm, then one way to limit this harm is to obtain food outside of these contexts. This is a production-specific environmental argument, as it largely hinges on criticisms of how food is produced. The main strategy for addressing these concerns is to opt into more environmentally friendly methods of farming. However, cropland deaths still happen in most large-scale operations. Hence, why ethical omnivores embrace the view that food stores should be supplemented through hunting and fishing. The less we rely on agriculture, the fewer deaths we will have in the fields. There are two assumptions here: First, that deaths caused by hunting will be fewer than those that occur in the field. The sheer number of animals killed in industrial production seems to support this position. One elk, for example, produces around 218–270 pounds of meat (Field et al. 2003) and the average American family consumes between 364 and 728 pounds of meat a year (Kuck and Schnitkey 2021). If you eat a relatively meat light diet, then two elk would meet a family's needs for 12 months. From this view, even supplementing your diet with hunting would help to limit your personal ecological and animal welfare impact, as fewer wild and domesticated animals would be killed. For ethical omnivores, this holds even if you embrace a vegetarian diet, due to cropland deaths.

However, not all hunting is the same. If ethical omnivores are serious about reducing environmental impacts, then one could argue that therapeutic hunting should be prioritized over sports hunting. The ethicist Gary Varner (2002) has gone so far as to argue that both animal rights activists and eaters who embrace an environmental ethic agree that therapeutic hunting is a moral necessity. But, what types of hunting fall under this category, beyond those loosely connected to ecosystem functioning? For Varner, therapeutic hunting mandates that we should target animals that fall into two specific categories. First, we should focus on hunting obligatory management species, or those species that regularly "overshoot the carrying capacity of its range, to the detriment of future generations and other species" (Varner 2002, 98). Examples include ungulates, or hooved animals, such as mule and white-tailed deer, bison, and elk. Second, we are also sometimes justified in targeting permissive management species, hence the term. Permissive management species are those that typically do not exhibit the tendency to overshoot carrying capacity, but still could suffer from overpopulation. These include animals such as cotton-tailed rabbits, squirrels, and quail, etc. It's not that this latter group doesn't produce more offspring than the ecosystem can support through the winter. Rather, they do not degrade habitats in ways that threaten future generations. Thus, it's "merely permissible" to hunt them, rather than obligatory or environmentally necessary. Therapeutic hunting largely focuses on maintaining appropriate populations of those animals where management is obligatory, yet there are some instances where it is permissible, on ecological or animal welfare grounds, to hunt others.

It should be noted here that environmentalists hold varying views on hunting. Several environmental groups have clearly stated their position on types of hunting. For instance, Sierra Club publicly stated that they oppose "any bill that will shift the proof from no hunting in state parks unless 'biologically necessary,' to hunting is allowed unless proven harmful to the areas resources" (Varner 2002, 99). The position here is that sport hunting shouldn't be allowed in state parks, unless it's required for biological reasons. This statement isn't clearly written, but it means that we should only allow hunting for ecological or animal welfare reasons. Washington State, for example, recently allowed the culling of elk infected by elk-hoof disease (TAHD), as it's highly contagious, very painful, and incurable. The Audubon Society also opposes sport hunting in state parks, unless it's for sound biological management purposes.

Sierra Club's and Audubon's position on hunting show that environmentalists tend to support "biologically necessary" culling, which is therapeutic hunting. Though, it should be noted here that there is some disagreement concerning how culling should be done. For instance, culling done by governmental agencies typically does not involve fair chase or the harvesting of meat, which is a violation of hunting ethics. There are also conflicts surrounding what constitutes "overpopulation," as farmers and biologists are often in disagreement here. With this being said, therapeutic hunting, in general, is largely considered to be ethical, when done properly. Groups are divided on sport hunting outside of protected areas, however. For example, as the name suggests, Backcountry Hunters and Anglers (BHA) support ecological conservation, as well as hunting on public and private lands. In fact, many environmentalists are avid hunters and anglers. The intersection between these two groups is not surprising, as the ability to hunt depends on protecting and maintaining habitat. As BHA states, "many treasured fish and wildlife species – such as cutthroat trout, grizzly bear and bighorn sheep – thrive in wilderness. Others, like elk and mule deer, benefit from wilderness" (BHA 2024). The mandate to preserve large tracts of wilderness has been a part of the hunting ethos since the time of Theodore Roosevelt, but today it takes on greater urgency, as land faces increasing development pressures to meet human needs. We also live in a technological bubble that isolates us from larger ecological realities. For BHA then, the culture of sport hunting places us back into the environment, galvanizing sportsmen, and women to advocate for wild country, and the wildlife that depends on it. They argue that the experience of hunting can unite individuals from diverse political backgrounds to support conservation efforts. Thus, for BHA and likeminded groups, sports hunting plays an important role in conservation efforts. After all, "without wild places for wild animals, there will be no place for sportsmen to hunt and fish" (BHA 2024). However, other environmentalists are not convinced that we should embrace sport hunting. Indeed, many would be happy if predator populations were restored, so that even therapeutic hunting was less necessary (Varner 2002).

The discussion surrounding sport and therapeutic hunting is an important one, especially for those eaters who are guided by ethics. The latter activity is largely supported by ethicists of all stripes, be those who prioritize animal welfare or those who emphasize ecological functioning. For example, Gary Varner (2002) famously argued that two important animal rights theorists, Peter Singer and Tom Regan, would support therapeutic hunting. This is surprising, as it seems like culling animals would violate their rights, even if this were done for ecological purposes. After all, even Regan's early writings railed against the idea that contextual factors should matter when discussing animal rights. For this thinker, "the fundamental wrong is the system that allows us to view animals as *our resources,* here for *us-to* be eaten, or surgically manipulated, or exploited for sport or money" (Regan 1983, 179). However, Varner argues that a more nuanced position emerges when we apply their specific theories to therapeutic hunting. For example, while Peter Singer is important for the animal rights movement, he is not a rights-based theorist like Regan. Singer is a utilitarian, meaning that he thinks that the right action is that which brings about the most pleasure and least pain. When applied to cases where species overpopulate, a utilitarian could justify culling animals. The argument could go as follows:

(1) We have a moral obligation to minimize pain.
(2) In the case of obligatory management species, more pain would be caused by letting nature takes its course than by conducting carefully regulated hunts.

(3)     Therefore, we are morally obligated to conduct carefully regulated therapeutic hunts of obligatory management species rather than let nature takes it course.

*(102)*

For Varner, the first premise is simply restating the hedonistic utilitarian principle, so it is not controversial. The point of contention is premise 2, but it isn't an ethical conflict. Rather, it's merely an empirical claim, meaning that any conflict between Singer and therapeutic hunters would concern current conditions, rather than moral principles.

Indeed, when you apply Singer's principles to hunting, his work could even support the harvesting of permissive management species. At first blush, it doesn't seem like this is the case though. For example, Singer (2011) argues in *Practical Ethics* that even his replaceability argument might not justify killing wild animals. According to him,

> The replaceability argument is severely limited in its application. It cannot justify factory farming, where animals do not have pleasant lives. Nor does it normally justify the killing of wild animals. A duck shot by a hunter… has probably had a pleasant life, but the shooting of a duck does not lead to its replacement by another.

*(1993, 133–134)*

This argument could limit the types of species that we can hunt. For example, those whose numbers are limited would not be on the menu. However, as Varner points out, hunting obligatory management species could be justified using this principle, as the animal would be replaced, and suffering would be reduced, by bringing populations into balance with ecological carrying capacity. It could even be used to justify permissible management species, when they produce more young than the environment can support. Thus, from a utilitarian perspective, both types of therapeutic hunting could be permissible. Another critique of Singer's argument is that it's too simplistic, not considering important contextual considerations in its application. While hunting doesn't produce another duck, per say, it does support a system of regulated therapeutic hunting which increases overall wildlife population numbers. Under the North American Model, the federal duck stamp required to shoot a duck funds duck habitat conservation. Although it may not be a 1:1 replacement, one could argue that virtually all game species populations are better-off today than they would be without a robust system to recover and conserve them. This argument can also be used to push back against Singer's criticism of sport hunting. He argues that sport hunting would cause more pain than can be justified by the pleasure of the hunter. However, when hunting is done in conjunction with a conservation-based regulatory structure, hunting practiced within this context can be considered therapeutic, as it supports wider conservation efforts.

As an important side note, conservation-based hunting models could also place species with limited numbers back on the menu, as well, further reducing the application of the replaceability argument. Limited regulated harvests of extirpated species, and those with small numbers, could be supported if money is used to bolster their populations going forward. For example, the National Wild Turkey Federation funded the reintroduction of turkeys into every state, except Alaska, using proceeds from hunters. This is one example of how game species have been restored from the brink of extinction, using the North American Model. As the conservation and hunting enthusiast Dan Curtis has stated in conversations, proceeds from hunting play a major role in bolstering populations of species, such as elk, mule deer, mountain goats, and wild sheep, to name a few. Western states auction off "governor's tags" for species with limited surplus populations that go for hundreds of thousands of dollars which is used to recover the species (Boone and Crockett 2024b).

But what about rights-based approaches? Tom Regan (1983) was highly critical of human activities that impact animals, from agriculture to hunting. From his perspective, all animals who are "subjects of a life," have inherent value. This category includes mammals, at minimum, or those beings sufficiently sophisticated to feel pleasure and pain, have a sense of self, etc. He compares his approach to utilitarian ones, where we are simply vessels for holding experiences, so the ethical question becomes how much happiness we can experience. In this way, we are, ourselves, instrumentally valued. In contrast, Regan and other rights-based theorists argue that we have value in ourselves, no matter our capacity for being happy. My grumpy aunt who is predisposed to hate everything and everyone is just as valuable as my cousin who finds joy in the smallest things, for example. I might want my aunt to find happiness, but her lack of capacity doesn't mean she's worth less. For Regan, maximizing aggregate happiness isn't the point of acting ethically. Any being that has the above basic capacities should be inherently valued.

But what does this have to do with hunting? If this is the case and the ducks, deer, elk, and moose are all valuable in and of themselves, then does this mean that they're off the menu? Regan (1983) certainly thought so, but Varner (2002) does not agree. Any ethical theory worth its salt will provide us with tools to address conflicts of interest. If both my brother and I have a claim to the car, a good ethical theory will help us determine who has the stronger claim. For example, if he needs to drive my mother to the hospital and I just want to get some popcorn, my brother's need will often be prioritized over mine. For hedonistic utilitarians, the action that brings about the most happiness would be the right one.

Regan provides two principles to help us determine the appropriate attitude towards individuals. First, is the worse-off principle, which mandates that when we must choose between violating the rights of individuals, we should not "override the rights of that worse-of individual or individuals" (Regan 2004, 308). Second, Regan also put forth the miniride principle. When we must "choose between violating the rights of the many and the rights of the few, and each of the individuals will suffer a comparable harm via those rights violations, then we ought to choose to override the rights of the few" (Regan 2004, 308). Regan does recognize that these principles will often lead to the same conclusions as utilitarianism, but the reasoning behind each is fundamentally different. Nevertheless, both will support similar conclusions concerning hunting, as we will see.

Let's apply the worse-off principle first. For Regan, death is the ultimate harm, as it ends our ability to form and satisfy desires. However, the death of a human is a worse harm than the death of a non-human animal, as we have a larger range of desires. Thus, subsistence hunting would be justified, if it were done to save the life of a human. However, in modern societies, Regan, and ethical vegetarians alike, would argue that we can thrive on plant-based diets. Thus, "we are not in a situation '[w]hen it is necessary to choose between violating the rights' of one group of individuals or those of another" (Anthony and Varner 2020, 214). We'll talk more about subsistence hunting below, as this analysis applies to only a narrowly defined subset of subsistence practices. Unlike the worse off principle, the miniride principle provides direction concerning therapeutic hunting. This rule demands that we violate the rights of a few, rather than the rights of the many. For Varner (2002), Regan is wrong that this principle would call for the abolition of all forms of hunting. If having moral rights means that certain things cannot be done to an individual for the betterment of the group, "then the basic rationale for therapeutic hunting- killing some in order that others may live- appears to be lost" (Varner 2002, 106). He went so far as to argue that wildlife managers should embrace the goal of defending "wild animals in the possession of their rights, providing them with the opportunity to live their own life, by their own lights, as best they can, spared that human predation that goes by the name of 'sport'" (Regan 1983, 357). However, Regan seems to collapse all forms of hunting into sport hunting and doesn't apply the miniride principle to this specific case.

For Varner (2002), therapeutic hunting is not only permissible, but ethically mandatory from an animal rights perspective. Responsible agents know the harms associated with nature taking its course. Allowing mandatory management species to proliferate and cause long-standing ecological harm would violate the rights of more animals than the culled few. For example, let's look at lionfish again. In areas where they have no predators, they eat approximately 460,000 prey fish per acre per year, including ecologically important species, like snapper and grouper. In some areas, they've reduced native fish populations by 90% (NCCOS 2024). The ecological impact of allowing their numbers to go unchecked is staggering, as are the numbers of beings whose rights are being violated. Unlike other species, we have the capacity to understand the gravity of the situation and change our behavior accordingly. Shouldn't we do so, recognizing an obligation to avoid overpopulation and the harms this would cause? For environmental ethicists like Gary Varner and Dale Jamieson, we should recognize this obligation, and the miniride principle can be used to support ecologically important hunting. Thus, ethical omnivore's commitment to hunting can be ethically justified, especially if we focus on eating invasive and mandatory management species.

Hunting and eating species prone to overpopulation is also supported by various ecological ethics. It's important to recognize ethical recommendations coming out of animal rights literature, but the ethical omnivore diet is firmly situated in ecological ethics. In fact, these ethical frameworks provide some of the strongest justifications for therapeutic hunting. For example, species management is often considered to be part of larger wildlife conservation plans (Noll and Davis 2020).

Many wildlife management and conservation projects are driven by underlying values, such as protecting ecosystem health, ensuring the continuation of species, and maintaining the wellbeing of individual animals (Gamborg et al. 2012). Utilitarianism and animal rights frameworks provide insights when making wildlife management decisions. However, for most wildlife conservation projects, "the wellbeing of individual animals matters less where species, ecosystems, or wild nature is emphasized –indeed, painful predation may be understood as promoting ecosystem health, or as applying the right kind of selective pressure on a species, as a whole" (Gamborg et al. 2012, 2). Environmental conservation historically embraced the twin goals of ensuring the continued use of nature and the preservation of natural areas, both of which move us beyond purely individual focused ethics (Minteer and Corley 2007; Rolston 2015). While these approaches provide different management recommendations, they stress the need to ensure the viability of ecosystems and species that have been or could be impacted by human activities and ecological changes (Sandler 2012, 47). Eating in line with ecological ethics demands that we think about the larger ecological impact of our food choices. While this brings the environmental impacts of agriculture into our purview, other factors should influence our plate, as well. For ethical omnivores, eating wild caught foodstuffs is another strategy important for eating in line with wider ecological realities, as one species among many.

The mandate to eat invasive and mandatory management species has its own strengths and weaknesses. Concerning the benefits, programs aimed at increasing human consumption to control species can help to increase public awareness of invasive species and environmental issues, improve their early detection and removal, and boost the local economy (Noll and Davis 2020; Nunez et al., 2012). However, from a policy perspective, there are several concerns that should be considered before adopting dietary focused wildlife management strategies. First, supporting the consumption of wild animals could lead to the creation of markets that create negative pressure on wild populations, potentially reducing their numbers below ecologically stable levels. As Nunez et al. (2012) argue:

> The ultimate goal in most eating invader campaigns is to eat the target species out of existence, just as humans have done for many native species. However, once a species becomes a genuine economic resource, it could be even harder to encourage complete removal of the monetarily valuable species.
>
> *(337)*

While this analysis largely focuses on invasive species, it would hold for any targeted wild species. These are important considerations, as there are many historical examples of hunting running contrary to wildlife management goals, especially when there are economic benefits (see Lambertucci and Speziale 2011; Fujimori 2003). Ethical omnivores should be aware of these practical concerns when hunting or purchasing wild-caught foodstuffs. These problems also bring us to another type of hunting: Subsistence hunting. Therapeutic hunting becomes a subsistence activity when we intentionally hunt to obtain foodstuffs for ourselves, families, and others.

## When Hunting Informs Culture

Ethical omnivores embrace ecological ethics, as their diet is built on the assumption that wild caught and harvested foodstuffs tend to be more environmentally friendly than those sourced from farms. As this is a diet, they also support subsistence hunting practices, as well as some sport hunting activities. Narrow definitions of subsistence hunting frame the activity as one where hunting is necessary for human survival. We harvest animals when eaters have few other options to obtain the calories necessary for life. For example, this activity has been defined as "hunt[ing] to provide nutrition that cannot be grown" (Woods et al. 2009, 500). Raymond Anthony and Gary Varner (2020) argue that many peoples practice subsistence hunting. Societies, such as "aboriginal Inuit peoples (the generic name for culturally related human groups that inhabit the Arctic Circle regions of Alaska, Greenland, and Canada), could not have survived on plant-based foods alone" (211). For these and similar groups, hunting is necessary to obtain adequate nutrition, and most people agree "that humans are justified in killing animals when it is *necessary* for human survival" (2012). When looked at from this position, there are very few contexts where humans engage in subsistence hunting. Many people living in industrial societies have access to sources of calories that do not involve hunting other species. Thus, we can argue that ethical omnivores living outside these specific communities are not subsistence hunters, when they have access to agriculturally produced foodstuffs.

We appear to be at an impasse, then. If we accept this definition, ethical omnivores living in modern industrial societies can engage in therapeutic and sports hunting, but not in subsistence hunting. This impasse is the result of a narrow understanding of what it means to hunt for food. According to Anthony and Varner (2020), there are two clearly demarcated positions concerning subsistence hunting. In addition to stressing human survival, narrow definitions also exclude the use of modern technology, which leads to the further othering of hunting groups. When discussing the seal hunting controversy in the Canadian Arctic in 1990, the geographer George Wenzel (1991) initially stated that subsistence hunting refers to when "human life is sustained at the barest possible margin," and is "a self-contained system," where humans do not take inputs from or send outputs out to larger socio-economic systems. In this context, as soon as individuals use imported tools and/or technologies, such as guns, or engage in the export of resources, they are no longer practicing subsistence hunting (Wenzel 1991, 57–58).

It follows that ethical omnivores who use rifles obtained through wider socio-economic channels may be engaged in therapeutic or sports hunting, but they are not subsistence hunters. This holds under the narrow definition even if the hunters are a part of a community where hunting is culturally significant, or their goal is to obtain foodstuffs for their families. This narrow definition is so restrictive that most hunting would fall outside the purview of subsistence. In fact, Tribal Nations hunting and fishing rights are hotly contested legal issues, in no small part due to the way subsistence activities have been framed by modern European societies. Definitions become ideologically harmful when they can be used to challenge the sovereignty of nations and the cultural significance of key practices, such as hunting and fishing. However, subsistence is difficult to conceptualize, as there are different definitions at play.

Wenzel and other scholars push back against the narrow definition of subsistence, arguing that hunting and fishing also play an essential role in maintaining communities, even after they are intertwined with modern North American and European economies. For many cultures, subsistence is not simply a matter of obtaining nutrition when we can't grow food, nor does it refer to only fishing, hunting, and gathering activities. As Anthony and Varner (2020) argue, even when "hunting is no longer necessary for physical survival, subsistence hunting is still necessary for the continuation of time honored practices (despite the use of some modern devices) and to the survival of aboriginal, subsistence *cultures*" (215).

Contemporary anthropologists also increasingly push back against narrow definitions, as historical interpretations were built on colonial assumptions, such as the demarcation between "natural" peoples fully dependent on nature and more culturally sophisticated farmers, who exercise control over nature (Moss 2010). In particular, scholars today emphasize the need to rethink concepts like subsistence in ways that are not static, minimalist, restrictive, and culturally insensitive to diverse groups. For instance, the anthropologists Polly Wheeler and Tom Thornton (2005) push back against these problematic definitions, arguing that societies, such as Alaska Natives, "typically define subsistence in dynamic, broad, and holistic ways, as 'our culture,' 'our way of being,' or 'our life'" (70). Subsistence hunters around the world employ sophisticated environmental management strategies and adapt those to changing environmental conditions. Narrow definitions fail miserably, to the point where they misrepresent what subsistence hunting means for a plethora of peoples. A broader understanding of subsistence cultures helps to correct these faults.

When we embrace a wider definition of subsistence that includes cultural and ecological commitments, hunting carries the "tremendous symbolic weight of sovereignty, respect, caring, and gratitude to subsistence animal species, and conveys a sense of connectedness to place and tradition" (Kawagley 1995). As a *Yup'ik* elder states so eloquently, "[s]ubsistence is directly related to and affected by everything that is happening … in the way of education, land use, economic development, wildlife management and other areas of public policy. Subsistence really is an entire way of life" (Harold Napoleon, quoted in *Yupiktak Bista* 1974, 2). Culturally based hunting practices are vital for ensuring the well-being of the practitioner, especially when they are connected to cultural beliefs, foundational narratives, specific customs, and focal practices (Anthony and Varner 2020). Here, hunting and fishing are not activities that can be replaced by the grocery store and tinned fish, but are deeply tied to self-determination, autonomy, and the rights to land and waterways. Narrow definitions contribute to the loss of subsistence hunting and foraging activities, which can lead to cultural loss and mourning (Barnhardt and Kawagley 1999; Cunsolo-Willox 2012). Thus, culturally appropriate definitions need to be a part of the conversation.

Eaters who embrace subsistence hunting push back against narrow definitions, as well as the ethical argument that we should rely on industrial agriculture for our foodstuffs. As we saw above, when there are adequate plant-based food stores, subsistence hunting is not ethical from an animal rights perspective. Though, it is ethical from an ecological perspective, if we primarily target mandatory and permissible management species. This latter position aligns with commitments guiding subsistence cultures. A holistic approach to hunting and eating ought to consider the whole and subsistence for that whole. Anthony and Varner (2020) apply culturally diverse understandings of subsistence hunting to current foodways. As we saw, they are highly critical of the narrow definition of subsistence hunting. These thinkers go on to place critiques of industrial agriculture into conversation with hunting narratives. Specifically, they argue that indirect harms caused by industrial agriculture supports the mandate to hunt for subsistence purposes, as a strategy to reduce overall harm. Plant-based foods available in grocery stores are not harm-free and thus ethically clean, so to speak. When you purchase that veggie burger, you're tacitly accepting a myriad of indirect harms caused during the production of the ingredients that went into making that product. From this perspective, replacing part of eater's diets with meat from respectfully hunted animals should be understood as a subsistence activity, broadly construed. These activities align with ethical omnivores environmental commitments and are also culturally sensitive to the myriad cultural backgrounds of these eaters. Hunting, fishing, and foraging play key cultural roles for many eaters, and they should be respected in any ethical diet.

In addition, these activities can also act as an experiential touchstone reinforcing the wider ethical omnivore heuristic. Placing food sourcing activities into social and cultural contexts highlights how focal practices reinforce specific customs, foundational narratives, and ethical orientations. Reo and Whyte (2012) argue that communities engaging in place-based, culturally specific hunting and fishing practices develop a sophisticated knowledge system that incorporates understandings of ecologies, biota, and place. We come to better understand the world, as we engage with it. This insight is important for many cultures and philosophies. For example, Henry David Thoreau (1995) is well known for his masterpiece *Walden*, which was built on the premise that going into the woods and living deliberately could provide valuable life lessons. Like many of his Transcendentalist contemporaries, he also recognized the value of wilderness, at a time when the Industrial Revolution began to take hold and transform American towns and identities. In this spirit, Thoreau wrote the following:

> we need the tonic of wildness...At the same time that we are earnest to explore and learn all things, we require that all things be mysterious and unexplorable, that land and sea be indefinitely wild, unsurveyed and unfathomed by us because unfathomable. We can never have enough of nature.
>
> *(205)*

This quote reminds me of the time I walked along the edge of the forest with my grandfather, as he pointed out a herd of deer bedded down in the brush for a nap. The environment has much to teach us and when we learn its ways, we see both its many gifts and its wounds, to paraphrase Aldo Leopold (Meine and Knight 2006). Hunting, in this context, includes myriad practices that bring us back into nature and help us to learn its rhythms and ways.

BHA embrace a similar view, connecting hunting to environmental care. They argue that engaging with nature is necessary for galvanizing individuals to protect wild country, and the wildlife that depend on it. As Aldo Leopold writes:

> This country has been swinging the hammer of development so long and so hard that it has forgotten the anvil of wilderness which gave value and significance to its labors. The momentum of our blows is so unprecedented that the remaining remnant of wilderness will be pounded into road-dust long before we find out its values.
>
> *(Leopold quoted in Meine and Knight 2006, 109)*

Thus, hunting practices lead us towards an ethic of care, so to speak, and help to place wilderness and wildlife into the ethical sphere. Through hunting and foraging specific customs and practices, we begin to recognize our connection to nature and, therefore, it's worth. We begin to realize that food comes from nature, rather than a grocery store. These insights then reinforce a general environmental ethic, where protection becomes a priority. For BHA and other groups, this is because hunting practices are about more than simply going out into the environment to obtain foodstuffs. There are cultural and ethical components of this activity that lead us towards a general ethic of care, built on our engagement with the natural world. Aldo Leopold captures the importance of praxis well in the first section of Sand County Almanac, where he provides vignettes or windows into daily life on the farm.

## Hunting as an Ethic of Care

Beyond increasing engagement, care ethics are often used to justify the three types of hunting we discussed, even sport hunting. In fact, care justifications feature prominently in the hunting literature, though traditional ethicists in this domain may find these arguments concerning. For example, justifications for sport hunting can be defined as a practice important for maintaining cultural and religious traditions, performing historical focal practices, and securing trophies (Varner 2002). This definition is broad, but this is because it's hard to capture the many motivations for hunting, in general. Some researchers insist on separating sports hunting from other types of hunting, though it's difficult to do so in practice. For example, hunters often enjoy the activity and even take trophies, while also providing food for their families and/or targeting obligatory management species. As we discussed earlier, one can simultaneously hunt for food and for sport, while maintaining cultural traditions. As such, hunting ethics tend to apply to many different types of hunting in praxis. Hunters and fishers often use care-based justifications to defend myriad types (McLeod 2007). The argument typically goes as follows: They care about wildlife and wilderness, unlike industrial farmers, and urban populations reliant on grocery stores, who are alienated from the modes of food production (Callicott 2014). This defense is largely a response to criticisms from various groups, including animal rights activists and some environmentalists, who argue that hunters are blood-thirsty, and that hunting is unnecessary for survival or an inefficient management strategy (Essen and Allen 2021; Cartmill 1993). Defenders meet these challenges by using "care" terminology to describe their interactions with nature.

The wildlife researcher Erica von Essen (2018) analyzed popular hunting magazines from the 1960s to today and found that hunters are significantly more concerned with animal welfare and environmental management than they were 50 years ago. Prior decades framed hunting ethics in terms of territorial disputes and respecting landowners. Today, sports hunters use distinct, yet overlapping understandings of care to justify their activities. Broadly, care can be defined as "everything we do to maintain, contain and repair our 'world' so that we can live in it as well as possible" (Tronto 1994, 40). It is a type of labor that is built on specific types of relationships. Care practices can be further divided into four elements, each emphasizing a social and relational dimension of concern. These are: (1) responsibility, (2) attentiveness, (3) competence, and (4) responsiveness (Hamington 2003). Each overlapping meaning informs arguments made to justify hunting activities, shifting ethical considerations to relationships, context, and relational knowledge. As Essen and Allen (2021) argue, we develop an ethic of care through praxis:

> …interacting with animals in a multisensory capacity…rather than viewing them through a distant gaze… or through a plastic wrap at the supermarket and caring for animals as stewards… by contributing to environmental improvement such as by habitually feeding game, constructing bird boxes, and sparing land for more destructive land-uses like agriculture and development. This is argued by hunting defenders to forge a better sense of community with animals.
>
> *(Essen and Allen 2021, 182)*

Hunters have gone from being overly focused on subsistence, to embracing "eco-buddy" and "compassionate transcendental" models of praxis, where watching wildlife grow and thrive is an important aspect of engaging in the activity (Makoto and Cheon 2017; Littlefield and Ozanne 2011). In these ways, hunting is framed as a type of active stewardship where practitioners are emotionally connected to the world around them and exercise situational ethics to ensure that animals do not suffer, by providing them with a quick death. This type of relationship is placed in juxtaposition with the impersonal and professional relationships in agriculture, where farmers are separated from their livestock at death and consumers of meat from the animals (Colling

2013, 6) to neutralize any psychological discomfort they may feel. However, factory farm workers and meat packers involved in animal death could face immense psychological discomfort. For hunters using care language, to kill dispassionately is ethically problematic (Mcintyre 1996). A care ethic that stresses connection and active stewardship is normatively superior.

## Hunting as Connection

While traditional care ethicists would be skeptical of how hunters' use this framework, ethical omnivores tend to embrace many of the justifications we just discussed. For these eaters, hunting is a way to interact with and 'repair' our world, as we attempt to embrace our role as one species among many in an interconnected ecosystem. This is an act of care. In fact, connection is a common thread uniting justifications of therapeutic, subsistence, and even sports hunting, if it's framed as a stewardship activity. Ethical omnivores care about how their food is produced and the wider harms associated with agriculture and foraging activities. As such, it makes sense that hunting and fishing would feature prominently in this diet. Most ethical diets, from vegetarianism to ethical omnivorism, recognize the deeply flawed nature of our contemporary agricultural system, and the harms that it causes to domesticated and wild animals, alike. When faced with the challenge of mitigating these harms, eaters tend to embrace different strategies. Vegetarians and vegans usually opt out of animal production systems, voting with their dollars, as they support vegetable production. Similarly, by embracing hunting and fishing, ethical omnivores are also opting out, reducing their support of animal agriculture, by harvesting and eating wild foodstuffs. Supporting regenerative organic production methods is another strategy that aligns with hunting, as it signals that current animal production systems are problematic. What we eat, and the way we obtain food, matters. It deeply connects us to our environment and each other. In short, hunting and fishing, for ethical omnivores, are ways to: (a) opt out of current systems and (b) re-ground eaters in the ecological realities of life. It is a panacea for modern life, where we're divorced from the environment and food production activities, alike.

This chapter provided an overview of the ethical dimensions of hunting and fishing, trying to capture the reasons why ethical omnivores embrace these practices. As we saw, ethical omnivores largely support hunting and fishing within certain parameters. Unsurprisingly, these eaters embrace therapeutic and subsistence hunting for animal welfare and environmental reasons, as both subsistence and therapeutic hunting provides an alternative way to obtain meat products. We ended with a discussion of care ethics, as these eaters gain important knowledge about food systems by interacting with nature and these insights bolster personal ethical growth. Ethical omnivorism is built on a heuristic, where eaters are encouraged to know more about food systems. Within this larger project, foraging activities are important for reconnecting people to the land. In our modern world, where wilderness is being lost, a sense of connection and responsibility is needed now more than ever. Food doesn't come from a grocery store. We lose more than we think when environments are harmed.

## References

Anthony, Raymond, and Gary Varner. 2020. "Subsistence Hunting." In *The Routledge Handbook of Animal Ethics,* 211–22. New York: Routledge.

Archer, M. 2011. "Slaughter of the Singing Sentients: Measuring the Morality of Eating Red Meat." *Australian Zoologist* 35 (4): 979.

Barnhardt, R., and A.O. Kawagley. 1999. "Education Indigenous to Place: Western Science Meets Indigenous Reality." In *Ecological Education in Action*, edited by G. Smith and D. Williams, 1–17. New York: State University of New York Press.

BHA. 2024. *Our Mission and Values*. Back Country Hunters and Anglers. www.backcountryhunters.org/mission_and_values.

Boone and Crockett Club. 2024a. *Fair Chase Statement*. Boone and Crockett Club. www.boone-crockett.org/fair-chase-statement.

Boone and Crockett Club. 2024b. *"B&C Position Statement- Governor's Tags."* Boone and Crockett Club. www.boone-crockett.org/bc-position-statement-governors-tags.

Callicott, J. Baird. 2014. "Environmental Ethics: I. Overview." In *Encyclopedia of Bioethics*, 994–1006. New York: Macmillan Reference.

Cartmll, M. 1993. *A View to a Death in the Morning: Hunting and Nature through History*. Cambridge, MA: Harvard University Press.

Colling, S. 2013. Animals without Borders: Farmed Animal Resistance in New York. Ontario: Faculty of Social Sciences, Brock University St. Catharines. https://dr.library.brocku.ca/handle/10464/5229.

Cunsolo-Willox, A. 2012. "Climate Change as the Work of Mourning." *Ethics & the Environment* 17 (2): 137–64.

Davis, S.L. 2003. "The Least Harm Principle May Require That Humans Consumer a Diet Containing Large Herbivores, Not a Vegan Diet." *Journal of Agricultural & Environmental Ethics* 16 (4): 387–94.

Demetriou, Dan, and Bob Fischer. 2018. "Dignitarian Hunting." *Social Theory and Practice* 44 (1): 49–73.

Essen, Erica von, and Michael Allen. 2021. "Killing with Kindness: When Hunters Want to Let You Know They Care." *Human Dimensions of Wildlife* 26 (2): 179–95.

Essen, Erica von. 2018. "The Impact of Modernization on Hunting Ethics: Emerging Taboos among Contemporary Swedish Hunters." *Human Dimensions of Wildlife* 23 (1): 21–38.

Field, R.A., F.C. Smith, W.G. Hepworth, and W.J. Means. 2003. *The Elk Carcass*. University of Wyoming, Agricultural Experimental Station b-594R:1–6.

Fischer, Bob, and Andy Lamey. 2018. "Field Deaths in Plant Agriculture." *Journal of Agricultural & Environmental Ethics* 31 (4): 409–28.

Fujimori, L. 2003. *Honolulu Star-Bulletin Hawaii News*. News Paper. The Star Bulletin. 2003. http://archives.starbulletin.com/2003/05/04/news/story2.html.

Gamborg, C, C Palmer, and C Sandoe. 2012. "Ethics of Wildlife Management and Conservation: What Should We Try to Protect?" *Nature Education Knowledge* 3 (10): 8.

Gruen, Lori, and Robert Jones. 2016. "Veganism and Aspiration." In *The Moral Complexities of Eating Meat*. Oxford: Oxford University Press.

Hamington, M. 2003. *Embodied Care: Jane Addams, Maurice Merleau-Ponty and Feminist Ethics*. Chicago, IL: University of Illinois Press.

Kawagley, A.O. 1995. *A Yupiaq World View: A Pathway to Ecology and Spirit*. Prospect Heights, IL: Waveland Press.

Kuck, Gretchen, and Gary Schnitkey. 2021. "An Overview of Meat Consumption in the United States." *Farmdoc Daily, Department of Agricultural and Consumer Economics, University of Illinois at Urbana-Champaign* 11:76.

Lambertucci, Sergio A., and Karina L. Speziale. 2011. "Protecting Invaders for Profit." *Science* 332 (6025): 35–35. https://doi.org/10.1126/science.332.6025.35-a.

Littlefield, J, and J Ozanne. 2011. "Socialization into Consumer Culture: Hunters Learning to Be Men." *Consumption Markets and Culture* 14 (4): 333–60.

Makoto, S.N., and E Cheon. 2017. "Reconsidering Nature: The Fialectics of Fair Chase in the Practices of American Midwest Hunters." *Proceedings of the 2017 CHI Conference on Human Factors in Computing Systems, Denver, Colorado, USA*, ACM.

Mcintyre, T. 1996. *The Way of the Hunter: The Art and Spirit of Modern Hunting*. New York: E.P. Dutton.

McLeod, C. 2007. "Dreadful/Delightful Killing: The Contested Nature of Duck Hunting." *Society and Animals* 15 (2): 151–67.

Meine, Curt, and Richard Knight. 2006. *The Essential Aldo Leopold: Quotations and Commentaries*. Madison, WI: University of Wisconsin Press.

Minteer, Ben A., and Elizabeth A. Corley. 2007. "Conservation or Preservation? A Qualitative Study of the Conceptual Foundations of Natural Resource Management." *Journal of Agricultural and Environmental Ethics* 20 (4): 307–33. https://doi.org/10.1007/s10806-007-9040-2.

Moss, M.L. 2010. "Rethinking Subsistence in Southeast Alaska: The Potential of Zooarchaeology." *Alaska Journal of Anthropology* 8 (1): 121–35.

NCCOS. 2024. "*Impact Assessments and Management Strategies for Invasive Lionfish in the Atlantic.*" NOAA. https://coastalscience.noaa.gov/project/management-strategies-lionfish-atlantic/.

Noll, Samantha, and Brittany Davis. 2020. "The Invasive Species Diet: The Ethics of Eating Lionfish as a Wildlife Management Strategy." *Ethics, Policy, and Environment* 23 (3): 320–35.

Nunez, A, S Kuebbing, R Dimarco, and D Simberloff. 2012. "Invasive Species: To Eat or Not to Eat, That Is the Question." *Conservation Letters* 5:334–41.

Regan, Tom. 1983. *The Case for Animal Rights*. 1st ed. Berkeley, CA: University of California Press.

Regan, Tom. 2004. *The Case for Animal Rights*. 3rd ed. Berkeley, CA: University of California Press.

Reo, Nicholas James, and Kyle Powys Whyte. 2012. "Hunting and Morality as Elements of Traditional Ecological Knowledge." *Human Ecology* 40 (1): 15–27.

Rolston III, Holmes. 2015. "After Preservation? Dynamic Nature in the Anthropocene." In *After Preservation*, edited by Ben Minteer and Stephen Pyne, 32–41. Chicago, IL: University of Chicago Press.

Sandler, Ronald L. 2012. *The Ethics of Species: An Introduction*. Cambridge University Press.

Singer, Peter. 2011. *Practical Ethics*. Cambridge: Cambridge University Press.

Thoreau, Henry David. 1995. *Walden*. New York: Dover Publishing.

Tronto, J. 1994. *Moral Boundaries: A Political Argument for an Ethic of Care*. New York: Routledge.

Turner, Shelley. 1989. "The Native American's Right to Hunt and Fish: An Overview of the Aboriginal Spiritual and Mystical Belief System, the Effect of European Contact and the Continuing Fight to Observe a Way of Life." *New Mexico Law Review* 19 (2): 377–423.

Varner, Gary. 2002. "Can Animal Rights Activists Be Environmentalists?" In *Environmental Ethics: An Anthology*, edited by Andrew Light and Holmes Rolston III, 94–113. New York: Blackwell Publishing.

Wenzel, G. 1991. *Animal Rights, Human Rights: Ecology, Economy, and Ideology in the Canadian Artic*. Toronto: University of Toronto Press.

Wheeler, P, and T Thornton. 2005. "Subsistence Research in Alaska: A Thirty Year Retrospective." *Alaska Journal of Anthropology* 3 (1): 69–103.

Woods, M, A.S. Gunn, G Varner, J.C. Evans, and C Preston. 2009. "Hunting and Fishing." In *Encyclopedia of Environmental Ethics and Philosophy*, edited by J. Baird Callicott and Robert Frodeman, 559–560. Farmington Hills, MI: Gale Cengage Learning/Macmillan Reference.

Yupiktak, Bista. 1974. "Does One Way of Life Have to Die so That Another Can Live?" In *A Report on Subsistence and the Conservation of Yup'ik Lifestyle*, edited by A Davidson, 6. Bethal, AK: Yupiktak Bista.

# 9

# EATING FOR A HEALTHY PLANET

## Agriculture in an Age of Disruptions

The COVID-19 pandemic lock-down was a difficult time for many people around the world. I was working as a professor at Washington State University, teaching food ethics and other classes. The students were worried, but we initially hoped that life would return to normal. As readers know, it did not. By mid-year 2020, The CDC was rethinking options for controlling the spread of this pathogen within and across borders (Cohen and Kupferschmidt 2020; Jacobsen and Jacobsen 2020). Non-essential works were told to "stay at home" and spent at least a year in isolation. I remember the many rules we had to follow, especially during the times when we left home for essential purposes, such as obtaining food, medical care, and exercise. There was so much collective anxiety in public spaces that it felt palpable. I keep a fully pantry and garden, so I didn't have to leave the house for food until later than most individuals. The grocery stores were a mess during this time. Shelves were mostly empty, with only a few products here and there. It was difficult to buy the essentials, as families stocked up for the long haul. Toilet paper was so scarce that people made memes about it. Fresh vegetables looked quite sad, as well, wilted and small. Meanwhile, mountains of potatoes rotted in the fields of Idaho, just miles away, as there weren't enough farm workers and packers to handle the harvest.

The pandemic impacted the world's agricultural systems and food security more than any other event over the last 50 years. The massive global epidemic disrupted the supply chain and exposed structural weaknesses in the world food system concerning "production, distribution, access, and stability," all culminating in acute hunger (Kakaei et al. 2022). Worker hours were limited due to the pandemic, which then caused farms and food factories to slow

DOI: 10.4324/9781003215189-9

down their production. At the same time, airline closures, the lack of truck drivers, national restrictions, and lockdowns also caused disruptions. Finally, many citizens were unable to obtain enough calories, due to limited access to the food supply, including grocery stores and food banks. All these failures combined to greatly increase global rates of insecurity. The good news is we are recovering but we can learn from this experience. Global and national food systems have weaknesses and can fail, especially during times of crisis. Consolidation is great for increasing efficiency and output, but not very good for ensuring that systems are resilient.

## From COVID to Climate Change: Agriculture in an Age of Disruptions

We live in an age where many events, like COVID, could impact the resilience of food systems around the world. In addition to pandemics, climate change is projected to negatively harm agricultural production. According to the EPA (2017), "Some areas will become colder, some will become warmer, overall variability is likely to increase... precipitation levels will change" (n.p.). For farmers, drastic shifts in weather mean uncertainty on the ground. More harvests will fail due to these factors. There are two ethical horns to this dilemma concerning food and agricultural systems. One the one hand, changing weather patterns are negatively affecting crop yields and thus reducing global food security. We live in a world where many people don't have enough to eat, where three-quarters of a billion people are going hungry, and this number is rising as climate change negatively harms our means of food production (Anzellini 2022). In this context, it seems prudent that we focus on addressing impacts to production. Thus, we are committed to improving food security (Borlaug 2002; Navin 2014.

On the other hand, ecological resilience is also being exacerbated by climate change. Entire species are now going extinct at unprecedented speeds, to the point where scientists are saying that we're in "Earth's Sixth Mass Extinction" (Barnosky et al. 2011). This is frightening, not only because they used capital letters, but also because paleontologists define mass extinctions "as times when the Earth loses more than three-quarters of its species in a geologically short interval, as has happened only five times in the past 540 million years" (Barnosky et al. 2011, 51). In addition to losing many species, including keystone species, others are migrating to stay in their ideal temperature zones, disrupting ecological stability. For food systems, the reduction of ecological resilience means that ecosystem services are eroding. These are the services that agriculture relies on to produce food and, more generally, to support life (Palmer and Larson 2014; Urban 2015). From this perspective, then, we should focus on reducing negative environmental impacts rather than increasing crop yields. If we want to continue growing food, we need to ensure that ecosystem services continue. Climate change is reinforcing the tension between the goals of increasing yields and ensuring sustainable harvests. Agricultural lands are already stressed, and population pressures are increasing demand for foodstuffs, bringing this conflict to the forefront (Malhi et al. 2021, FAO 2009).

The aim of this chapter is to explore ethical omnivores' recommendations concerning where we go from here. What should agriculture and our food systems look like going forward? The debate is heated and contentious. Considering climate pressures, it's easy to argue that we should prioritize food security, potentially sacrificing other goals at the altar of increased yields. Depending on how we define food security, as we will discuss, improving efficiency could be the main value guiding food production. Even the United Nations recommends the use of technological advances and greater consolidation in food systems to combat climate change impacts (FAO 2017). These measures are meant to improve efficiency. However, greater consolidation means that fewer people will have the opportunity to produce their own food and that local production systems could further fall into the hands of powerful conglomerates, which was Marrisa Landrigan's (2011) worry in *The Vegetarian's Guide to Meat Eating*. As fields become larger, technologies could be employed to maximize commodity production. Just last month, I attended an event where artificial intelligence (AI) systems were being implemented in Washington orchards. Climate-smart, precision agriculture, enabled by hyper-localized agriculture sensors, "smart" devices, and AI platforms, is harkening in a new age of agricultural efficiency. In this context, everything is monitored, from the sap running through trees to the bees to ensure maximum efficiency. This is the next technological frontier on the farm, where data are the new crop, but it is predicated on a specific vision of what agriculture is.

As we grapple with how best to mitigate climate change impacts, we are confronted with Wendell Berry's (1977) plea that farmers think about which ethos they want to embrace, that of the exploiter or that of nurturer. If farms are simply production zones, then embracing technological innovation to improve crop yields makes sense. From this perspective, the ethical omnivore diet, with its focus on regenerative organic agriculture, is quint. It's reflective of an earlier era of agriculture, where farmers had the luxury to care about biodiversity and animal welfare. But today, we need to feed the world and local food systems aren't going to do that. We must push our farmland to brink, eking out every ounce of productivity they can muster. Alternatively, the nurturer argues that we should embrace a standard of care and prioritize the health and carrying capacity of the land. Rather than giving in to the exploiter mentality, the ethical omnivore diet is firmly grounded in maintaining ecological resilience. As we will see, this goal isn't in conflict with food security but is necessary to maintain food production now and in the future. In other words, it's important for sustainability. However, before we explore ethical omnivore's vision of agriculture, we must better understand the shocks to the system that are prompting calls for greater efficiency.

## Climate Change, Agriculture, and Food Security

Climate change is one of the most important, yet complex, problems of the modern age. The Intergovernmental Panel on Climate Change (IPCC) emphasized the extraordinary scope of this crisis in their 2018 and 2021 reports—Reports that urged countries around the globe to make drastic changes to avoid dire environmental and social consequences (Shukla et al. 2018). Changing weather patterns are already impacting agricultural production, and this situation is only expected to worsen in the years to come. According to the National Climate Assessment, "many regions will experience declines in crop and livestock production from increased stress due to weeds, diseases, insect pests, and other climate change induced stresses" (Melillo et al. 2014, 1). Similarly, The EPA argued that "climate change could make it more difficult to grow crops, raise animals, and catch fish in the same ways and same places as we have done in the past" (EPA 2017, n.p.). IPCC doubled down on the dire predictions, connecting agricultural production impacts to global food security. According to their latest report, food security will be impacted by climate change in the following ways: First, global crop and economic models projected a cereal price increase in 2050 due to weather fluctuations, which could raise food prices globally (Shukla et al. 2018). These price hikes place low-income consumers at risk, potentially causing large numbers of additional people to become food insecure. Second, increased $CO_2$ levels are projected to lower the nutritional quality of foodstuffs. The distribution of diseases and pests will also change which could impact overall yields. Due to the increase in extreme weather events, the IPCC is highly confident that food system disruptions will become more frequent. The above predictions are concerning to say the least. Impacts to crops, livestock, and fisheries translate to disruptions in food availability on the ground, as well as food quality. Agricultural systems and larger food systems could face substantial shocks in the future. As we saw from the pandemic, there are serious flaws that limit the resilience of current food systems. Farmers, scientists, NGOS, and governments are currently working to determine the best ways to mitigate impacts. However, the fact remains that climate change is one of the biggest threats of our lifetime to local and global food security. As global populations increase, the human cost of agricultural failures could be staggering.

These threats to food security prompted calls for the adoption of preventative measures, such as increasing efficiency and using techno-fixes to mitigate harms. In this way, climate change impacts are pushing large organizations to double-down on extractive tendencies in the name of feeding the world. As the IPCC states:

> Agriculture and the food systems are key to global climate change responses. Combining supply-side actions such as efficient production, transport, and processing with demand-side interventions such as modification of food choices, and reduction of food loss and waste, reduces GHG emissions and enhances food system resilience.
>
> *(Mbow et al. 2019, 440)*

With three-quarters of a billion people going hungry, there are good reasons for these recommendations. Eaters have greatly benefited from technological innovations driving modern agriculture. Between 1960 and 2015, production more than tripled, resulting in an abundance of low-cost food and averting global food shortages (FAO 2017). During this time, systems also saw improvements in the efficiency of food delivery systems, and increased food quality and safety. These innovations led to the reduction of hunger and poverty globally. Considering current supply side stressors, it seems only prudent that we continue down the path of industrial agriculture, further refining, consolidating, and automating our food systems.

The IPCC recommendations connect greater efficiency with food system resilience (Mbow et al. 2019). However, greater efficiency does not always translate into resilience, as this depends on what strategy we employ to bolster efficiency. While the report is sensitive to food system complexity, the need to increase the efficiency of production, transport, and processing often prompts calls for consolidation throughout the food system. According to the agricultural economist James MacDonald (2017), "there are powerful movements toward consolidation throughout the food system and toward high concentration— with only a few buyers or sellers—in many of its markets. Some consolidation follows from economics of scale and innovation and can therefore be a channel for productivity growth" (85). Historically, key players in agribusiness used efficiency to justify the increasing concentration of our most basic processing industries, as well as those that provide important farm services and inputs, such as seeds, chemicals, and machinery. Agriculture also experienced "consolidation" in farms, as shifts in production led to the creation of larger farms owned by a handful of producers, thereby shouldering out small-scale farmers.

This trend towards higher concentration is not unique to the agricultural sector, but it is especially concerning. High concentration of control can lead to the creation of monopolies, accompanied by higher prices for sellers and lower prices for buyers, thereby distorting consumption and production decisions, reducing efficiency (MacDonald 2017). Reduced competition could also lead to reduced innovation, slower productivity growth, and lower productive efficiency in the impacted industries (Holmes and Schmitz 2010; Bloom et al. 2017). Farm consolidation is especially problematic, as it impacts the effectiveness and design of the farm, undermining environmental policies not directly concerned with consolidation or concentration. What this means is that greater consolidation could undermine environmental policies aimed at resilience. There are also equity concerns surrounding this practice, as fewer families can obtain the resources needed to grow and produce foodstuffs, thereby reducing community resilience and self-sufficiency.

If we embrace the call further consolidate our food systems, in the name of efficiency, then we could undermine environmental stewardship, equity, and innovation in the food sector. Policies not directly concerned with consolidation and concentration will be de-prioritized, even though increased efficiency is not ensured. These are a lot of values to sacrifice for the promise of greater efficiency. This brings us back to Berry's (1977) criticisms of farmers who embrace a strip-mining, or exploiter approach. Indeed, eking out every ounce of productivity is one strategy that we could employ to help bolster food security going forward, but it's not the panacea we're looking for. Berry uses provocative language to describe this type of farming, but his words are meant to prompt readers to think about what we sacrifice when we prioritize yields above other goals. It's clear from their recommendations that the Food and Agriculture Organization (FAO) and IPCC are worried about food insecurity moving forward. The twin concerns of climate change and rising population levels fuel their recommendations. In this agricultural future, farmers must maintain agricultural production levels to feed populations, *and increase production*, all while weathering climate induced shocks. Thus, it's not surprising that this prompts some producers to ask, "of a piece of land only how much and how quickly it can be made to produce," in Berry's words. By stressing efficient production and consolidation, one could argue that the above recommendations are built on the tacit assumption that agricultural lands are primarily for commodity production. They are what Paul Thompson (2010) calls "sacrifice zones," or areas of little value beyond their human use value. We cleared the land and now create increasingly controlled environments with the single goal of producing desired products. Indeed, with AI, even the bees are being optimized for maximum efficiency. Climate change is yet another reason why we need to ask more of our land and expect it to deliver, irrespective of other uses, besides production.

### From Efficiency to Sustainability: Eating for Future Generations

But, efficiency can only take us so far. Ethical omnivores ask us to think about what we are sacrificing when we prioritize efficiency and production over all other goals. As we discussed throughout this book, many values guide the way that we farm. Yes, farms should be productive, but producers embrace all sorts of normative goals, such as improving biodiversity, maintaining high animal welfare standards, improving the soil, feeding their local communities, saving heritage seeds and breeds, etc. One of the main goals of The Organic Movement is to challenge the myopic vision of agriculture guiding the above recommendations. When placed in this larger conversation, the push for even greater efficiency and consolidation are knee jerk reactions to stressors, and predicated on the idea that agricultural lands are sacrifice zones, where human needs should dominate land-use decisions. This is precisely what early figures in organic agriculture were fighting against. The stressors may be different, but the response is similar. Today, we talk about AI and Smart Agriculture, which is simply another technology in a long line of technologies transforming farming. Historical leaders in The Organic Movement wisely asked farmers and eaters to consider how new techniques could impact the land, soils, farm animals, wildlife, and human communities (Rodale Institute 2024; Conford 2001). This question is more important than ever, as 38% of the world's total landmass is used for agriculture (FAO 2017). And, 42% of U.S. water withdraws were used for crop irrigation (USDA 2022). The push for ever greater yields could carry a monumental equity and environmental price tag, if we're not careful.

We already know that the price of industrial agriculture is high. As the United Nations Environment Programme (2023) argues, "the low retail cost of industrialized food can obscure its very high environmental price tag" (1). Founding voices, such as Lady Eve Balfour, Sir Albert Howard, and J.I. Rodale spent their lives developing alternative methods of production that prioritized environmental health and sustainability (Noll 2024). For the founders of The Organic Movement and ethical omnivores, alike, any benefits that conventional agriculture produces should be weighed against environmental, community, and health costs. This is why the ethical diet advocates that we grow our food locally and eat organic produce and environmentally sustainable and ethically raised meats, poultry, fish, dairy, and eggs. When looked at wholistically, how and where we grow, raise, and harvest our food is the foundation of the ethical omnivore diet. Environments matter. What we eat and how we grow our food has a large impact on nature. Nature, in turn, impacts the quality and nutritional content of our food. So, what does this tell us about where to go from here, especially when climate-induced system failures and food insecurity looms?

## Regenerative or Bust: Farming for Sustainability

Some research suggests that we only have approximately 60 years of topsoil left if we continue to farm using current practices (Arsenault 2014). Thus, it's not enough to increase production. We must also ensure that foodstuffs can be produced for years to come. This is why the IPCC also stresses the need for greater resilience in food systems. However, we don't just need to improve resilience, or the ability of a system to handle various shocks. We also need to prioritize sustainability. People use this term in so many ways that it's sometimes difficult to figure out what they mean. Our most basic understanding of whether something is "sustainable" is a factual matter (Thompson 1997). Is a practice sustainable? My brother might be an excellent sprinter, for example, but that pace isn't sustainable, especially if you're running a marathon. A store selling items below cost is also not sustainable, if the owner wants to stay in business. For advocates of regenerative organic agriculture, our current farming practices are worrisome, as resources become scarce. In an age where shocks to food systems are increasing, our farms need to be managed in ways that increase resilience. Regenerative farming systems use practices like crop rotation, cover crops, and conservation tillage to build organic matter and promote biodiversity in soils (Khangura et al. 2023). In certain areas, these techniques can improve the health of crops, increase their nutritional value, and guard against droughts. In fact, regenerative methods are often touted as important strategies for achieving the United Nations Sustainable Development Goal #2. This goal is lofty, as it pushes producers to "ensure sustainable food production systems and implement resilient agricultural practices that increase productivity and production, that help maintain ecosystems, that strengthen capacity for adaptation to climate change, extreme weather, drought, flooding and other disasters" all by 2030 (United Nations 2015, n.p.). While there is no agreed upon definition of regenerative agriculture, five principles guide this approach. These include the commitments to: (1) reduce soil disturbances, (2) keep soil covered, (3) ensure that roots and live plants are kept in the soil as long as possible, (4) improve biodiversity, and (5) incorporate animals into farming systems (Khangura et al. 2023). Supporters argue that following these principles will have several benefits, just discussed. In fact, many of these practices are already used and overlap with other systems of agriculture, including organic farming, low-input farming, sustainable agriculture, etc. They are important for maintaining the yields and fecundity of farming systems for years to come. So, are these practices sustainable? Factually, they are.

However, this analysis depends on how we define sustainability. A factual understanding of sustainability brings us back to the twin horns of our original dilemma. While supporters argue that these techniques could produce high yields (Rhodes 2017), many researchers are quite concerned that adopting regenerative agriculture could have negative consequences for producers and food security. Most cropland in the United States is managed as large monocultures, where productivity is maintained using tillage, external fertilizers and pesticides (Schipanski et al. 2016). Alternative regenerative models of production promote biodiversity and soil health, and the growth of nutrient-dense foodstuffs (Khangura et al. 2023), but these goals come at a cost. For example, some research suggests that regenerative fields had approximately 29% lower yields than conventionally managed lands (LaCanne and Lungren 2018). This is a substantial drop in productivity, which is particularly troubling when placed in conversation with climate change impacts. The goal is to increase production, while weathering climate induced stressors, not reduce productivity. As populations double ever 25 years or so, a 29% reduction in yields could undermine that lofty goal of achieving global food security.

While yields are an important metric for farmers, this decrease doesn't capture the whole story. Ecologically based farming systems have several advantages over conventional production systems. First, they produce food while simultaneously conserving the natural resource base needed for sustainable harvests. Rather than depleting topsoil reserves, these methods could improve soil fertility, store carbon, and increase biodiversity levels (Khangura et al. 2023). These practices help to maintain ecosystem functioning and increase the resilience of agricultural zones, as they're better able to weather climate impacts, such as droughts. In this way, regenerative agriculture could help to improve environmental sustainability on the farm. Second, while yields dropped, incomes rose. Using corn as an example, regenerative farms had 78% higher profits than their conventional counterparts. This is due to the fact that regenerative agriculture requires fewer external inputs, such as seeds and fertilizer. Modern farmers must grapple with an increasingly consolidated agricultural landscape, where a few companies control the industries providing important farm services and inputs, such as seeds and chemicals (MacDonald 2017). From this perspective, regenerative agriculture may be more financially sustainable for producers, even when we take lower yields into account, as it shields farmers from the predatory practices of monopolies. Pushing back against the trend of consolidation is beneficial, if we want to increase community resilience and self-sufficiency. Increased profits means that fewer farmers will go bankrupt and must sell their land to their larger neighbors. Thus, from a factual sustainability position, regenerative agriculture has several benefits. After all, if our practices lead to the collapse of farming systems, be that for environmental or economic reasons, then they are not sustainable practices (Thompson 1997). The twin forces of consolidation of our agricultural lands and increasing industrial agricultural production might be effective for increasing efficiency, but not sustainability, if they incentivize questionable practices.

Critiques of regenerative agriculture are typically built on the tacit assumption that we value yields above environmental health and farm equity, if the latter are reduced to increase productivity. Here, recommendations aimed at increasing productivity are connected to the goal of improving food security, which is also an equity issue. Though, of course, we can question whether global hunger is really a matter of quantity, or the result of access to resource bundles (Sen 1987, 1999). The recognition of values driving these positions shifts the conversation from factual matters, such as which system is more sustainable, to the muddied water of normative questions. As we can see, different agricultural systems prioritize different outcomes, and these are guided by what we value. Conventional systems value efficiency and productivity, while regenerative systems place more emphasis on environmental health and resilience. This picture is overly simplistic, as producers must often juggle competing values on the farm. However, it is useful for better understanding the heated debates surrounding both regenerative methods and what agriculture should look like going forward, considering climate change.

## Eating for a Healthy Planet: Food Security Reconceptualized

The wider sustainability literature can help us to address normative conflicts, as it is sensitive to the interconnections between values. For example, discussions surrounding sustainability have been quite lively for the last 40 years, with several approaches vying for attention. For instance, the 1987 meeting of the United Nation's World Conference on Environment and Development (or WCED) was a key moment for the definition of the concept (Van Horn 2013). The definition proposed in WCED's report (popularly called "the Brundtland Report") is often used as a baseline today: "Sustainable development is development that meets the needs of the present without compromising the ability of future generations to meet their own needs" (quoted in Van Horn 2013, 2). This definition is broad, however, and can support several interpretations and interests. But for many scholars and organizations, it helped to bolster the idea that environmental impacts, human equity, and economic security are interconnected subjects (Kates et al. 2005). Since this report, much work has been done to clarify sustainability goals, standards, models, and definitions (Waas et al. n.d.). Yet, in agriculture, discussions often harken back to Gordon K. Douglas's (1986) early categorization of sustainably (Thompson 1997). In this early work, there are three types of sustainability: Resource sufficiency, or the idea that a practice is sustainable if we have the resources needed to do this practice for the foreseeable future. Ecological sustainability, or the idea that practices need to be constrained or align with biological functioning. Finally, there's social sustainability, or the view that practices should be sensitive to equal opportunity and justice. Wholistically, Douglas's:

> slicing emphasizes the wholeness or integrity of systems. Ecological sustainability addresses biological systems, while social sustainability considers social and political systems... In each case, it is the functional

integrity of the system that must be understood and respected, though the nature and boundaries of the systems being described vary tremendously.

*(Thompson 1997, 77)*

From a functional integrity standpoint then, each of these dimensions are necessary to ensure the functioning of food and agricultural systems.

Arguments concerning sustainability are ongoing and there are many definitions (Norton 2005; Davidson 2001; Zagonari 2022). However, I find Douglas's (1986) original taxonomy to be quite helpful, especially when we're trying to address conflicts. It's not that one group is right, while the other group is wrong. Each vision of the future of agriculture, with respect to climate change, emphasizes one aspect necessary for the health of the larger whole. Agriculture is not a monolith. It's contextual, by its very nature, as different practices and methods are best in different regions. It's also an activity embedded in both natural and social systems. This systems-focused understanding of agriculture, through the lens of sustainability, pushes us to move beyond technical or economic metrics of success. Rather than choose between resource sufficiency and functional integrity, we need an updated understanding of agriculture that recognizes the interconnections and interdependence between the two. Thus, IPCC was right to argue that we need to combine "supply-side actions such as efficient production, transport, and processing with demand-side interventions such as modification of food choices, and reduction of food loss and waste, reduces GHG emissions and enhances food system resilience" (Mbow et al. 2019, 440). When placed in conversation with Douglas' taxonomy, efficiency here is balanced with food system resilience. It's not that we're once again torn between farming as exploiter versus farming as nurturer. Rather, we need to embrace agricultural methods that are guided by these twin goals. If our farming practices incentivize questionable practices (Thompson 1997), then they are not truly sustainable from a systems perspective. Depending on contextual factors, certain practices may be better than others for balancing resource sufficiency, ecological sustainability, and social equity.

A thin layer of topsoil is all that stands between us and famine. Returning to regenerative agriculture, the 29% reduction of yields (LaCanne and Lungren 2018) is not a deal breaker for these agricultural methods. If the research is correct that we that we have approximately 60 years of topsoil left (Arsenault 2014), then conventional systems could indeed be a type of strip-mining. Here, I mean that if an agricultural practice removes the resources necessary to continue farming, then it is unsustainable, both factually and normatively. The FAO estimates that:

the global food system produces 17% more calories per person than it did 30 years ago, even after factoring in for the 70% population increase. Yet these 'gains' have come at tremendous cost to the environment, individual and societal well-being, human health, and the food sovereignty of nations.

*(Carolan 2013, 177)*

In fact, here I argue that the tension between efficiency/productivity and resilience is a false dichotomy, which can be resolved by updating our understanding of food security. After all, the goal of achieving global food security is what ultimately motivates the IPCC and FAO agricultural recommendations. If we are using problematic definitions, then potential solutions could also be problematic. As we will see, the tension breaks down when efficiency is balanced with food system resilience, as part of a sophisticated food security index.

The sociologist Michael Carolan (2013) is highly critical of conventional understandings of food security, arguing that they cannot be relied on to feed the world. Two of his critiques are particularly important for our discussion of food and agricultural systems. First, Carolan argues that definitions of food security underwent a "calorie-ization," meaning that definitions were guided by the view that insecurity occurs when a country lacks sufficient calories to feed their citizens (177). For developing nations, this meant that agricultural production needed to be increased, while affluent nations were encouraged to intensify agriculture, or risk food shortages in the future (Carolan 2013). The historical solution to the problem of hunger was simple: We must push our agricultural systems to produce more. The green revolution is an excellent example of how calorie-ization-informed policy and research surrounding food security. The goal of these initiatives was to develop high-yield varieties of cereals to feed the world. Second, prominent understandings of food security "are remarkably silent on the subject of sustainability" (Carolan 2013, 184). To be sure, organizations in the past acknowledged that "natural resources" and "natural capital" are valuable when discussing food security (Flora 2010). Yet, Carolyn is concerned that food security, as defined and measured by large organizations such as the FAO, places little importance on ecological sustainability. He provides various other critiques, ultimately arguing that we need to push back against food security as framed by conventional agri-food practices and policy. These pay lip-service to our desire to end hunger, while simultaneously ensuring that we never achieve this goal. He ends with an elaboration of a more comprehensive model called the Food and Human Security Index (FHSI), where several important factors are considered, such as societal and individual wellbeing, ecological sustainability, nutritional access, etc.

Carolan's critiques and FHSI align well with our earlier discussion of the three different definitions of sustainability: resource sufficiency, ecological health, and social equity (Douglas 1986; Thompson 1997). Each of these frameworks implicitly or explicitly accept the idea that we cannot ensure resource sufficiency without ecological health. In fact, he goes so far as to argue that:

> from a long-term food security perspective… large ecological footprints are fundamentally unsustainable and therefore ought to be avoided. Even in the shorter term, an excessive ecological footprint for a country can suggest (among many other things) dietary patterns that can have a negative impact of both life expectancy and life satisfaction.
>
> *(184)*

The latter concern is also an ecological indicator, as diets consisting of highly processed foods are environmentally harmful, in that their production consumes significant amounts of water, energy, and other resources (Carolan 2011). Thus, for Carolan (2013), "it is impossible to define a nation as 'food secure' when its food comes at great expense to the ecological productive base that makes agriculture possible" (184). When we adopt a definition of food security that moves away from "calorie-ization," and instead recognizes the importance of protecting ecological services, regenerative organic production becomes more attractive as a strategy for achieving food security. As we can see, broader concepts of sustainability inform this robust definition of security. From this perspective, regenerative agriculture is a better strategy for achieving the twin goals of efficiency and resilience.

### Eating for Resilience beyond the Farm

So, what does this mean for the future of agriculture? As we've been discussing, agricultural systems and larger food systems could face substantial shocks in the future. These threats to food security prompted calls for the adoption of preventative measures, such as increasing efficiency and using techno-fixes to mitigate harms. Let us return to the IPCC recommendations a third time:

> Agriculture and the food systems are key to global climate change responses. Combining supply-side actions such as efficient production, transport, and processing with demand-side interventions such as modification of food choices, and reduction of food loss and waste, reduces GHG emissions and enhances food system resilience.
>
> *(Mbow et al. 2019)*

In this paragraph, increasing efficiency is linked to reducing emissions and enhancing food system resilience, but this is not always the case. One interpretation could be used to justify the adoption of extractive tendencies in the name of feeding the world. As we discussed, there are good reasons for prioritizing efficiency. Considering current supply side stressors, it seems only prudent that we continue down the path of industrial agriculture, further refining, consolidating, and automating our food systems. However, as we saw from the analysis of food security definitions, agri-businesses are expert at co-opting calls to feed the world to justify greater consolidation and productivity at the cost of ecological resilience. Strategies grounded in a vision of agriculture as an extractive activity often fail to meet high sustainability and food security standards, when these standards include environmental components. As we saw, greater efficiency does not always translate into resilience, as this depends on what strategy we employ to bolster efficiency.

At the most basic level, ethical omnivores care about how food is produced and desire to eat food that was grown or harvested in ecologically healthy ways. In this way, the diet is sensitive to eating in tune with the world around us. As weather patterns shift, this means that we need to eat in ways that support greater ecological resilience on the farm, and beyond it. However, buying local and supporting organic agriculture is not enough to ensure food security and sustainability going forward. As we learned, all organic agriculture is not the same. Producers embrace various production methods on their farms, which could differ widely. Large organic production still embraces many practices common in industrial farming, such as conventional tillage and monocrop planting. In contrast, regenerative organic takes the organic standard as a starting point but pushes producers to go beyond it in their management practices, looking for even better ways to improve biodiversity levels, soil health, animal welfare, and the flourishing of farm systems. This is simply one example of how farming can be guided by myriad values beyond efficiency and productivity. We must ask more of our agricultural standards and systems. In a world where even weather patterns are changing, we need to eat for environmental sustainability and resilience on the farm and for our planet.

## Wildlife Corridors and Resilience

By supporting agricultural production systems that bolster biodiversity levels, ethical omnivores are also helping to mitigate wider environmental disruptions. As we will see, maintaining biodiversity levels and wildlife corridors on the farm, could help to maintain ecosystem functioning in wilderness areas. As readers know, agriculture dominates the world's total landmass. The sheer amount of land used for agricultural production led Paul B. Thompson (2010) to argue that agriculture plays a major role in the way humans impact the environment. Climate changes are severely impacting ecosystem health and species survival rates, and exacerbating environmental stress factors, such as habitat destruction, food and water scarcities, and the reduction of wildlife corridors (Bellard et al. 2012; Noll 2018b). In fact, "one influential review predicts that, depending on the rate and magnitude of planetary warming, up to 35% of the world's species could be on the path to climate-driven extinction" (Minteer and Collins 2010, 1801; Thomas et al. 2004). More recently, Urban stated that "if we follow our current, business-as-usual ...., climate change threatens one in six species (16%)" (2015, 571). While estimates vary, even a small reduction (especially of keystone species) could impact biodiversity levels (Botkin et al. 2007; Palmer and Larson 2014) and thus ecosystem resilience (Noll 2017).

As biodiversity levels fall, ecological processes are also threatened. This, in turn, negatively impacts ecosystem services (Nelson et al. 2013). Once again, we return to agriculture, as ecosystem benefits include "provisioning services (production of foods, fuels, fibers, water, genetic resources), cultural services (recreation, spiritual and aesthetic satisfaction, scientific information), and regulating services (controlling variability in production, pests and pathogens, environmental hazards, and many key environmental processes)" (Perrings 2010, 2). While this list is varied, a key takeaway for our analysis is the following: Several processes important for agriculture could be threatened (Nelson at al. 2013). As the EPA (2017) stated, climate changes are already impacting our ability to grow crops, raise animals, and catch fish using the same methods that we used historically (1). In short, the loss of biodiversity impacts: (1) systems that food production is built upon and (2) ecological resilience. Beyond food production, as species go extinct, this reduction impacts the ability of our planet to support life.

By embracing agricultural practices that bolster biodiversity levels and maintain wildlife corridors, farmers could help reduce the number of species going extinct. Like humans, other species respond to environmental "push" factors, including extreme weather events and other slow-onset events, by migrating to new areas (Angetter et al. 2011; Palmer and Larson 2014). Species also respond to "pull" factors or geographical features that entice individuals to migrate, such as an abundance of food, water, or habitat (Gemenne 2012). In ecology, "this is frequently described as species following their 'ecological niches' or 'climate niches,' which can approximately be defined as the identifiable limits of a species' range or the range in which a species can flourish" (Palmer and Larson 2014, 641). Unlike annual migrations, climate-induced species migrations are caused by shifts not part of "seasonal" behavioral patterns. Today, many species are shifting their ranges, as a response to environmental push and pull factors (Botkin et al. 2007; Bellard et al. 2012). But, according to the FAO (2016):

> food production has only exacerbated this problem, as agriculture and intensive forest cultivation (in conjunction with urban development) created 'barriers (physical, chemical and ecological) [that]...prevent the natural movement of individual animals in the short term and prevent the

gradual shift of populations of plants and small territorial animals in the medium term.

*(FAO 2016, 32)*

Coupled with the sheer amount of land used for agriculture, the probability is high that species could be: (a) barred by or (b) attempt to move though agricultural zones, as their ranges shift (Noll 2018a). The result is a vicious loop, where biodiversity loss is exacerbated by agricultural production, while climate induced species migration, which may, in turn, impact agricultural production. Thus, agricultural production areas could exacerbate existing pressures on the environment by undermining ecosystem functioning and acting as barriers to species migration.

Regenerative agriculture reminds us that all agricultural systems are not the same. We could and should, considering the above impacts, manage our farms to mitigate these impacts.

Several farming management strategies can be used to bolster biodiversity levels and restore habitat, while still maintaining agricultural yields. Wildlife experts David Macdonald and Ruth Feber's (2015) research on conserving biodiversity in agricultural areas illustrates how farming zones are not "only" areas of production, and they do not have to act as barriers to species migration. Farms could be understood as part of a larger mitigation strategy. However, this view pushes back against the twin forces of increasing efficiency and productivity, as areas are set aside for conservation. Corn fields as far as the eye can see, while efficient, are highly problematic from a wildlife management perspective. As is draining our rivers and wilderness areas of water to irrigate these fields. From a wholistic perspective, modern agricultural paradigms need to shift, especially when placed in larger ecological contexts that are stressed due to climate change. As weather patterns shift, large organizations are beginning to realize that industrial agriculture's price tag is too high. As the FAO (2024) so poignantly notes, "climate change threatens food security and our ability to achieve sustainable development. Agriculture both suffers from climate change but also contributes to it as a significant amount of greenhouse gas emissions come from the agrifood sector" (n.p.). What we need going forward are more sustainable agricultural practices—Ones that are committed to climate change adaptation and mitigation and contribute to the reduction of greenhouse gas emissions.

## Conclusion

Ethical omnivores embrace the idea that agricultural zones are valuable, and they think about the environmental costs of the food on their plates. Industrial agriculture might, at one point, have been able to feed the world. Today, however, food and agricultural systems are facing unprecedented stressors. As food system failures loom, consumers no longer have the luxury of ignoring the true costs of present-day consumption. In many ways, the ethical omnivore diet is an answer to Paul B. Thompson's (1995) concerns discussed at the end of *The Spirit of the Soil: Agriculture and Environmental Ethics*. As he argues "the moral collapse that gives rise to the shopping mentality is already a system failure, a breakdown in the interconnections among daily work, habitus, and the mechanisms that reproduce and reinforce an environmental ethic at the cultural and personal level" (213). He is doubtful that consumers can be persuaded to look to the future and ask if the resources they need to continue their consumption are foreseeably available. For Thompson, consumer's habits of shopping shape their moral lives. "As decision makers, expressing preferences in the milieu of consumer goods... their preferences come to define their human condition" (213). In this context, there is no reason why eaters should know where their consumable foodstuffs come from. Warnings of catastrophe, of stressed and failing agricultural systems, fall outside of their moral world. In the world of the shopper, the wider environmental and social costs of feeding their habits and preferences are experienced as abstractions. However, the modern world demands a morality that pushes eaters to realize the true cost of today's consumption. By pushing eaters to think more critically about how their food is produced, the ethical omnivore diet is one strategy to reconnect consumers with the wider realities of food production. It's not a perfect fix and doesn't replace the contextual expertise of farmers, but it is a first step—A step that can hopefully push eaters to think beyond habits and preferences and embrace an agrarian ethic of seeing.

Understanding how and where we grow, raise, and harvest our food is the foundation of the ethical omnivore diet. As Dalrymple and Hilliard (2020) plainly state, ethical omnivores grapple with which food production systems they want to support. Farms are very different places when they're managed using sustainable and environmentally friendly methods. Environments matter. What we eat and how we grow our food has a large impact on nature. Nature, in turn, impacts the quality and nutritional content of our food. Considering climate pressures, it's easy to argue that we should prioritize food security as "calorie-ization," sacrificing other goals at the altar of increased yields. But, as we grapple with climate change, we are once again confronted with Wendel Berry's (1977) plea that eaters come to know how their food is produced. After all, "sane and healthy agriculture requires an informed urban constituency" (Berry 1977, ix). These eaters have taken up the call to influence the way that we produce food and, thus what is on our plates. Beyond the plate, our decisions can change agricultural systems and even ecosystems. So, we are back to our original question: What should agriculture and our food systems look like going forward? As you practice an ethic of seeing, that is up to you. But, remember that ethical omnivore's vision of farming is one that prioritizes the health and carrying capacity of the land. It is a vision where farmers are nurturers, not exploiters. Please take that piece of advice with you, as you decide what's for dinner.

## References

Angetter, Lea-Su, Stefan Lötters, and Dennis Rödder. 2011. "Climate Niche Shift in Invasive Species: The Case of the Brown Anole." *Biological Journal of the Linnean Society* 104 (4): 943–54. https://doi.org/10.1111/j.1095-8312.2011.01780.x

Anzellini, Vicente. 2022. *Global Food Insecurity Is on the Rise, so Is Internal Displacement. What Is the Relationship?* Internal Displacement Monitoring Center. www.internal-displacement.org/expert-analysis/global-food-insecurity-is-on-the-rise-so-is-internal-displacement-what-is-the/

Arsenault, Chris. 2014. *Only 60 Years of Farming Left If Soil Degradation Continues.* Reuters. www.reuters.com/article/us-food-soil-farming-idUSKCN0JJ1R920141205/

Barnosky, Anthony, Nicholas Matzke, and Susumu Tomiya. 2011. "Has the Earth's Sixth Mass Extinction Already Arrived? Nature." *Nature* 471 (7336): 51–57.

Bellard, Céline, Cleo Bertelsmeier, Paul Leadley, Wilfried Thuiller, and Franck Courchamp. 2012. "Impacts of Climate Change on the Future of Biodiversity." *Ecology Letters* 15 (4): 365–77. https://doi.org/10.1111/j.1461-0248.2011.01736.x

Berry, Wendell. 1977. *The Unsettling of America: Culture & Agriculture.* Oakland, CA: Sierra Club Books.

Bloom, Nicholas, Erik Brynjolfsson, Lucia Foster, Ron Jarmin, Megha Patnaik, Itay Saporta-Eksten, and John Vvan Reenen. 2017. "What Drives Differences in Management?" *National Bureau of Economic Research working paper no. 23300.* Available at https://doi.org/10.3386/w23300

Borlaug, Norman. 2002. "Feeding a World of 10 Billion People: The Miracle Ahead." *In Vitro Cellular & Developmental Biology* 38 (2): 221–28.

Botkin, Daniel B., Henrik Saxe, Miguel B. Araújo, Richard Betts, Richard H. W. Bradshaw, Tomas Cedhagen, Peter Chesson, et al. 2007. "Forecasting the Effects of Global Warming on Biodiversity." *BioScience* 57 (3): 227–36. https://doi.org/10.1641/B570306

Carolan, Michael. 2011. *The Real Cost of Cheap Food.* New York: Routledge.

Carolan, Michael. 2013. "The Food and Human Security Index: Rethinking Food Security and 'Growth.'" *International Journal of the Sociology of Agriculture* 19 (2): 176–200.

Cohen, Jon, and Kai Kupferschmidt. 2020. "Strategies Shift as Coronavirus Pandemic Looms." *Science* 367:962–63.

Conford, Philip. 2001. *The Origins of the Organic Movement.* Glasgow: Floris Books.

Dalrymple, Laura, and Grant Hilliard. 2020. *The Ethical Omnivore: A Practical Guide and 60 Nose-to-Tail Recipes for Sustainable Meat Eating.* Sydney: Murdoch Books.

Davidson, Aidan. 2001. *Technology and the Contested Meanings of Sustainability.* Albany, NY: State University of New York Press.

Douglas, Gordon. 1986. "Introduction." In *Agricultural Sustainability in a Changing World Order,* edited by Gordon Douglas. Boulder, CO: Westview Press.

EPA, OA. 2017. "Climate Impacts on Agriculture and Food Supply." *Overviews and Factsheets.* 2017. /climate-impacts/climate-impacts-agriculture-and-food-supply

FAO. 2009. *Coping with a Changing Climate: Considerations for Adaptation and Mitigation in Agriculture.* Rome, Italy: FAO.

FAO. 2016. *Wildlife in a Changing Climate.* Food and Agricultural Organization of the United Nations. www.fao.org/4/i2498e/i2498e00.htm

FAO. 2017. *Future of Food and Agriculture: Trends and Challenges.* Food and Agricultural Organization of the United Nations. https://openknowledge.fao.org/server/api/core/bitstreams/2e90c833-8e84-46f2-a675-ea2d7afa4e24/content

FAO. 2024. *Transforming Agriculture to Combat Climate Change.* Food and Agricultural Organization of the United Nations. www.fao.org/europe/news/detail/transforming-agriculture-to-combat-climate-change/en

Flora, C. 2010. "Food Security in the Context of Energy and Resource Depletion: Sustainable Agriculture in Developing Countries." *Renewable Agriculture and Food Systems* 25:118–28.

Food and Agriculture Organization of the United Nations. 2020. *Sustainable Food and Agriculture: Land Use in Agriculture by the Numbers.* 2020. www.fao.org/sustainability/news/detail/en/c/1274219/

Gemenne, F. 2012. *An Introduction to International Migration Studies: European Perspectives.* Stockholm: Amsterdam University Press.

Giller, Ken, Renske Hijbeek, Jens Andersson, and James Sumberg. 2021. "Regenerative Agriculture: An Agronomic Perspective." *Outlooks in Agriculture* 50 (1): 13–25.

Holmes, Thomas, and James Schmitz. 2010. "Competition and Productivity: A Review of the Evidence." *Annual Review of Economics* 2:619–42.

Jacobson, Grant, and Kathryn Jacobsen. 2020. "Statewide COVID-19 Stay-at-Home Orders and Population Mobility in the United States." *World Medical & Health Policy* 12 (4): 347–56.

Kakaei, Hojatollah, Heshmatollah Nourmoradi, Salar Bakhtiyari, Mohsen Jalilian, and Amin Mirzael. 2022. "Effect of COVID-19 on Food Security, Hunger, and Food Crisis." *National Library of Medicine*, 3–29.

Kates, Robert, Thomas Parris, and Anthony Leiserowitz. 2005. "What Is Sustainable Development?" *Environment: Science for Policy and Development* 47 (3): 8–21.

Khangura, Ravjit, David Ferris, Cameron Wagg, and Jamie Bowyer. 2023. "Regenerative Agriculture—A Literature Review on the Practices and Mechanisms Used to Improve Soil Health." *Sustainability* 15 (3): 2338.

LaCanne, Claire, and Jonathan Lundgren. 2018. "Regenerative Agriculture: Merging Farming and Natural Resource Conservation Profitably." *Peer Journal.* 26 (6): 1–12.

Landrigan, Marissa. 2011. "The Vegetarian's Guide to Eating Meat." *Iowa State University Digital Repository*, Graduate Theses and Dissertations, 251.

MacDonald, David, and Ruth Feber, eds. 2015. *Wildlife Conservation on Farmland.* Oxford: Oxford University Press.

MacDonald, James. 2017. "Consolidation, Concentration, and Competition in the Food System." *Federal Reserve Bank of Kansas City: Economic Review*, (September 2017): 85–105.

Malhi, Gurdeep, Manpreet Kaur, and Prashant Kaushik. 2021. "Impact of Climate Change on Agriculture and Its Mitigation Strategies: A Review." *Sustainability* 13 (3): 1–21.

Mbow, C, C Rosenzweig, L.G. Barioni, L.G. Benton, M Herrero, E Krishnapillai, P Liwenga, M.G. Rivera-Rerre, T. Sapkota, and F.N. Tubiello. 2019. "Food Security." In *Climate Change and Land: An IPCC Special Report on Climate Change, Desertification, Land Degradation, Sustainable Land Management, Food Security, and Greenhouse Gas Fluxes in Terrestrial Ecosystems*, edited by P.R. Shukla, E Skea,

Otávio Bueno, Buendia Calvo, H Masson-Delmotte, D.C. Portner, P. Roberts, et al., 437–550. Geneva: The Intergovernmental Panel on Climate Change.

Melillo, Jerry, Terese Richmond, and Gary Yohe. 2014. *Climate Change Impacts in the United States: The Third National Climate Assessment*. U.S. Global Change Research Program. https://nca2014.globalchange.gov/downloads/low/NCA3_Full_ Report_0a_Front_Matter_LowRes.pdf

Minteer Ben A. and Collins James P. 2010. "Move It or Lose It? The Ecological Ethics of Relocating Species under Climate Change." *Ecological Applications* 20 (7): 1801–4. https://doi.org/10.1890/10-0318.1

Navin, Mark. 2014. "Local Food and International Ethics." *Journal of Agricultural and Environmental Ethics* 27 (3): 349–68.

Nelson, Erik, Peter Kareiva, Mary Ruckelshaus, Katie Arkema, Gary Geller, Evan Girvetz, Dave Goodrich, et al. 2013. "Climate Change's Impact on Key Ecosystem Services and the Human Well-Being They Support in the US." *Frontiers in Ecology and the Environment* 11 (November): 483–893. https://doi.org/10.1890/120312

Noll, Samantha. 2017. "Climate Induced Migration: A Pragmatic Strategy for Wildlife Conservation on Farmland." *Pragmatism Today* 8 (2): 17.

Noll, Samantha. 2018a. "Balancing Food Security and Ecological Resilience in the Age of the Anthropocene." In *Food, Environment, and Climate Change: Justic at the Intersections*, edited by Erinn Gilson and Sarah Kenehan, 179–93. New York: Rowman & Littlefield.

Noll, Samantha. 2018b. "Nonhuman Climate Refugees: The Role That Urban Communities Should Play in Ensuring Ecological Resilience." *Environmental Ethics* 40 (2): 119–34.

Noll, Samantha. 2024. "Environmental Ethics Down on the Farm: Hargrove's Weak Anthropocentrism and the 'Agricultural Blindspot.'" *Environmental Ethics* 46 (3): 247–54.

Norton, Bryan. 2005. *Sustainability: A Philosophy of Adaptive Ecosystem Management*. Chicago, IL: University of Chicago Press.

Palmer, Clare, and Brendon M. H. Larson. 2014. "Should We Move the Whitebark Pine? Assisted Migration, Ethics and Global Environmental Change." *Environmental Values* 23 (6): 641–62.

Perrings, Charles. 2010. *Biodiversity, Ecosystem Services, and Climate Change: The Economic Problem*. 58165. The World Bank. http://documents.worldbank.org/cura ted/en/241621468149401563/Biodiversity-ecosystem-services-and-climate-cha nge-the-economic-problem

Rhodes, Christopher. 2017. "The Imperative for Regenerative Agriculture." *Science Progress* 100 (1): 80–129.

Robinson, John. 2004. "Squaring the Circle? Some Thoughts on the Idea of Sustainable Development." *Ecological Economics* 48:369–84.

Rodale Institute. 2024. *Regenerative Organic Certified*. Rodale Institute. https://roda leinstitute.org/regenerative-organic-certification/

Schipanski, M.E., G.K. MacDonald, S. Rosenzweig, M.J. Chappell, R.B. Kerr, J. Blesh, T.F. Crews, L.E. Drinkwater, and J.G. Schnarr. 2016. "Realizing Resilient Food Systems." *Bioscience* 66:600–610.

Sen, Amartya. 1987. *Hunger and Entitlement*. Helsinki: World Institute for Development Economics Research, United Nations University.

Sen, Amartya. 1999. *Development as Freedom*. New York, NY: Knopf.

Shukla, P.R., E Skea, Buendia Calvo, H Masson-Delmotte, D.C. Portner, P. Roberts, R. Zhai, et al. 2018. "IPCC, 2019: Climate Change and Land: An IPCC Special Report on Climate Change, Desertification, Land Degradation, Sustainable Land Management, Food Security, and Greenhouse Gas Fluxes in Terrestrial Ecosystems." Governmental Website. *IPCC Climate Report. 2018.* www.ipcc.ch/

Thomas, Chris D., Alison Cameron, Rhys E. Green, Michel Bakkenes, Linda J. Beaumont, Yvonne C. Collingham, Barend F. N. Erasmus, et al. 2004. "Extinction Risk from Climate Change." *Nature* 427 (6970): 145–48. https://doi.org/10.1038/nature02121

Thompson, Paul B. 1995. *The Spirit of the Soil: Agriculture and Environmental Ethics.* Routledge.

Thompson, Paul B. 1997. "Sustainability as a Norm." *Philosophy and Technology* 2 (2): 75–94.

Thompson, Paul B. 2010. *The Agrarian Vision: Sustainability and Environmental Ethics.* University Press of Kentucky.

United Nations. 2015. "Sustainable Development Goals. Transforming Our World: The 2030 Agenda for Sustainable Development." *A/Res/70/1.* New York: United Nations. https://sustainabledevelopment.un.org/content/documents/21252030%20Agenda%20for%20Sustainable%20Development%20web.pdf

United Nations Environment Programme. 2023. *Ten Ways You Can Help Fight the Climate Crisis.* United Nations. www.unep.org/news-and-stories/story/10-ways-you-can-help-fight-climate-crisis

Urban, Mark C. 2015. "Accelerating Extinction Risk from Climate Change." *Science* 348 (6234): 571–73. https://doi.org/10.1126/science.aaa4984

USDA and National Agricultural Statistics Service. 2022. *Farms and Land in Farms: 2021 Summary.* United States Department of Agriculture. www.nass.usda.gov/Publications/Todays_Reports/reports/fnlo0222.pdf?>

Van Horn, Gavin. 2013. *Ethics and Sustainability: A Primer with Suggested Readings.* Center for Humans and Nature. https://iseethics.wordpress.com/wp-content/uploads/2013/09/ethics_and_sustainability_primer.pdf

Waas, Tom, Jean Huge, Aviel Verbruggen, and Tarah Wright. n.d. "Sustainable Development: A Bird's Eye View." *Sustainability* 3:1637–61.

Zagonari, Fabio. 2022. *Environmental Ethics, Sustainability and Decisions.* New York: Springer.

# INDEX